Cutting Rhythm.

"Karen's insights about the flow of story, emotion, image and sound have helped me at all stages of filmmaking, from onscreen drafting to fine cutting."

Genevieve Clay-Smith, multi-award winning Director

"A great resource! Karen's out-of-the-box thinking about editing brings a new level of insight and articulation to describing what editors do and how we do it."

Jason Ballantine, ASE

There are many books on the technical aspects of film and video editing. Much rarer are books on how editors think and make creative decisions.

Filled with timeless principles and thought-provoking examples from a variety of international films, the second edition of Karen Pearlman's *Cutting Rhythms* offers an in-depth study of the film editor's rhythmic creativity and intuition, descriptions of the processes and tools editors use to shape rhythms, and insight into how rhythm works to engage audiences in film. While respecting the importance of intuitive flow in the cutting room, this book offers processes for understanding what editing intuition is and how to develop it. This fully revised and updated editio

- New chapters on collabora
- Advice on making onscreen dr

- Tips on how to create and sustain audience empathy and engagement;

- Explanations of how rhythm is perceived, learned, practiced and applied in editing;

- Updated discussions of intuition, structure and dynamics;

- An all-new companion website (www.focalpress.com/cw/pearlman) with video examples and links for expanding and illustrating the principles of key chapters in the book.

Dr Karen Pearlman is a director of the multi-award winning Physical TV Company where she directs, produces and edits drama, documentary and dance film. Currently a lecturer in Screen Production at Macquarie University, Karen is a former President of the Australian Screen Editors Guild and a four-time nominee for Best Editing at the Australian Screen Editors Guild Annual Awards.

Cutting Rhythms
Intuitive Film Editing

Second Edition

Karen Pearlman

Focal Press
Taylor & Francis Group

NEW YORK AND LONDON

Second edition published 2016
by Focal Press
711 Third Avenue, New York, NY 10017

and by Focal Press
2 Park Square, Milton Park, Abingdon, Oxon OX14 4RN

Focal Press is an imprint of the Taylor & Francis Group, an informa business

First edition published by Focal Press in 2009

Library of Congress Cataloging in Publication Data
Pearlman, Karen.
 Cutting rhythms : shaping the film edit / Karen Pearlman.—Second edition.
  pages cm
 Includes index.
 1. Motion pictures—Editing. 2. Motion pictures—Philosophy. 3. Motion picture plays—Editing. 4. Rhythm. I. Title.
 TR899.P42 2016
 778.5'35—dc23   2015016843

ISBN: 978-1-138-94608-8 (hbk)
ISBN: 978-1-138-85651-6 (pbk)
ISBN: 978-1-315-71958-0 (ebk)

Typeset in Giovanni Book
by Keystroke, Station Road, Codsall, Wolverhampton

Contents

Preface to the Second Edition

There have been a lot of changes to industry, technology and audiences since the first edition of *Cutting Rhythms, Shaping the Film Edit*. Forms, formats and distribution have changed. Editing gear has changed. Audience access and viewing patterns have changed. All of these will continue to change, and these changes all impact on editing.

Change is not new, though. It has been a constant since the beginning of film. Even the word "film" doesn't mean what it used to. It used to mean a celluloid substance, now it is a generic word for a screen story experience. A filmmaker rarely works with film. She makes screen stories. But she is still a filmmaker. So, rather than changing the book to address particular changes to industry and technologies, which will change again before you read this, this new edition is looking at change as part of what we do.

Editing is change. It is transformation. Editing changes two shots into a juxtaposition. It changes movement into rhythm. Editing is the skill that transforms any mass of material into a coherent story.

If there is a new theme to this second edition it is this: editing is a transferable skill. It doesn't just work on celluloid, movies, and TV shows. Editors can transfer their abilities to new formats and platforms. We can apply our "editing thinking" to words, images, sounds, games, apps, series, events, experiences, and things as yet unknown or unnamed.

The new title reflects this theme. It used to be *Cutting Rhythms: Shaping the Film Edit*. Now it is *Cutting Rhythms: Intuitive Film Editing*. Cutting rhythms is what we do. Editing intuition is what we develop and take with us across forms, formats, media, and technologies as they and their audiences change.

Preface to the First Edition

My interest in writing this book began when I was finishing the practical course work for my M.A. in Editing at the Australian Film Television and Radio School (AFTRS). I was approached by the head of the editing department, Bill Russo, ASE, about the possibility of researching editing history and theory for the purposes of teaching incoming students. From that discussion, the idea was to base my research on words that are frequently used, but infrequently defined in the regular course of editing a film,[1] such as "structure," "montage," and "rhythm." Bill's expertise in editing came about through many years of practical experience. The AFTRS, in trying to train an editor in a few short years, was already very focused on providing a variety of practical editing experiences. Bill responded enthusiastically to my ideas for research because he wanted to know: What could film school offer that was different from working in the field? And, more importantly: Could principles be articulated and communicated that might otherwise be understood only through years of practice or experience?

In the course of my research I found that it was a relatively straightforward matter to draw together and teach many specific principles about Soviet montage theory, techniques of continuity cutting, structure, devices, and common scenes by studying films and books and talking to writers, directors, and editors. However, rhythm, as a topic, was elusive. A literature search yielded contradictory, limited, or inconclusive definitions. Experienced editors, although in agreement that rhythm (along with structure) is what an editor shapes in a film-making process, were reluctant to try to articulate a definition. Finally, David Bordwell and Kristen Thompson's *Film Art* threw down the gauntlet with the comment "the issue of rhythm in cinema is enormously complex and still not well understood."[2] Perhaps perversely drawn to the most ineffable, or at least the trickiest, topic of study I had yet found, I set out on my quest to understand rhythm in film editing.

Since discussion of rhythm in film editing is rare I have had the opportunity to draw on a range of disciplines, including film studies, dance, and neurology, to help me formulate some principles. In the first four chapters of this book I develop ideas about intuition, editing as a choreographic process, and the tools and purposes of rhythm. Then I look at the different kinds of rhythms with which editors work. In the new edition I have added chapters about collaboration and editing thinking. *Cutting Rhythms* is a book about editing theory and practice. It looks at the creative processes, tools, and functions of rhythm in film editing. *Cutting Rhythms* looks at something central to the art of filmmaking: rhythm, a word often used and rarely defined, and it aims to enhance rhythmic creativity and intuition.

ENDNOTES

1. In this book, I use the word "film" to refer to screen stories made with moving images.
2. Bordwell, D., and Thompson, K., *Film Art: An Introduction*, pp. 196–197.

Acknowledgments

This book is based on the doctoral thesis *Cutting Rhythms: Ideas about the Shaping of Rhythm in Film Editing*, by Dr. Karen Pearlman, University of Technology, Sydney, 2006.

An earlier version of Chapter 1 of this book was published as "The Rhythm of Thinking—speculations on how an editor shapes the rhythm of a film," in a special feature section on editing in *Metro Magazine*, a publication of the Australian Teachers of Media, 141, pp. 112–116, 2004.

Excerpts from Chapters 4, 5, and 6 were published in a series of three articles in the journal of the Dance Films Association, New York, 2005–2006 (*Dance on Camera Journal*, July–August 2005, 8(4); *Dance on Camera Journal*, September–October 2005, 8(5); and *Dance on Camera Ezine*, February 9, 2006).

An earlier version of Chapter 11 was published in *Lumina, The Australian Journal of Screen Arts and Business*, Issue 11, 2013.

The ideas in Chapter 12, *Editing Thinking and Onscreen Drafting*, are part of an ongoing research project being supported by a Macquarie University New Staff Grant, and there will be additional scholarly publications forthcoming on these topics.

The second edition of this book owes a debt to my colleagues at Macquarie University: Kathryn Millard, Iqbal Barkat, Tom Murray, Maree Delofski, Gill Ellis, Joseph Pugliese, Catharine Lumby, and Nicole

Anderson who have all contributed to supporting my research and writing. Thank you to all of the Dept. of Music, Media, Communications and Cultural Studies for welcoming me into your community and creating such a collegial and stimulating environment.

I'd like to acknowledge the skill, commitment, and excellent advice of my doctoral supervisor, Sarah Gibson, and my co-supervisor, Professor Ross Gibson, whose own writings have been so significant in shaping my ideas. I'd like also to acknowledge the influence and inspiration provided by my original supervisor, Dr. Patrick Crogan. Acknowledgment and thanks are due to Bill Russo, ASE, former Head of Editing at the Australian Film Television and Radio School (AFTRS), for his curiosity, challenges, and discussions. I would also like to acknowledge Paul Thompson, professor at the NYU Tisch Film School, for his articulation of ideas about "hope and fear." A thank you to Philippa Harvey, Mark Warner, Matthew Campora, and all of my colleagues at the AFTRS for their insights and interest, as well as my former and current students at Macquarie University, the AFTRS, and at the University of Technology, Sydney (UTS), whose energy and passion for their work have been so inspiring.

While doing my doctorate, the lecturers at UTS in the Department of Media Arts and Production, were all influential and often, perhaps without knowing it, dropped in a remark or an idea that set me thinking. Special thanks to the then Dean of the Faculty of Arts and Sciences at UTS, Professor Theo van Leeuwen, for his work on rhythm in film and for bringing key texts to my attention.

My highly esteemed colleagues at the Australian Screen Editors Guild have been a great inspiration for me, and I'd particularly like to acknowledge the input, advice, and encouragement of Henry Dangar, ASE; Emma Hay, ASE; Peter Whitmore, ASE; Jane St. Vincent Welch, ASE; Dany Cooper, ASE; and Jason Ballantine, ASE. I also acknowledge the advice and assistance of Dr. Stephen Malloch, Dr. Greg Hooper, and Dr. Mark Seton in discussion of particular problems and in locating particular texts. Dr. Christopher Allen, Michelle Hiscock, Dierdre Towers, Darmyn Calderon, J. Gluckstern, and Ross Murray have all been kind enough to read some parts of the manuscript, and I thank them for their comments and suggestions.

At Focal Press, I am also indebted to the editor of the first edition Elinor Actipis, the editor who commissioned the second edition Dennis McGonagle, and editors of the second edition: Elliana Arons, Emily McCloskey, and Peter Linsley. Thank you to the Focal Press readers Cari Ann Shim Sham and Jerry Hofman for your insights and suggestions.

Finally, for having gotten this far I owe a debt to my family: my father, Dr. Alan Pearlman, whom I "mirror" in all of my thinking, and his wife, Gail Bass, whose knowledge of music has provided stimulating debates about rhythm; my mother, Joan Pearlman, an endless source of enthusiasm and loving support, and her husband, Professor Peter Kivy, who gave me my first books on film theory. To the memory of my father-in-law, Robert Allen, and special thanks to my mother-in-law, Jocelyn Allen, who lifted the burdens of all my daily cares and held them aloft so graciously while I sheltered with her and wrote. Then there are the gorgeous ones, my children Sam and Jaz, my *raisons d'être*, who inspire me to get up in the morning and in absolutely everything else, and my wonderful partner, Richard, the astounding river of energy, vision, and love running through it all. With love and thanks to you all, here it is!

Introduction

Cutting Rhythms is about rhythm in film editing. It begins with the question: What can be said about the shaping of a film's rhythm in editing beyond saying "it's intuitive"? This question leads to an in-depth study of editors' rhythmic creativity and intuition, the processes and tools editors work through to shape rhythms, and the functions of rhythm in film. *Cutting Rhythms* covers ideas about what rhythm in film editing is, how it is shaped, and what it is for. Case studies about creating rhythm in films edited by the author and examples of rhythm in a range of other films describe and illustrate practical applications of these ideas.

Cutting Rhythms begins in Chapter 1 by asking about intuition. What kinds of thinking and practice are editors referring to when they say the processes of creating rhythm are "intuitive"? Can the capacity to cut "intuitively" be developed? *Cutting Rhythms* proposes that it can. It draws on diverse sources of knowledge about intuition, including science, philosophy, education, film theory, and even dance theory to define ways of strengthening, supporting, and refining rhythmic intuition. Chapter 1 describes the editor's intuition about rhythm as something developed from mindful awareness of the rhythms of the world and the rhythms of one's own body. These are the sources of the editor's embodied expertise and implicit intelligence about rhythm, and they are also the triggers that activate the editor's creativity in cutting rhythms.

Chapter 2 of *Cutting Rhythms* builds on the ideas in Chapter 1 about physical thinking and movement. It puts forward the notion that editing is a form of choreography, because, like choreographers, what editors do is manipulate the composition of moving images and sounds to shape a meaningful flow. This chapter looks at some of the ways in which choreographers and dancers work with movement and finds that these provide some quite useful crafting tools for shaping a film's rhythms.

The tools for cutting rhythms are discussed in Chapter 3, which breaks down and defines "timing" and "pacing." This chapter also introduces "trajectory phrasing," a term devised to describe some of the key operations an editor performs that are not precisely covered by timing or pacing. "Trajectory phrasing" is what we are doing when choosing different takes of a performance to join together, to create the impression of a single flow of energy and intention. It is a useful way of thinking about some key editing decisions.

Chapter 4 looks at the purposes for which movement in film is shaped into rhythms. It describes the effect of rhythmic cycles of tension and release on the viewer's mind and body, and the effect of synchronization that a film's rhythm can have on the rhythms of a viewer.

These four chapters cumulatively propose that: *Rhythm in film editing is time, movement, and energy shaped by timing, pacing, and trajectory phrasing for the purpose of creating cycles of tension and release.*

With that definition in hand, *Cutting Rhythms* then applies its ideas about intuition, choreographic approaches, and the tools and purposes of rhythm to different types of rhythm that editors encounter. The terms "physical rhythm," "emotional rhythm," and "event rhythm" are used as ways of describing kinds of rhythm and some of the approaches that editors might take to work with them.

Finally, *Cutting Rhythms* offers a series of chapters that address particular editing issues and opportunities. It starts with a chapter on style, looking at the kinds of decisions an editor makes about thematic montage, continuity cutting, collision, and linkage when establishing and sustaining a style. Chapter 10 looks at parallel action, slow motion, and fast motion—things an editor can use to vary the rhythmic texture of a film—how they work best and when they descend into cliché. Chapter 11 looks at one of the editor's most complex issues and opportunities—collaboration—and playfully describes the intuitive process of collaborating with directors as a "Vulcan Mind Meld." The book ends with a new idea being developed for the new filmmaking processes that we are being offered by low-cost digital technology. It proposes that we can use a process of "onscreen drafting" to bring an editor's unique and intuitive "editing thinking" into the filmmaking process much sooner, for much better results.

Cutting Rhythms is written to address editors and filmmakers who are learning their craft and more experienced practitioners who find their work benefits from discussion of their craft. Knowledge about rhythm helps students and editors to shape rhythms and maximize their material's rhythmic potential. It is also relevant to the screen studies scholar who is interested in the connection of theoretical ideas to practical methods and outcomes. Its purpose is to stimulate ways of thinking and talking about rhythm in film and to understand and deepen rhythmic creativity.

METHODOLOGY: THEORY

A survey of recent literature about editing[1] shows that the question of rhythm in film editing is rarely addressed as a topic in and of itself. One notable exception is the work by Theo van Leeuwen, who notes in the introduction to *Rhythmic Structure of the Film Text* that:

> There was a time when few works of film theory failed to address the role of rhythm in film . . . More recently the study of rhythm in film has been all but abandoned. Since the publication of Mitry's *Esthetique et*

Psychologie du Cinema (1963) little if any original thought has been contributed to the subject.[2]

Handbooks on editing craft sometimes supply rules about the rhythm-making tools of timing and pacing. These books and interviews with editors may also provide examples of rhythms from specific films, but say that there are no rules for editing rhythms and do not offer any substantial definitions of rhythmic creativity in film editing.

In his book *The Technique of Film and Video Editing: Theory and Practice*, Ken Dancyger describes rhythm as part of pace, and says, "The rhythm of a film seems to be an individual and intuitive matter."[3] *The Technique of Film Editing*, by Karel Reisz and Gavin Millar, positions rhythm as an attribute of timing.[4] In *Film Art*, Bordwell and Thompson describe a number of attributes of rhythm in their discussion of the "Rhythmic Relations between shot A and shot B,"[5] but most of them are subsumed under the operations I will call pacing as in frequency of cuts. Bordwell and Thompson preface their remarks by saying that "cinematic rhythm as a whole derives not only from editing but from other film techniques as well." Unlike their discussion, mine is an effort to consider cinematic rhythm as a whole inasmuch as the editor devises its final shape and form. In other words, although I am focused exclusively on editing operations, my question concerns their impact on the larger aspects of cinematic rhythm that they shape. I will define, therefore, a number of considerations the editor has in the affective shaping of cinematic rhythm, and frequency of cuts is only one of those operations.

Don Fairservice, author of *Film Editing: History, Theory and Practice*, gives a summary view of the literature available on rhythm in film editing when he says:

> Any discussion about film editing will inevitably sooner or later raise the matter of rhythm. It tends to be used rather as a compendium word, a sort of catch-all which tends to obscure as much as it reveals about something that is difficult to define.[6]

Cutting Rhythms avoids putting forward any rules about rhythm or creativity in rhythm. Instead, it articulates some principles of rhythm in film editing as questions that editors, filmmakers, or film studies scholars can ask themselves and of their material in order to expand the scope and sensitivity of their rhythmic intuition. This approach, to articulate questions that editors can ask themselves or ask about their material, is a way of tying theory to the more pragmatic and pressured moments of practice. When working on a film, and someone in the edit suite says "it isn't right," "it doesn't feel right," or "the rhythm is off," ideas about rhythm may present possibilities an editor can consider for herself to make it "right."

Given this practical, craft-based purpose and my interest in connecting theory to practice, I have chosen, primarily, a cognitive approach to my discussion of the properties and processes involved in working with rhythm in film editing.

Cognitivists consider the physiological makeup of humans when they are studying how we understand and are affected by something like film. The underlying principle is that there are certain things hardwired into all human beings, things that are part of our makeup before we are shaped by our particular moment in time or upbringing, such as "the assumption of a three dimensional environment, the assumption that natural light falls from above, and so forth. These contingent universals make possible artistic conventions which seem natural because they accord with norms of human perception."[7]

These assumptions are present in most editing practice—we do not spend our time in the editing suite wondering about the nature of being or the universe; rather, we are trying to shape an experience that resonates with the knowledge and beliefs many people hold. The ability to tap into those aspects of human experience that are physiological or deeply ingrained in perception and knowledge is an asset in trying to create resonant stories or experiences. So the discussions between working collaborators about a film project are generally grounded in this cognitive approach, and the cognitive approach will be used as a practical basis from which to work with the vocabulary in the filmmaking process in order to expand and refine it.

In particular, this book seeks to understand rhythm in film editing and the process of creating rhythm "through the physiological and cognitive systems 'hardwired' into all human beings."[8] *Cutting Rhythms* makes numerous references to "physical thinking." By taking this approach, I follow, to some extent, the great Soviet director and montage theorist Sergei Eisenstein, who believed that "in its fullest manifestation, cognition becomes kinaesthetic."[9] In other words, deep knowledge is not just something you know, but something you are and you feel. In saying that the mind is physical and the body thinks, I am not making any comment about what else the mind may be, if anything. There is no revelation about consciousness or Consciousness, and no material versus extra-material value judgment implied. I don't know what else the mind may be, or how else it may function, and I do not intend to address that question. My ideas rely on the evidence that the mind is a physiological entity as well as, despite, without regard for, and without implication of, anything else it may or may not be. And given that the mind is physical and the body thinks, I am developing an idea about cutting rhythms that looks at the way an editor shapes the flow of a film as a unified action of mind, emotion, and body.

The cognitive approach is effective in making my arguments accessible to practitioners; however, there is an anomaly in this approach for my particular topic. The study of rhythm is a study of something that is not, or is not primarily, apprehended cognitively. Dictionary definitions of the word "rhythm" frequently emphasize that "rhythm is a *felt* phenomenon."[10] This quality of being felt and created through feeling is a substantial thread in my overall inquiry. It is this quality that causes rhythmic creativity to be characterized as subjective and ineffable in writings on the craft of editing. It is also this quality that finds expansive, sympathetic discussion in the phenomenological and Deleuzian approaches to the study of cinema. For more information on this approach to understanding film, readers may find it interesting to go directly to the source and read Deleuze, *Cinema 2: The Time Image*, in which they will find a discussion of "the sensory (visual and sound), kinetic, intensive, affective, rhythmic" from another perspective.[11]

However, through an analysis of the shaping of "the sensory (visual and sound), kinetic, intensive, affective" into rhythms through various procedures and for particular purposes, *Cutting Rhythms* makes the case that, although rhythm is a felt phenomenon, it is not *just* felt. Creativity in rhythm and spectators' expectations about rhythm are also learned, and the process of creating and learning rhythms can be described.

Cutting Rhythms draws on recent discoveries in neuroscience to explain the actual physical processes of experiencing and creating rhythm. In particular, it draws on ideas about the functioning of mirror neurons in the recognition of intentional movement. By describing the processes through which the brain apprehends rhythm and phenomenological theories of the ways that living bodies have kinaesthetic empathy with movement they perceive, *Cutting Rhythms* develops a model of a thinking body, a body that gathers, stores, and retrieves information about rhythm and uses it strategically—in other words, a body that thinks, but does so primarily through a directly physical, experiential process.

I make use of work by the philosophers, scientists, and various scholars, However, my objective is not to "create new concepts" or to "alter our modes of thinking about time and movement,"[12] but to engage in what Bordwell and Carroll describe as "problem driven research."[13] The problem is to find a way to describe the materials, processes, and purposes of rhythm and modes of physically thinking about rhythm so that rhythmic creativity in film editing can be understood and extended.

METHODOLOGY: PRACTICE

A substantial portion of my research into rhythm is necessarily practical. I have edited a number of short dramas, short and longer form documentaries, and the occasional educational or promotional video. Each of these has provided insights into the editing process. I have made observations and notes about each project I've worked on, so all of them have had an impact, in some way, on this book. By integrating theory with practice, testing my own and others' ideas against the practical experience of cutting to discover and articulate knowledge about rhythm, my intention has been to produce a set of ideas that are useful to practitioners and that may also provide useful ideas for other inquiries.

ENDNOTES

1. In *Editing: The Art of the Expressive,* Valerie Orpen discusses various kinds of books available on editing, saying, "The existing literature on editing can be divided into three categories: textbooks or general studies on film, either solely on editing or with a section on editing; editor's handbooks; and interviews with editors, which include autobiographies, transcripts of lectures, essays, anthologies of interviews and individual interviews in periodicals." See Orpen, V., *Film Editing: The Art of the Expressive,* p. 10. My literature survey includes texts in all three categories.

2. Van Leeuwen, T., "Rhythmic structure of the film text," in *Discourse and Communication: New Approaches to Analysis of Mass Media Discourse and Communication,* p. 216.

3. Dancyger, K., *The Technique of Film and Video Editing: Theory and Practice,* pp. 307–315.

4. Reisz, K., and Millar, G., *The Technique of Film Editing,* pp. 246–247.

5. Bordwell, D., and Thompson, K., *Film Art: An Introduction,* pp. 278–280

6. Fairservice, D., *Film Editing: History, Theory and Practice,* p. 273.

7. Bordwell, D., and Carroll, N., *Post-Theory: Reconstructing Film Studies,* p. xvi.

8. Stam, R., *Film Theory: An Introduction,* p. 236.

9. Bordwell, D., *The Cinema of Eisenstein,* p. 125.

10. Brogan, T.V.F., "Rhythm," in *The Princeton Encyclopedia of Poetry and Poetics,* p. 1068.

11. Deleuze, G., *Cinema 2: The Time Image,* p. 29.

12. Wartenburg, T.E., and Curran, A., *The Philosophy of Film: Introductory Text and Readings,* p. 7.

13. Bordwell, D., and Carroll, N., *Post-Theory: Reconstructing Film Studies,* p. xvii.

CHAPTER 1

Rhythmic Intuition

How does an editor make decisions about where and when to cut in order to shape the rhythm of a film?

When asked, most editors will say something along the lines of "by intuition" or "you just know when it's right." For example, in *First Cut, Conversations with Film Editors* by Gabriella Oldham, editors are quoted talking about rhythm and editing as "magic" (Sheldon Kahn), "feels right" (Carl Kress), "it's intuitive" (Bill Pankow), "it's intuition" (Paul Hirsch), "having a sense" (Donn Cambern), "you just know" (Sidney Levin), "exclusively in the realm of intuition" (Merle Worth), "an internal sense" (Richard Marks), and "we go by intuition" (Alan Heim).[1] These are extraordinary editors, and there is no question they are right: editing, especially the shaping of rhythm in editing, is highly intuitive.

But is there anything else that can be said? Anything that can provide an idea of what this kind of intuition really is and how it can be developed? This chapter aims to paint a picture of what an editor's intuition may be and how it can be developed.

But first it is important to dispel some myths about the dangers of discussing intuition.

Many people, especially editors, shy away from speaking about things they consider to be "intuitive." The fear is that analyzing intuition will disrupt it. Since no creative person wants their intuition disrupted, it is important to separate out talking about intuition and engaging in an intuitive practice. They can both happen, they just can't happen at the same time, because trying to break down and observe an action at the same moment as doing it causes the brain's attention to be split and diffused. Doing and analyzing at the same time disrupts the action. Or the analysis. Or both.

Neurologist Richard Restak explains:

> In terms of brain performance, "just doing it" involves the smooth non-self-conscious transfer of learned actions from working memory, stored in frontal lobes, to the pre-motor and motor areas that transform the working memory into those effective, winning plays that result from thousands of hours of practice . . .[2]

This doesn't mean we can't develop an understanding of what intuition is and how it can be strengthened, in fact quite the opposite. We need to understand the kinds of knowledge and support the brain needs to be able to do an action "unselfconsciously." Our intuition can be developed, strengthened, and enhanced by all kinds of knowledge, as long as the process of consciously acquiring knowledge is at a different time, in a different place, or as a different action from the expert execution of a task that intuition supports.

Intuition is not the same as instinct. People are born with instincts, but intuition is something we develop over time, through experience. In other words, it is learned. Scientists, educators, and even artists are clear: the knowledge and analysis that underpins expert action has to be gathered. Explicit knowledge is an essential support to intuition. It is the learned knowledge that gets transferred from working memory into intuitive action. The more that is explicitly known, the more readily accessible intuitive responses will be. "Geniuses . . . share a similar talent for storing vast amounts of information in long-term memory and then retrieving the information as circumstances demand."[3]

So, the aim of this chapter is simple: explore what an editor's intuition is, where it comes from, and how it is developed so that it can be accessed when working with the editing strategies and ideas that come up in subsequent chapters.

INTUITIVE THINKING

Six Components of Intuition

Guy Claxton, educator and co-editor of *The Intuitive Practitioner*, articulates six types of things that are at work when we say something is intuitive: expertise, implicit learning, judgment, sensitivity, creativity, and rumination. Each of these things could be at work at any moment that intuition is activated and often in complex combinations. But to pull them apart for a moment and see how they work in the process of editing, I have listed them below, first with Claxton's definition,[4] followed by my thoughts about some of the ways they apply specifically to an editor's intuitive processes.

1. *"Expertise*—the unreflective execution of intricate skilled performance"

   An example of expertise is the way a professional editor with years of experience uses her gear. It's like touch-typing or riding a bicycle; she doesn't have to think about what button to push in order to do an operation, and this frees her concentration to focus on the material she's working with. I call it "breathing with the Avid," but it's not restricted to Avid. It's a matter of knowing your gear of choice so expertly that its operation doesn't require conscious thought.

   Another important instance of expertise is that which arises from years of experience with the editing process. Editors often say that each new project is like learning to edit all over again, and in my experience this is an accurate description of what it feels like. However, after accruing a degree of experience in shaping a story or scene, an editor becomes expert, in the sense that she can see a possible organization or flow very quickly and without conscious thought. Note, however, that there is practice and learning at work in acquiring this expertise that, just like learning the gear, can be made explicit. Later chapters in this book break down some of that learning into principles and tasks that can be practiced.

2. *"Implicit learning*—the acquisition of such expertise by non-conscious or non-conceptual means"

A lot of implicit learning about editing is acquired by watching films. There are conventions of filmmaking that show up in most TV programs, ads, and movies. An editor may not know the names of these conventions or techniques but has seen them enough to know what they are without ever having consciously learned them.

An editor also accrues a substantial amount of implicit learning about the world through observation and participation in the movement and rhythms of the world. This is something that all humans do, of course, but as will be discussed below, doing it mindfully is a useful tool for enhancing an editor's rhythmic intuition.

3. *"Judgment*—making accurate decisions and categorizations without, at the time, being able to justify them"

Judgment can be seen at work whenever an editor makes an adjustment to a cut and it works better. Once the "working better" is visible, an editor is rarely called upon to explain why or how. In fact, there are reasons why something works better that can be articulated, but the use of judgment implies making good decisions without going through the process of justifying them. Judgment is, however, acquired by having a thorough understanding of the material, the story, the conditions, and the traditions within which you are working. The capacity to make judgments is a good example of something no one is born with, but which can be enhanced and developed through explicit teaching and learning.

4. "*Sensitivity*—a heightened attentiveness, both conscious and non-conscious, to details of a situation"

   An editor has sensitivity or heightened attentiveness to movement and emotion in the material. Developing sensitivity is a matter of learning to see the potential of movements and moments before they are shaped—a subject that will be taken up at length in this book!

5. "*Creativity*—the use of incubation and reverie to enhance problem solving"

   Creativity is a complex and much discussed notion, sometimes understood to mean generating new ideas or concepts, but just as often considered to be the process of making new associations or links, which, of course, is exactly what an editor does. Editing creativity is the lateral association of images or sounds to solve the problem at hand, which is the shaping of the film and its rhythms. The editor's reveries yield connections between images, sounds, and movements in the raw material, which will create new and coherent meanings. Practice, and trial and error, informs these reveries, of course, but also the editor's acquired knowledge of the world, herself, and her sensitivity to movement and emotion give her the basis from which to make creative connections and associations.

6. "*Rumination*—the process of 'chewing the cud' of experience in order to extract its meanings and its implications"

   Rumination is what is at work when you are washing the dishes and suddenly the solution to an intractable sequence is clear to you. It is the kind of thinking that happens when you're thinking about something else, and you have immersed yourself so deeply in your material that it inhabits a part of your brain even when you're not actually looking at it or working on it. Rumination is what happens on the weekend or while you're making a cup of tea and can yield some of your best solutions and ideas, which is why healthy work/rest cycles are so important to editing: they enhance your intuition!

Looking at intuition as these six types of thinking clearly demonstrates that intuitive thinking need not draw a protective veil around itself. The ecology of mind that allows these kinds of thinking to flourish is nourished by explicit acquisition of skills and knowledge. In short, intuition isn't something you just have. It is something that can be developed, enhanced, and even acquired through practical and theoretical experience and education. The question implied by Claxton's list is this: Where, specifically, does the experience and education of rhythm, which editors use as fodder for their intuition, come from?

MOVEMENT AND INTUITION

The editor's intuitive thinking is based in movement: movement of story, movement of emotion, movement of image and sound. The rest of this book will develop ideas about shaping rhythm by shaping movement. Chapter 2 will look at how choreographers do it. Chapter 3 will unpack the specific tools of timing, pacing, and trajectory phrasing of movement. Chapter 4 is about the tension and release of movement. Chapters 5, 6, 7, and 8 break it down into physical, emotional, and event movement, and then put it back together again. This book is all about movement, and the rest of Chapter 1 is about why movement isn't just what an editor thinks about, it is how an editor thinks.

Here is how the argument will go:

1. Editors shape movement. Physics, filmmakers, and philosophers all weigh in here to say that movement is what we perceive and what we are.

2. Editors' brains are especially tuned to movement. We use kinaesthetic empathy and mirror neurons to understand movement's expressive potential. (These terms will be unpacked below.)

3. Editors respond with their own internal sense of movement to the movement they see and hear. Or as Dany Cooper, ASE, multi award winning editor and former President of the Australian Screen Editor's Guild says: "It's a body thing."[5]

RHYTHM IS MADE OF MOVEMENT

The universe is rhythmic at a physical, material level. Seasons, tides, days, months, years, and the movement of the stars are all examples of universal rhythms, and our survival depends on us oscillating with these rhythms and functioning as part of a rhythmic environment.

Waking/sleeping, eating/digesting, working/resting, and inhaling/exhaling are just some of living beings' ways of following the rhythms of the world, of surviving by oscillating or moving with the rhythms of their physical world.

Going beyond rhythmic survival and into rhythmic creativity is partly a matter of developing awareness of rhythm. If we actively see and hear and feel the world's rhythms, what we are actually seeing, hearing, and feeling is *movement*. Movement happens in time, and it is impelled by energy, but we can't see time and energy. We see movement and use it to understand time and energy. Russian filmmaker Andrey Tarkovsky uses the metaphor of a reed quivering to describe the way that movement shows us time and energy in life and in film:

> Cinema . . . is able to record time in outward and visible signs, recognizable to the feelings . . . Rhythm in cinema is conveyed by the life of the object visibly recorded in the frame. Just as from the quivering of a reed you can tell what sort of current, what pressure

there is in a river, in the same way we know the movement of time from the flow of the life-process reproduced in the shot.[6]

When Tarkovsky writes, "we know the movement of time from the flow of the life-process," he describes movement as the means by which we perceive life's time and energy.

NOTICING MOVEMENT AS RHYTHM

As living beings, editors inherently have knowledge of rhythms of the world. However, it is also possible for us to develop and enhance our rhythmic intuition by engaging an *active* or *mindful* awareness of rhythms of the world. For example, almost every one of the twenty-three distinguished editors interviewed in *First Cut, Conversations with Film Editors* mentions music, their love of music, or their musical training.[7] These editors' experience of music, their awareness of rhythm in the movement of sound has been specifically and consciously activated. This activation educates their intuition about rhythms more generally—in life and in film. It may even cause them to perceive rhythms in the world around them quite actively, to become consciously aware of the rhythms with which people walk and talk, with which nature ebbs and flows. Music is an intentionally formed instance of rhythm, but knowledge of music has developed these editors' capacity to perceive any rhythm.

I have also heard editors speak about surfing, rowing, dancing, painting, and cooking as experiences of rhythm that help them to develop their rhythmic intuition. These editors draw on their direct experiences of the movement of these rhythms to accrue a cache of rhythmic knowledge.

FEELING MOVEMENT'S RHYTHMIC POTENTIAL

In the process of shooting a film, a small, specific "world" is created. Watching the uncut material of a project activates the editor's rhythmic intuition about the project and its rhythmical world. The same active

PRACTICAL EXERCISE

Becoming Aware of Rhythms of the World

Becoming aware of the rhythms of the world is a way of adding to your rhythmic knowledge. We all behave rhythmically all of the time—how else would we avoid being hit by cars, for example, if we didn't judge their speed and our trajectory in relation to their speed? By recognizing our everyday lives as rhythmic entities, we can refine our sense of the rhythms of the world from rhythmic survival into rhythmic creativity.

Choose something that you do often, something physical that you do without thinking about it, something that is not dangerous; for example, brushing your teeth or locking and leaving the car once you've parked it. As you go through the motions of this activity, notice the speed of movements relative to each other, the efforts, the sounds, the emphasis points or punctuation points in gestures and actions, and particularly their relationship to one another. You could map this flow with a line drawing of accents, or hum it to yourself, or just see it in your mind's eye as a flow of energy, directions, and actions.

When I pull into the garage at night I do a very polished rhythmic routine, and I do it without conscious thought—but it is not instinctive; I have trained myself to do it. It goes: ignition off, key out, parking brake on, seatbelt click, door open, relock door, keys into bag, and slam. Each of these actions has duration, a sound, an amount of effort required (mostly very small!), and together they make a rhythm, a flow, a pattern with lulls and accents. This is a rhythm of the world, one of thousands, that informs my sense of what feels right as far as duration, emphasis, and rate of movement are concerned.

Do this exercise only outside of the cutting room, where analysis won't disrupt action. The objective is to develop a heightened sense of rhythms of the world, happening and intersecting all around you, all of the time. Later, in the cutting room, this sense will support and inform intuition or the "unreflective execution of intricate skilled performance."[8]

awareness that editors use to accumulate a rhythmic sense of the larger world is employed, but now in a very specifically directed way, to accumulate information about rhythms in the rushes or dailies.

The editor finds specific cues to rhythmic possibilities in the uncut material, in the movement inherent in the recorded images and sounds. This may be movement of the frame, movement within the frame, or movement of the eye around the frame. And, as will be discussed in greater detail later, it may also be movement of events or emotions. The editor who tunes her awareness to movement in the rushes or dailies—its pulse, effort, speed, shape, size, causes, purposes, and so forth—gathers information about the rhythmic potential of the film.

Movement is what we perceive, what we are, and what we shape into a film's rhythm. If willing to accept that premise, it is possible to skip now to other chapters to find principles and processes for shaping movement into affective rhythms. If curious about the brain and body and why movement is so important to intuitive rhythmic thinking, the next section is all about this phenomenon.

EMPATHY WITH MOVEMENT: EXPERIENCE, BODY, AND BRAIN

This section will look briefly at body and brain responses to movement that editors are using when they cut "intuitively."

Kinaesthetic Empathy

"Kinaesthetic empathy" is a term often used to talk about dance. It suggests that what we are doing when we watch dance is empathizing with the movement we see. We are experiencing a feeling for the dance in our own bodies, a kind of "inner mimesis."[9] As we'll see below, in the discussion of mirror neurons, this is literally how we process movement at a neurological level, by mirroring it. But first some explanation of what kinaesthetic empathy is as an experience and how we develop it throughout our lives.

- *Kinaesthetic*: the esthetic emotion or sensation connected with kine.

- *Kine:* Greek for move, or set in motion, it is also the root word of "cinema."

- *Empathy:* feeling with, or sharing another person's feeling.

So kinaesthetic empathy is feeling *with* movement.

Kinaesthetic empathy is a sensitivity all people develop to a greater or lesser extent. We can't help learning what movement feels like and empathizing when we see or hear movement because life is movement, change is movement, we are movement ourselves.

Neuropsychologist Arnold Modell describes it this way: "The perception of feelings relies on the corporeal imagination, which in turn is determined by the history of the self."[10] In other words, our own bodies' history of movement allows us to imagine what movement feels like when we see or hear movement of other bodies. Modell's phrase "corporeal imagination" suggests that the body not only thinks, it imagines, in this case imagining how another body feels. And it imagines in relation to its own experience, drawing on remembered sensations to recognize feeling in movement.

Our physical response to movement is based on direct or indirect experience of movement, the history of our individual bodies in movement, and physically innate reflexes connected to movement. In other words, even if we ourselves have not moved in a particular way, for example, if we have not fallen in a fast, straight, hurtling trajectory, our bodies know to duck if something comes hurtling at them, just as they know to brace for impact if they themselves are falling. We know the laws of physics in our bodies because we live them. So, movement speeds, directions, and energies have meaning when we see them, even if we have not experienced them.

The ways that editors use kinaesthetic empathy to shape movement in films include:

1. first experiencing and empathizing with the movement they see in the uncut material;

2. then identifying the movement or moments in that material that evokes the most appropriate sensation or emotion;

3. then trimming and connecting that movement or moment with others to create a coherent flow of movement, a coherent experience of kinaesthetic empathy for the audience.

In other words: an editor makes the movement of a film feel right by using their own capacity to feel with movement. And given that the editor's capacity to feel with movement is accrued through lived experience, there is no reason why an editor could not choose to heighten their own ability to shape movement by increasing the experience of kinaesthetic empathy.

Mirror Neurons

When movement is intentional, our responsive attention to its rhythms is augmented by a special feature of our advanced brains: mirror neurons. Mirror neurons are explained in layperson's terms by neurologist Richard Restak:

> Neuroscientists have recently discovered the existence of "mirror neurons" in the brains of monkeys that discharge both when the monkey performs certain movements and when the animal merely observes another monkey performing the movement. Strong evidence suggests a similar mirroring process in humans—certain nerve cells are activated both during an activity and while observing another person performing the activity . . . the brain is a powerful simulating machine designed to detect and respond to a wide range of intentions on the part of other people. Neuroscientists are further exploring how our observations of another person's behavior allow us to infer his or her conscious or even unconscious intentions.[11]

This breakthrough discovery of mirror neurons by neuroscientists accounts for empathetic engagement with intentional movement. Neurologically speaking, we physically participate in the movement of people we see, even if we are sitting still. Moving with intention lights up certain neurons in our brains, and watching someone do the same movement lights up the same neurons.[12] So, watching movement really is a physical thing; it is a special brain process that interacts differently with differently intended movements. Scientist V. S. Ramachandran writes:

> With knowledge of these neurons, you have the basis for understanding a host of very enigmatic aspects of the human mind: "mind-reading" empathy, imitation, learning and even the evolution of language. Anytime you watch someone else doing something (or even starting to do something) the corresponding mirror neurons might fire in your brain, thereby allowing you to "read" and understand another's intentions, and thus to develop a sophisticated "theory of other minds."[13]

One of the ways the editor knows how to cut rhythm is through her mirror neurons. Mirror neurons allow us to participate in another person's intentional movements. Our neurons do the movement with them, whether they are live or on the movie screen.

So, what an editor may be doing in making rhythm in moving pictures is engaging her corporeal memory and/or mirroring, neurologically, parts of what she sees and hears. Some part of what she sees or hears in the movement of the rushes will light up the editor's mirror neurons or her kinaesthetic memory, and that part will be selected and juxtaposed with another part that also lights up her lights, so to speak.

PRACTICAL EXERCISE

Mirroring Intentions

The purpose of this exercise is to recognize how much you already know about movement, emphasis, energy, and intention.

Sit in a café and observe a conversation between two people—observe, but don't listen in. You don't want to know what the conversation is actually about, you just want to become aware of how much you know by seeing movement dynamics rather than hearing dialog. Watch the movements of your subjects' heads, eyes, posture, and hands, and notice how much you know about their intentions just by their body language. You know, for example, when one person leans forward whether they are leaning forward conspiratorially or aggressively. And you know, just by watching the energy and quality of movement, whether the other person is delighted (leaning in to catch the gossip) or ambivalent (shifting to one side, looking away) or scared (leaning back warily).

The people you are watching may not lean forward and back but they will, without fail, use their hands, eyes, posture, speed, and attack on movement to express things—things they themselves may not even be aware of. Furthermore, they will also read each other's intentions and respond through movement. If one leans forward aggressively and the other leans back warily, the first person will, consciously or unconsciously, make a decision to pursue (lean farther forward) or retreat (relax, back off, withdraw . . .). The decisions made and expressed in movement are arrived at through interpretation of the information being provided by mirror neurons, by the neurological readings of each other's intentions as expressed in movement.

Observing the conversation from the outside, you are not called upon to make decisions about how to respond, but your mirror neurons are activated just by watching the two people move. You know what they mean because you yourself have done similar movements, and your neurons recognize the intentions that drive those movements. If you were constructing the same conversation from a number of available takes in the editing suite, you would be making decisions about which nuances of the movement to emphasize and which to elide to create a rhythm that feels right. The intuition about what feels right, and what doesn't, comes, in part, from mirror neurons doing their work of interpreting intentions in movement. The shaping of the flow of these movements is the editor's work of creating the appropriate interchange for a given moment in a film.

Putting two shots together, each of which inherently has rhythm, makes a third rhythm, which is not the same, or even just the sum of the first two. So the edit begins to have a rhythm of its own. At this point the editor cannot simply recognize a "right" rhythm. Her own internal rhythms must come into play to shape rhythm through an editing process. As editors begin to do more than neurologically imitate existing rhythms, we draw on rhythms inside ourselves, *as well as* those things captured in the rushes, to create the film's rhythm.

BEING RHYTHM AND THINKING RHYTHMICALLY

So far this chapter has proposed that movement is what we shape into a film's rhythm, and that we develop knowledge or intuition about shaping movement through our kinaesthetic empathy and mirror neurons. Building on those ideas, the final section of this chapter looks at how the editor's living, breathing body is influential on the shaping of a film's rhythm.

Roland Barthes' discussion of playing music in his essay "Musica Practica" could also be a description of the way in which the editor's body participates in the creation of rhythms: "the body controls, conducts, coordinates, having itself to transcribe what it reads, making sound and meaning, the body as inscriber and not just transmitter, simple receiver."[14]

The musician's, or in this case the editor's, physical presence and physical engagement with the material becomes part of the creative process. Her own rhythm of blinking, breathing, heartbeat, synapses firing, as well as the rhythm of her cycles of sleeping, eating, thinking, and feeling, shape the film's rhythm.

Thinking rhythmically is what I will call the intersection of the rhythms of the world and the rhythms of the editor's body with the editor's craft skills. The three—the world, the body, and the craft— are deeply entwined. The entwining occurs while learning to edit.

FIGURE 1.1

In this scene from Quentin Tarantino's film Pulp Fiction *(1994), Tim Roth's character Ringo is trying to convince Yolanda (Amanda Plummer) to do something. In the first image (a) he is leaning forward, arms open to her in a gesture that reads as sincere, serious, and intent. She is focused on him, but her arms are clenched close to her body, shoulders slightly hunched, and face turned very slightly to the side so that she would have to look at him out of the corner of her eye. Her posture in relation to his is protective, maybe unwilling or skeptical. In the next image (b) Ringo looks as though he is about to jump out of his seat with vehemence. Yolanda has opened her arms and is leaning farther forward, looking straight at him; in other words, she has physically and psychologically opened up to his plan and is moving toward it. Even without hearing the dialog, we know what these characters mean because we recognize the intention in their movement. [Photo credit: Miramax/Buena Vista; The Kobal Collection; Linda R. Chen]*

During this process the body develops a new rhythm, a rhythm of editing as physical movement and work.

Also during this process some of the editor's significant neural mirroring patterns are formed. To quote Walter Murch on learning rhythms from working closely with other editors: "You pick up the good things that other editors are doing and you metabolize those approaches into what you're doing, and vice versa."[15]

Murch describes a process of embodied learning. The picking up of good things is "metabolizing" i.e., taking the crafting knowledge into your body. In Murch's description of learning from other editors, the rhythms of the world and the rhythms of the body become entwined with the skills of editing.

Murch also talks about blinking and tuning oneself to the rhythm of the filmed material:

> One of your tasks as an editor is sensitizing yourself to the rhythms that the (good) actor gives you, and then finding ways to extend these rhythms into territory not covered by the actor, so that the pacing of the film as a whole is an elaboration of those patterns of thinking and feeling. And one of the many ways you assume those rhythms is by noticing—consciously or unconsciously—where the actor blinks.[16]

I propose that an editor doesn't just notice where the actor blinks, she imitates it. This might mean that the editor literally imitates it, or at least tries to, by syncing up her own blinking rhythm with that of the actor and making a cut. Then, in playing back that cut, if the rhythm of her own blinks and the rhythm of the actor's blinks don't sync up, perhaps the rhythm of the film doesn't "feel right." So, the editor will have a look, adjust the cut, and then try re-syncing her rhythm to the rhythm in the material she has just cut into place. The editor needn't literally blink with the actors (although some do), her mirror neurons imitate the blinks. They mirror the movement of the actor, and perhaps, on the first rough assembly, the blinks fail to light up all the mirror neurons they could. In which case, the cut gets adjusted. The rhythmic material (blinks in this case) and our rhythmic bodies both have a shaping influence on the rhythm of the film.

In his essay "Acting and Breathing" Ross Gibson picks up on Murch's ideas about blinking and extends them into a discussion of performer's breath rhythms:

> When we watch a body in performance, we watch its breathing, and most crucially we also imbibe its breathing. Performers with strong presence can get us breathing (and blinking also) in synch with them. As we experience the patterns of their corporeal existence, we also get gleamings (*sic*) of their thoughts and feelings—we get these gleamings in our bodies, nervously, optically, and cardio-vascularly . . . we feel ourselves occupied and altered by the bodily rhythms of another.[17]

Gibson is writing about live performance at this point in the essay, but the same "imbibing" of breath can take place in the cinema. The difference is that in cinema the actor's breath rhythms have passed through the hands, or perhaps the lungs, of the editor.[18] Gibson goes on to write about being physically and emotionally moved by a performance:

> By blinking and breathing in synch with the performer, you can feel the actor representing you in the world of the drama. And through the proxy of the actor . . . you can feel the imaginary world course through you. Your representative breathes you and blinks you and thereby helps you imagine experiences other than your own.[19]

Before the spectator can have this wonderful experience of blinking and breathing with the performer in the cinema, the editor has to do it. She has to use her own physical presence as a stand-in for the spectator's and measure the rhythms of the film's breath by comparing it with the feeling of her own breathing. To do so, the editor has to imbibe the breath first. Then she deploys her rhythmic intuition: the rhythms she experiences in the world and in the filmed material pass through the rhythms of her own body, her own breathing and blinking.

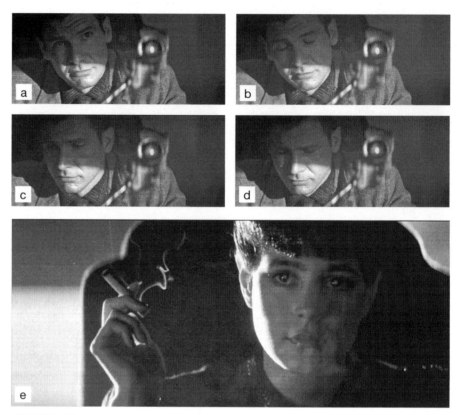

FIGURE 1.2

In this scene from Blade Runner (Ridley Scott, 1988) Deckard (Harrison Ford) puts Rachael (Sean Young) through a test to determine whether she is a human or a "replicant." The test measures her eye movement as a way of determining her thoughts. So the scene, in a sense, illustrates Murch's premise about blinking revealing thinking. Interestingly, Harrison Ford blinks fairly often in this scene, shifting his thoughts and focus from himself to his job, to his subject, to his concerns about the whole operation, and so on. Sean Young blinks not at all, an impenetrable presence, until, toward the end, when she becomes confused and flustered by the test results, she uncharacteristically blinks three or four times in one shot. [Photo credit: Warner Bros]

To take this idea one step further, Murch's ideas about blinking and Gibson's about breathing can be extended to take the actor's whole body and the whole of the mise-en-scene into account. Everything in the film that moves has some resonances with the editor's kinaesthetic empathy or mirror neurons. As an editor, my body tenses and relaxes responsively to what I see because my kinaesthetic empathy and

FIGURE 1.3

In this scene from American Beauty *(Sam Mendes, 1999) there is a quartet of breath rhythms carried on the voices of the four actors, each of whom has a different pattern and different state of mind and different objective. But the scene is unmistakably driven by the breathing of Lester (Kevin Spacey), who is overwhelmed by desire for his daughter's friend, Angela (Mena Suvari). Each of his utterances is borne on a particular breath expressing his desire, and each of his exhalations and inhalations adds to the sense of his purpose and intent. The other three characters each respond: Lester's wife (Annette Bening), with a chirpy, high-pitched insistence that glosses over everything; Janie (Thora Birch), with a strangled breath and sound that barely escapes through gritted teeth; and Angela, with an easy poise, a breath rhythm that promises much but gives little away. [Photo credit: DreamWorks/Jinks/Cohen; The Kobal Collection]*

mirror neurons are activated by all of the sources of movement on the screen. If I can tune to these physical responses to what I see and hear, then I can use them to make the rhythm feel right.

In this case, the method editors use for constructing a rhythm is this: we feel our way through a shot, a performance, a scene, and the whole film. We tune our awareness of the movements in the film to the rhythms of our own bodies. Some even hear the film's movement as a song in their heads. Others sway, shrug, nod, or squint with the energies made visible by movement passing before their eyes. Maybe something is off. The sigh of the actor doesn't feel long enough—literally. I know because I can feel his sigh in my body.

Because the editor is conducting rhythms of the whole world of the rushes, Murch suggests "sensitizing yourself to the rhythms that the (good) actor gives you, and then finding ways to extend these rhythms into territory not covered by the actor."[20] The editor uses her empathetic intuition to make decisions about when and where to cut the performance to shape its rhythms. During this process a rhythm of the film begins to take shape in the rushes, and in the editor there awakens a physical experience of this nascent rhythm. This physical experience is used to map the rhythms in the film where the actor is not present, to give the story, emotions, and images and sounds a coherent rhythm of their own.

SUMMARY

Intuition in editing includes creativity, expert judgment, sensitivity, and "unreflective execution of intricate skilled performance."[21] It also includes activation of implicit learning, (which is learning acquired through non-conscious means). The learning that supports intuition about rhythm in film editing is acquired through living in a rhythmic body and in a rhythmic universe. However, although this learning *is* implicit in being alive, it is not necessarily *only* implicit. Just as Murch suggests that we can sensitize ourselves to the rhythms a good actor provides, we can also sensitize ourselves to the rhythms of the world and of the body to expand and enhance our intuitions about cutting rhythms.

ENDNOTES

1. Oldham, G., *First Cut: Conversations with Film Editors*, p. 27 ("magic," Sheldon Kahn), p. 91 ("feels right," Carl Kress), p. 177 ("it's intuitive," Bill Pankow), p. 194 ("it's intuition," Paul Hirsch), p. 209 ("having a sense," Donn Cambern), p. 301 ("you just know," Sidney Levin), p. 320 ("exclusively in the

realm of intuition," Merle Worth), p. 372 ("an internal sense," Richard Marks), p. 381 ("we go by intuition," Alan Heim).

2. Restak, R., *The New Brain,* p. 22.

3. Ibid.

4. Claxton, G., "The anatomy of intuition," in *The Intuitive Practitioner,* p. 40.

5. Rowe, C., "Dany Cooper interview," *Inside Film Magazine,* p. 43.

6. Tarkovsky, A., *Sculpting in Time,* pp. 119–120.

7. Oldham, G., *First Cut: Conversations with Film Editors.*

8. Claxton, G., "The anatomy of intuition," in *The Intuitive Practitioner,* p. 40.

9. For more on this, visit www.watchingdance.org.

10. Modell, A.H., *Imagination and the Meaningful Brain,* p. 145

11. Restak, R., *The New Brain,* pp. 35–37.

12. The meaning of "intentional" has significant potential for variation when moving between scientific studies and philosophical studies. As Robert Sokolowski says in *Introduction to Phenomenology,* "The core doctrine of phenomenology is the teaching that every act of consciousness we perform, every experience that we have is intentional: it is essentially 'consciousness of' or an 'experience of' something or other . . . We should note that this sense of 'intend' or 'intention' should not be confused with 'intention' as in purpose we have in mind when we act" (p. 8). In the phenomenological sense, all human movements are intentional. In the "practical" (p. 34) sense of having purpose in mind, not all human movements have intention. The discussions of mirror neurons that I have researched do not specifically address this question of the philosophical versus the practical sense of intention. However, my readings do seem to suggest that any human movement can and will be mirrored by another human. When introducing the topic of mirror neurons, Restak begins by discussing how the brain can distinguish "biologically based movements, such as walking, from random other movements" (Restak, *The New Brain,* p. 34). Walking is an example of a movement that is potentially intentional in either sense. It may be that one walks with a specific intention or desire, or it may be that walking is intentional in the sense that the biological being, who is walking, has consciousness. What is important is that in *either* case, walking is mirrored by the mirror neurons. This book takes the point of view that other human movements, such as breathing and blinking, which may not be intentional in the sense of having a purpose in mind, are still intentional movements that trigger responses from mirror neurons.

13. Ramachandran, V.S., "Mirror neurons and imitation learning as the driving force behind 'the great leap forward' in human evolution."

14. Barthes, R., "Musica Practica," in *Image–Music–Text,* p. 149.

15. Ondaatje, M., *The Conversations: Walter Murch and the Art of Editing Film,* p. 62.

16. Murch, W., *In the Blink of an Eye,* 1992, pp. 62–63.

17. Gibson, R., "Acting and breathing," in *Falling for You: Essays on Cinema and Performance,* p. 39

18. These breath rhythms have also, of course, been considered, shaped, and captured through the rhythms of directing and shooting, passing through the lungs, as it were, of the director, the cinematographer, and the rest of the crew.

19. Gibson, R., "Acting and Breathing," in *Falling for You: Essays on Cinema and Performance,* p. 41–42

20. Murch, W., *In the Blink of an Eye,* 1992, p. 62.

21. Claxton, G., "The anatomy of intuition," in *The Intuitive Practitioner,* p. 40.

CHAPTER 2

Editing As Choreography

Rhythm in film is made from patterns of movement. Movement is what editors mirror neurologically, what activates their kinaesthetic empathy, and what they work with intuitively to shape the film's rhythm. Building on that premise, this chapter compares editing to another art of shaping movement: choreography.

Choreography is the art of manipulating movement: phrasing its time, space, and energy into affective forms and structures. In their work with rhythm, editors do similar things. This chapter compares editing to choreography and uncovers some principles that choreographers use which editors might also find useful in their work.

Before looking at choreography as a source of metaphors about editing, this chapter first pulls apart some more commonly used metaphors for editing, metaphors that compare an editor's craft to composing, conducting, or orchestrating music. One musical idea that does make it through scrutiny is "pulse." Pulse is looked at more broadly though, as something that runs through movement, time, and energy of many things, not just music. The pulse—the smallest expressive unit of the movement of time and energy—is discussed before looking at the choreographic processes of shaping pulses into phrases.

From there, the ways that choreographers construct dance movement phrases are compared to the ways an editor assembles movement into phrases and sequences when creating rhythms, and the questions choreographers can ask when shaping movement are reframed as questions editors can ask when shaping rhythm in film.

SHIFTING THE DISCUSSION FROM MUSIC TO MOVEMENT

Editing is often compared with music making. Many people understand the use of the word "rhythm" in film to be a musical metaphor. The discussion of rhythm in, for example, the 2004 book about the editing craft, *The Eye Is Quicker*, opens with the following quote: "'All art constantly aspires towards the condition of music.'—Walter Pater."[1] Another example is filmmaker Martin Scorsese's quote: "For me the editor is like a musician, and often a composer."[2] And "Eisenstein . . . often makes implicit appeal to musical analogies."[3] Music can be a rich source of language and ideas for the talking about rhythm; but its terms don't exactly match what editors do. This section looks at some of the comparisons of editing to music to see how they might or might not be useful.

Composing

Composing, in general, is more like writing than it is like editing. A composer delineates the form and structure on which the musicians base the performance of their craft. A screenwriter does the same for the cast and crew of a film. The composer makes up the music and its rhythms, whereas an editor doesn't exactly make anything up. Editors compose rhythms in the sense that someone might compose a flower arrangement: not by making the flowers, or in this case the shots, but by choosing the selections, order, and duration of shots.

Orchestrate

The use of the word "orchestrate" comes from the idea that there are many different elements within shots, and between them, that an editor coordinates. These might include performance, composition, texture, color, shape, shot size, movement energy and direction, and many more. Eisenstein called these "attractions," as in the different elements within shots and films that might attract the spectator's attention.[4] Orchestration, in this case, is a metaphor for giving each set of attractions consideration in relation to the others. However, orchestration is *actually* a distribution of parts to various instruments. In shots, framing, design, performance, and lighting have already been orchestrated in relation to each other. Using what Theo Van Leeuwen calls "initiating rhythms" might be more useful for describing what an editor does than orchestrating. Van Leeuwen suggests that there may be, and usually are, a few things attracting the attention in a shot, so that "editors are faced with the problem of synchronizing" the various elements into a coherent rhythmic experience. To do so, the editor chooses one of the lines of movement, energy, or emphasis "as an initiating rhythm and subordinates to this rhythm the other profilmic rhythms."[5] Shaping the flow and emphasis of "initiating rhythms" is a more precise description of the editor's decision-making process than orchestration.

Conducting

Conducting is perhaps the most apt musical metaphor because, like the conductor, the editor decides on the pacing, timing, and emphasis presented in the final composition. However, in music, conducting also suggests that a finished composition has already been submitted to the conductor and he *interprets* it, which is not really what happens in editing.

There is a nonmusical meaning to the word "conducting" that might be more useful for describing what an editor does. This is conducting in the sense of facilitating the flowthrough of rhythm like wires facilitate the flowthrough of electricity or, as filmmaker Andrei Tarkovsky suggests, pipes facilitate the flowthrough of water:

> Time, imprinted in the frame, dictates the particular editing principle; and the pieces that "won't edit"—that can't be properly joined—are those which record a radically different kind of time. One cannot, for

instance, put actual time together with conceptual time, any more than one can join water pipes of different diameter. The consistency of the time that runs through the shot, its intensity or "sloppiness," could be called time pressure: then editing can be seen as the assembly of the pieces on the basis of time pressure within them.[6]

Tarkovsky's comparison of shots to water pipes shifts the conversation about rhythm away from music and toward the more visible *movement* of time "imprinted in the shots." Although Eisenstein and Tarkovsky usually present oppositional ideas about the nature and purpose of the editing process, this shift from music to movement also has precedent in Eisenstein's writing. Eisenstein writes "in rhythmic montage it is movement within the frame that impels the montage movement from frame to frame."[7] Rhythm is not categorically or completely defined by Eisenstein's discussion of "rhythmic montage." However, it does, for our purposes, firmly shift the focus of the discussion of rhythm from music to movement.

The next question, then, is: What can we say about the art of shaping movement that can inform an editor's intuition? For insight into this, I turn to studies of the art of choreography, which, of course, is the art of shaping movement.

A team of Australian researchers, including psychologists, scientists, and choreographers, provides a useful starting point for looking at editing as a form of choreography. Their study, *Choreographic Cognitions*, talks about how dance is made and how it is perceived and understood by audiences. This cognition of dance is, I argue, similar to the cognition of rhythm in film.

The *Choreographic Cognitions* team explains that *time* is the artistic and expressive medium of contemporary dance. So, when we watch dance, we see movement, but we understand what movement *means* by how it expresses the otherwise invisible elements of time and energy dynamics. In the *Choreographic Cognitions* team's words:

the artistry of movement is in trajectories, transitions, and in the temporal and spatial configurations in which moves, limbs, bodies, relate to one another . . . change to a single component can affect the entire interacting network of elements. In a dynamical system, time is not simply a dimension in which cognition and behavior occur but time, or more correctly dynamical changes in time, are the very basis of cognition.[8]

Like choreographers, editors shape the trajectories of movement across shots, scenes, and sequences. We also shape the transitions of movement between the shots. Choreographers and editors both work with the temporal and spatial dynamics of movement. We create a flow of moving images that carries meaning. And, just like choreographers, editors will often describe the way a "change to a single component can affect the entire interacting network of elements."[9]

Editors less often describe rhythm and time as a basis of cognition. But in a sense, they are. Rhythm is part of the sensual experience of the film. It is an immediate and *felt* way for us to understand what we see and hear. So, the "dynamical changes in time"[10] that are core to the choreographer's art are also core to the editor's art.

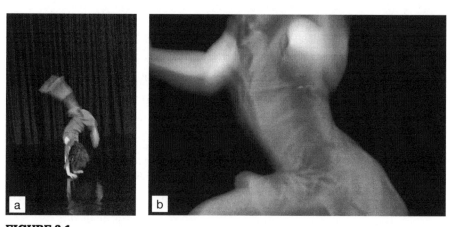

FIGURE 2.1
Jadzea Allen performing a phrase of movement from ". . .the dancer from the dance" (Karen Pearlman, 2014). [Photo credit: The Physical TV Company; Christophorus Verheyden]

The next section will look at the pulse, the smallest unit of movement shaped by choreographers and editors into rhythm, and the role of pulse in defining dynamical changes in time.

PULSE

Pulse is the smallest, the most constant, and perhaps the most ineffable unit of rhythm in film. It is ever present, just as it is in your body, and unnoticed, just as in your body. Pulse in film has a few other characteristics in common with a living body—it tends to stay within a certain range of speeds, it organizes the perception of fast and slow, and it keeps the film alive. Just as in a living body, if a film's pulse stops, slows, or speeds too much, the results can be dire for the rhythm, the story, or the experience of the film.

Pulse defines and demarcates what Tarkovsky calls "the consistency of time" or the "time pressure"[11] within shots. A single pulsation is the extra effort placed on one part of a movement compared to the less energetic other parts of the movement. Just as in the beating of a heart,

---

PRACTICAL EXERCISE

Feeling Pulse

Try speaking without placing an accent on any syllable.

Without training or practice this is very difficult to do because we learn language with emphasis points built into it. That is, we learn language in order to say what we mean, and without emphasis points, meaning is indistinguishable. If you can master the speaking of a couple of sentences with equal emphasis on each syllable and equal time between each syllable, try speaking these sentences to someone and see how well they understand you. Chances are they will focus a great deal more on how strangely you are speaking than on the meaning of the words you are uttering. This is because you have created a mono-dynamic utterance. Since the meaning of every interchange resides to some extent in the dynamic—your listener will focus more on the dynamic than the words.

An editor works with and shapes the dynamics of interchanges when shaping rhythm. She chooses takes or shots with different emphases, she places these shots in relation to one another to create a pattern of emphasis, and she curtails the duration of shots to shape the rate of the accents. Underlying all of these decisions, whether they result in maintaining or varying the film's pulse in a given moment, will be a feeling for the overall strength, speed, and consistency of the pulse being shaped in the film.

there is a continuous on/off of emphasis points. Accents on words, gestures, camera moves, colors, or any thing else that moves in a shot contribute to the film's pulse. Pulses are shaped by the energy or intention behind movement, including speech. (Actors may sometimes develop a character by giving their performance a distinctive pulse.) Pulses make energy or intention something we can feel, hear, and see.

The film editor does not necessarily set the pulse of a shot—the director and actors do that mostly. But the editor has choices to make about the sustaining, changing, and coordinating of pulses. These choices are made through the selection of takes and the choice of cutting points. Pulse accents can also be emphasized or de-emphasized and even shifted by cuts.

Pulses in movement are shaped by choreographers into phrases. They are also shaped by editors into phrases, we just don't usually call them phrases. We call them exchanges between characters or sequences of shots, but seeing them as pulses and phrases of movement is helpful to seeing how they can be shaped expressively. The next section of this chapter describes two choreographic methods for shaping phrases and compares them to two kinds of editing challenges.

MOVEMENT PHRASES

A movement phrase in dance (and in film editing) is a rhythmically coherent sequence of moves or shots that convey some feeling or idea through their rhythm.

For example, imagine your film has a scene in it where a man comes home. You could make a series of different phrases from the sounds or images in different shots that you have, and each of these phrases would have a different rhythm. The rhythms, made through the juxtapositions of different movement energies, timings, and directions, would each express something different.

Start with a shot of the door closing behind him. What does the door sound like? Is it a slam because he is angry? A stealthy click as though he is trying not to disturb anyone? Does it stick in the doorframe as though the house is a bit rundown? Does it close behind him with an efficient click just as it closes everyday?

He walks in. What does the house sound like? Is it noisy with kids? Did he leave the TV on in the morning? Is there a fridge hum but all else is quiet? Is there a spooky supernatural atmosphere?

What is the first thing he does when he gets in the house? Does he open that humming fridge and grab a beer with a smooth, practiced gesture? Does he step on the dog's tail and make it howl? Does he throw the mail and his keys down on the dining table? Does he drop, exhausted, on to the sofa?

If you chose the sound of a slamming door, screaming kids and a heavy sigh as he drops, exhausted, onto the sofa we would understand this story world and character as completely different than if you chose a stealthy click, a humming fridge, and the sound of a beer! If you are becoming adventurous with your juxtapositions you could try combining the stealthy click, humming fridge, and the drop, exhausted, onto the sofa or the stealthy click, humming fridge and step on the dog's tail. Each of these last two options would begin the phrase of movement in the same way, and end it differently, creating a different phrasing of movement and a different meaning.

We are used to seeing costume express character—we ascribe different characteristics, moods, and contexts to people in business suits or gym clothes, however we are not so much in the habit of recognizing that movement expresses world and character. Thinking about phrasing is one way of broadening our perspective on how movement works expressively.

There are lots of approaches a choreographer might take to shaping movement phrases in dance. What follows is a description of just two approaches, chosen to illustrate what the art of choreography and the art of editing might have in common.

One choreographic approach is for the choreographer to create a movement sequence with inherent timing, spatial organization, and emphasis, and then teach that phrase to the dancers. This approach to choreography has an affinity with Tarkovsky's water pipes. If a film director works in this way, he provides the editor with material that has immutable, self-contained phrases of movement. So, the editor's job is not to *create* the phrase's rhythm, but to *respect* the phrase's rhythm. This would be the equivalent of shooting the man coming into the house (in the example above) all in one shot, and with only one take. In this approach the editor's choreographic input comes in extending these rhythms to the construction of the larger sequences. She does

FIGURE 2.2

Birdman: Or (The Unexpected Virtue of Ignorance) *(Alejandro G. Iñárritu, 2014) In* Birdman *the phrasing is not created in the editing, rather it resides in the shots. The movement of the camera, the actors, the dialogue, and the sound are all coordinated in the rehearsal and shooting process to create the flow of time through very long takes. The editor joins these pieces of time like water pipes, selecting the takes that join together time, movement, and energy into a coherent phrasing of story, emotion, image, and sound. [Photo credit: Fox Searchlight Pictures]* this by shaping the *joins* of phrases. So, she is still grappling with the shaping of movement "trajectories, transitions . . . and temporal and spatial configurations,"[12] but the smallest unit for transitioning or configuring is not the pulse or the single gesture or the movement fragment, but whole movement phrases.

A different approach a choreographer might take is to give her dancers "movement problems" to solve, such as, "Invent five gestures of frustration." These five gestures are fragments, like a series of short shots. The choreographer connects the fragments into phrases and in doing so designs their temporal flow, spatial organization, and emphasis. In film, the connecting and shaping of fragments into phrases is done by the editor. This approach has more affinity with Eisenstein's sense of montage than Tarkovsky's. Tarkovsky's approach to rhythm considers time to be present in the shot, and the editor's job is to construct the film so that time flows effectively in spite of cuts. In Eisenstein's view the course of time is *created* in the cutting. The editing process actively choreographs rhythms; i.e., editing connects bits of movement on film to *create* the passage of time.

WHY BOTHER WITH PHRASING?

Choreographers often work with abstract or non-naturalistic movement, and editors often work with naturalistic movement of actors or subjects, so why bother with phrasing? Because the choreographic principles can still be applied. A movement phrase is not just a unit of rhythm in abstract movement. A naturalistic character's movement in narrative drama is also shaped choreographically into phrases. To expand on the example above, assume that the action in the script calls for a character to enter the house. The director and actor have decided, in blocking, that he will enter, put his keys on the table, and get a beer, so all of the shots that you have are only of those three actions. There may still be a lot of different ways to phrase this sequence. There may, for example, be variations in the actor's performance. Does he drop the keys on the

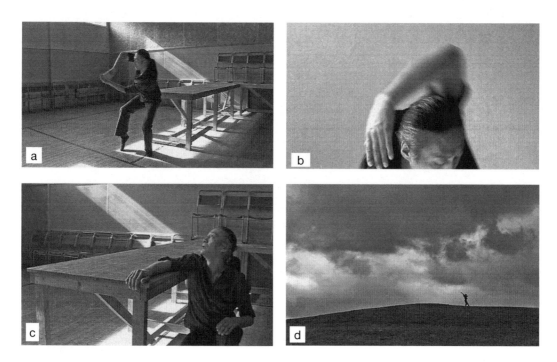

FIGURE 2.3

In There is a Place *(Katrina McPherson, Simon Fildes and Sang Jijia, 2010) shots are cut together to form phrases. McPherson & Fildes' films make use of cutting as a form of movement, along with camera movement and performer movement. So each cut is a move to a different shot, a move of the spectator's mind and eye, a move that contributes to the phrasing. In this approach, the editor takes fragments of movement and designs them into phrases. Rises and falls of emphasis, direction and speed changes, size, shape, and performance are all shaped into the dynamic flow that is the "cine-phrase's" meaning. [Photo credit: Goat Media, Katrina McPherson, www.youtube.com/watch?v=DicA-jC1gS8]*

table? Place them hesitantly? Toss them casually? Slam them down? There may be variations in how he opens the fridge. Does he pull it open distractedly? Pry it open deliberately? Yank it open? Sneak it open? Developing your eye to see the differences in these kinds of movement is a way of developing your intuition about rhythm. It makes it possible for you to shape rhythms that *"feels right"* for the emotional moment of the film, and express something in the phrasing of their movement without necessarily even consciously doing so. When you put together a series of expressive gestures into a sequence that "feels right" the phrasing of the movement's rhythm will have impact and meaning.

FIGURE 2.4

Michael Sheen and Frank Langella in Frost/Nixon *(Ron Howard, 2008).* Frost/Nixon *is just one example of hundreds that follow a 'middle way' between Tarkovsky's and Eisenstein's views, creating some of the phrasing in the shots and some through the cuts. Ron Howard's films have a very silky smooth (some would say slick) feel to them, with every aspect of movement, including camera movements, performers' movements, and movements between shots expertly gauged to propel the narrative and not to draw the eye away from story. Editors Daniel P. Hanely, Mike Hill, and Robert Komatsu tuck cuts almost imperceptibly between similarly composed shots, with the performance movement motivating the cut or used as punctuation at the beginning or end of phrases. [Photo credit: Universal Pictures, Imagine Entertainment, Working Title Films]*

Once it is phrased, the movement becomes the emotional content in the context of the story. If the character comes home very late in a domestic drama and rushes in the door, the hesitation before dropping the keys might be a questioning, "Is everyone asleep?" or more melodramatically, "The house feels deserted, has my wife left me?" A "deliberate" opening of the fridge then becomes thoughtful, maybe even anxious, depending on the story context. The story context tells us the focus of the emotional content—what the questioning and the anxiety are directed *toward*—but it is the hesitation and the deliberateness that gives us the *feeling* of questioning and anxiety.

This is important because we don't go through a conscious process in our thoughts to understand the feeling we are seeing. We feel *with* it, we use our mirror neurons and our capacity for kinaesthetic empathy to grasp the pulsation of the movement directly. When a movement phrase is well "choreographed" by an editor, it gives us the kinaesthetic information the story requires. It does so without confusing us or making us stop feeling and start asking questions about what we're supposed to be feeling, and it does so immediately—it lets us feel and move on to what happens next.

PHRASING CONSIDERATIONS

One reason to compare editing to choreography is to use knowledge about the craft of choreography to extend ideas about the crafting of rhythm in editing. Some of the questions choreographers grapple with may be useful questions an editor can ask herself in the process of shaping a film's rhythm.

The following ideas about crafting dance are presented as questions editors can ask themselves for two reasons: First, because they are not rules. Second, because they are not meant to be prescriptive. Since they are lateral ways of looking at the flow of movement, they're most likely to be useful when the more standard questions of story construction are failing the editor in her effort to make a film feel right.

American dancer and choreographer Doris Humphrey wrote about the craft of choreography in her book *The Art of Making Dances*. The following topics are Humphrey's chapter subheadings; the questions they raise are mine and represent just a sampling of the line of questioning raised by taking a choreographic approach to rhythm in film editing.[13]

Symmetry and Asymmetry

The tension between symmetry and asymmetry can be manipulated by an editor to create or disrupt style. A smooth, classical style will tend to emphasize symmetry in the composition of frames and the evenness of pulse. Disruption of symmetry then becomes an important dramatic break. For the editor, the questions of the overall film may be: Should the rhythm, and its movement phrasing, emphasize balance or imbalance? Even or uneven patterns? Measured or manic paces? These questions can also be applied to a specific break in a rhythmic pattern, as in the question of when to switch from even to uneven or from measured to manic.

FIGURE 2.5

The Grand Budapest Hotel (Wes Anderson, 2014) *gets its tonal character in part from relentlessly flat and symmetrical framing that David Bordwell calls "planimetric" framing (www.davidbordwell.net/ blog/2014/03/26/the-grand-budapest-hotel-wes-anderson-takes-the-43-challenge/). Bordwell describes the cutting between shots that are framed this way as 'compass point edits', which move 180 degrees to make shot–reverse shot configurations. This jump from flat and centered to flat and centered has a comically disruptive effect, lessening the sense that this is an actual interchange between people and heightening the absurdity of the characters. [Photo credit: Fox Searchlight Pictures]*

FIGURE 2.6

The fractured lives of the characters in Incendies *(Denis Villeneuve, 2010) free fall through asymmetrical compositions that express the imbalance of powerful forces. Cutting these together across jagged shifts of time period creates a series of disorienting 'shocks' and aligns us with the characters and their emotional lives in a visceral cinematic way. [Photo credit: micro_scope]*

One and More Bodies

FIGURE 2.7

Movement is scattered and diffuse in this image of a community mourning the deaths they feel sure are coming in Whale Rider *(Niki Caro, 2002). [Photo credit: New Zealand Film Comm.; The Kobal Collection]*

FIGURE 2.8

But the individual movements of Keisha Castle-Hughes in Whale Rider *(Niki Caro, 2002) are, in contrast, focused and directed as she saves the whales and reunites the community. [Photo credit: New Zealand Film Comm.; The Kobal Collection]*

For an editor, the question of one and more bodies is concerned with the choice of shots and the concentration of movement they contain. In the shaping of an expressive moment an editor may, for example, have choices between tightly framed individuals or looser frames of groups. Or she may have choices about the concentration of movement within different takes. Her questions about a given moment or an overall film might be: Is the concentration of movement high or low, scattered or unified, moving toward chaos or order? To shape these variations into an affective flow, the editor may consider the distribution of movement at a given moment and whether to amplify movement or personalize it by emphasizing a group or an individual.

The Phrase

As discussed above, the phrase is a composition of movement into a rhythmically expressive sequence. The questions at work in shaping phrases of rhythm in editing include: What is the cadence of this rhythm? What is the rate and strength of its pulse? Where are its rests and high points? Where are its breaths and shifts of emphasis? Does it have even or dynamic variation of accent by stress? What about accent by duration?

The Stage Space

In this section of *The Art of Making Dances*, Humphrey asks choreographers to consider the use of space as an affective tool. The same questions apply for an editor faced with the frame and working to determine rhythm through the use of various shots. Of course the director and cinematographer have already given in-depth consideration to the frame and movement in the frame by the time the material reaches the editor. So, the editor's concern is with the choreographic composition of the joins of frames and the impact the material has when seen in a flow rather than as individual shots. The questions are: Are shots put together to progress smoothly from wide to close, jump from close to wide, or jump around in size? Does movement flow in a consistent direction, in alternate directions, collide from all screen directions, or are there different patterns at different times? What about angles? What kind of effect are they having and is it to be used sparingly or relentlessly?

Humphrey's ideas about the art of making dances are helpful to me in demonstrating the principles at work in rhythm, and they may be helpful to an editor if she is stuck. But, as we have seen in Chapter 1, these questions don't necessarily have to be consciously articulated to be the ones you are grappling with. There are other ways to solve problems than to articulate them. If an editor is working with the movement of time and energy in a film, she is working with these principles of movement distribution, concentration, phrasing, and spatial organization whether she knows it or not. Where these questions may be useful is if the editor *knows* she is working with movement to create rhythm and wants to know how to engage with choreographic principles of composition.

A choreographer will build up phrases of dance movements, vary them, juxtapose them, interpolate them, and otherwise manipulate them, shaping them within themselves and in relation to one another to make an overall experience of time, energy, and movement called a dance. In film editing, an editor is rarely simply making an experience

FIGURE 2.9
Bill Butler, the editor of Stanley Kubrick's A Clockwork Orange *(1972), cuts extremes of shot sizes hard together at certain moments, creating a jarring, destabilizing rhythm. [Photo credit: Warner Bros., The Kobal Collection]*

of time, energy, and movement; she is also shaping story, character relationships, and other kinds of information. Furthermore, film editors rarely work exclusively with human movement. However, in shaping the rhythm of the film, time, energy, and movement are the salient factors. They shape the qualitative experience of the story and information. The movement through time and energy of all of the filmed images is shaped into phrases of related movements and grouped emphasis points. These phrases are then varied, juxtaposed, interpolated, and shaped within themselves and in relation to each other to make the overall experience of time, energy, and movement in a film that is known as rhythm.

SUMMARY

In this chapter the metaphor for editing rhythms has been shifted from music to movement, and we have compared the art of editing to the art of choreography. Choreographers talk about movement pulses and movement phrases and these two words have been applied to editing to see how they may be useful. In editing, sometimes the movement phrase is within the shot and sometimes it is created by juxtaposing shots. Either way, its rhythmic coherence carries the expressive qualities of time and energy. The movement of a steady, inexorable press of a stranger through a bedroom door expresses one kind of time. Sharp flashes of knife points, blood, water, and shower curtain create another. Movement is how we see time and energy. Editing phrases the movement into an expressive rhythm.

The next chapter will examine the specific tools an editor has for the shaping of rhythm in film.

PRACTICAL EXERCISE

Time, Space, and Energy: Part 1

This exercise requires at least five people. It demonstrates the affective power of time, space, and energy and shows how much impact an editor's manipulation of just these three things can have on the emotion and the story.

To set up the exercise, ask two people within the group to enact the following scene:

A: sits at a table, reading.

B: walks in and stops, looking at A.

A: looks up.

B: shakes head "no."

A: looks away.

B: sits down.

A: looks back at B; they lock eyes.

A: stands up and starts to walk out, pauses near B, and then leaves.

Once they have the script staged, three other people each get a chance to direct the scene, but each person gets to direct only *one* quality.

The first director can give directions only to do with time. He may say anything to do with speed—faster or slower; and anything to do with duration—for a longer time or a shorter time. Give the director and performers a few minutes to work and then watch the results. Notice how the whole feeling and meaning of the scene changes when things are given different emphasis by being done more quickly, or slowly, or for a longer or shorter time. This is what an editor does when she decides which take to use, the quicker or the slower one, and where to cut into the action, after a short time or a long time.

Now the second director gets a chance, and this one gets to direct only space. He can change stage directions, proximity, or direction of gestures or movements and nothing else. Again, after this director and the performers work for a few minutes, there is a marked difference in the meaning and emotion of the scene. This is the element the editor is manipulating when choosing whether to use the close, medium, or long shot of a given moment. Proximity and distance can create intimacy, discomfort, isolation, and a range of other feelings. Stage direction moves the eye around the space and can create smooth or abrupt flows of the action and a range of dynamics in between.

Time, space, and energy are all considerations in phrasing. The tools an editor has for manipulating them will be discussed in greater detail in the next chapter. The completion of this practical exercise, the directing of energy, can be found in the next chapter after the discussion of energy and trajectory phrasing.

ENDNOTES

1. Pepperman, R.D., *The Eye is Quicker, Film Editing: Making a Good Film Better*, p. 207.

2. Scorsese, M., as quoted in *Motion Picture Editors Guild Newsletter*, www.editorsguild.com/newsletter/specialjun97/directors.html.

3. Stam, R., *Film Theory: An Introduction*, p. 43.

4. Eisenstein also uses "orchestration" in a discussion of the relationships of sound and images. This is a more accurate use of orchestration in the sense of distribution of parts—the sound plays one part in creating affect, the images another, and Eisenstein et al. exhort us to use the parts contrapuntally, not redundantly. See "A statement on the sound-film by Eisenstein, Pudovkin and Alexandrov," in Eisenstein, S., *Film Form: Essays in Film Theory*, pp. 257–260.

5. Van Leeuwen, T., "Rhythmic structure of the film text," in *Discourse and Communication*, p. 218.

6. Tarkovsky, A., *Sculpting in Time*, p. 117.

7. Eisenstein, S., *Film Form: Essays in Film Theory*, p. 75.

8. Stevens, K., et al., "Choreographic cognition: composing time and space," in *Proceedings of the 6th International Conference on Music Perception & Cognition*, p. 4.

9. Ibid.

10. Ibid.

11. Tarkovsky, A., *Sculpting in Time*, p. 117.

12. Van Leeuwen, T., "Rhythmic structure of the film text," in *Discourse and Communication*, p. 218.

13. See Humphrey, D., *The Art of Making Dances*, p. 11.

CHAPTER 3

Timing, Pacing, and Trajectory Phrasing

What are the tools editors use to shape rhythm? This chapter introduces three: timing, pacing, and trajectory phrasing.

Timing, pacing, and trajectory phrasing are each broken down in quite a lot of detail in this chapter, and the question may well arise for an editor: How could all of this information be useful to me? Well, like much of the information in this book there are two points in an editor's process where so much detail may be useful, and neither of them will be in the edit suite while in the full flow of editing.

As mentioned in Chapter 1, when working well with intuitive flow, analysis is not useful—it may even get between the editor and her feeling for the material. However, as also discussed in Chapter 1, that "intuitive" flow is not something a person is born with. It comes from stoking the storehouse of learned knowledge with the information and ideas that can support immediate and unreflective action. Knowledge about timing, pacing, and trajectory phrasing is precisely the kind of knowledge that can support your intuition unconsciously in the edit suite. It can help sensitize you to the flow of the movement of story, emotions, image, and sound, and give you tools that you can deploy expertly, without justifying why or how you deploy them. So one way of using this information will be to absorb it and then, on a conscious level, forget about it, and allow it to simply support your intuition.

The other place that some depth of knowledge of timing, pacing, and trajectory phrasing may be useful is when things are not going well in the edit suite. One of the most common experiences collaborators have when the edit doesn't "feel right" is difficulty in pinpointing what feels wrong. At these moments, since one is not in full flight of intuitive flow anyway, it is possible to step back and deploy the tools and vocabularies this chapter describes. By the end of the chapter you will be able to identify three things that could be addressed when someone says the timing is off; three different things that they might be talking about when they say the pacing is off; and three things that you could ask yourself about the trajectory phrasing.

A word of caution when deploying the trajectory phrasing tools though: trajectory phrasing is a new expression that is exclusive to this book and rarely used in edit suites. It is, in a sense, secret editors' business. This doesn't mean it isn't useful knowledge, just that no one else will use those particular words to describe what doesn't feel right. So, the opportunity this chapter offers is for the editor to simply nod sagely when someone says it "doesn't feel right" and quietly use one or all of the nine aspects of timing, pacing, and trajectory phrasing described herein to address the issues.

TIMING

There are three aspects of timing to be considered when discussing rhythm in film editing:

1. choosing a frame;

2. choosing duration;

3. choosing the placement of the shot.

Choosing a Frame

Choosing which frame to cut on is one sense of timing. It creates the specific frame-to-frame relationship of two shots and their contents. "Etymologically the word [rhythm] probably implies 'not flow, but the arresting and firm limitation of movement'."[1] Timing is the tool at work in firmly limiting the movement of one shot by choosing the precise frame on which to begin and end it. If, for example, the editor is constructing a conversation in a shot–reverse shot configuration, and there is a shot in which a man looks up and then smiles, followed by a shot in which a woman looks away, the editor might choose to cut on the frame before the smile starts. In that case the scene would play as "the man looks up, then the woman looks away." As little as one frame later, the smiling becomes perceptible, so cutting exactly one frame later would make the scene play as "the man looks up and starts to smile, but the woman looks away." A world of different meanings can unfold if the woman seems to look away because the man is smiling or because the man looked up.

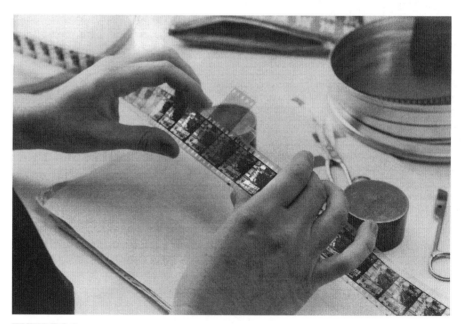

FIGURE 3.1

In the days when "cutting film" meant actually cutting pieces of film, you could hold up a film strip to the light and choose the precise frame on which to cut. The process of editing was altogether more physical, and, when holding those strips of film, you actually had the sensation of holding time in your hands. [Photo credit: The Kobal Collection]

Choosing Duration

"Timing" frequently refers to duration or the length of time a shot is held. It is the aspect of rhythm being referred to when one says something feels long or short. Holding a shot for a long time or for what *feels* like a long time are both functions of timing. Choosing duration is distinct from choosing the precise frame on which to cut because, although a shot may change meaning quite dramatically by holding or dropping one frame, the feeling of its *duration* is not really affected by one frame (which is only a small fraction of a second). A 10-second shot will feel long if it is juxtaposed with a series of 1-second shots. The same 10-second shot, used in the same context, will still *feel* just as long if it is actually only 9 seconds and 20 frames. And the same 10 (or so)-second shot will *feel* quite short if juxtaposed with a series of 60-second shots. The feeling of a shot's duration is created by the relative durations of the shots near to it and the concentration of information, movement, and change within it.

Choosing the Placement of a Shot

The decision about *where* to use a shot is also called timing. This sense of timing refers to "where" as in *when* to reveal the punch line or the surprise. It is related not so much to duration or precise frames; rather, it shapes rhythm in broader strokes by determining trajectories and

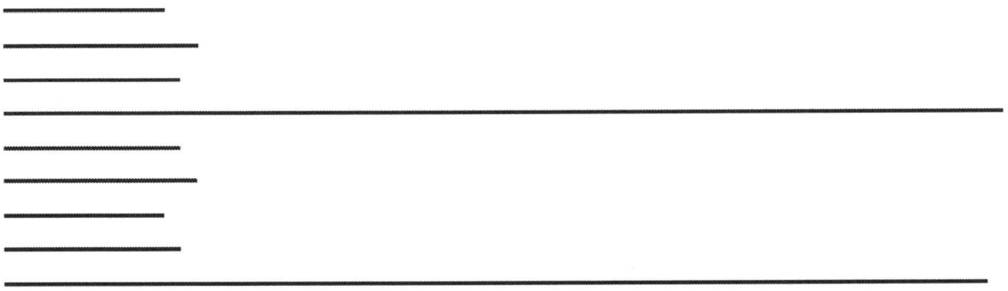

FIGURE 3.2

Even though the long lines are not exactly the same length, they both feel long compared to the short lines. Similarly, the short lines all feel short; although their shortness varies in relation to one another, they are roughly the same in relation to the long lines.

emphasis. If, for example, the plot is moving toward the discovery of a clue, does the detective stumble over traces of gunpowder in the foyer or discover a smoking gun first? The movement of the plot—direct or indirect—is determined by the timing of *where* the shots are placed. The detective's sequence of movements reveals something of his character, such as how astute or dimwitted he seems to be, by placing shots in an order that makes him move directly to the clues or meander, bumbling, toward them.

This is also a way of placing emphasis by repetition.[2] If an editor has standard coverage for a scene (for example a single on each character and a two-shot of both characters), she will be able to use repetition of shot setups expressively. A common repetition, for example, is to alternate between the singles of the two characters as they discuss something and then to cut to the two-shot, introducing change, at the moment at which their discussion is resolved.

Movement qualities within shots can also work with patterns of repetition for emphasis. An editor does not have to repeat three gestures of hesitation *exactly* to emphasize hesitancy; she can cut together a hesitant glance, a hesitant reach, and a hesitant step to place a big emphasis on hesitancy, or she could drop all three of those shots and go straight to the smoking gun to remove any hesitancy from a detective's timing.

All of the uses of timing—the precise frame on which cuts are made, the duration of shots, and the sense of timing as in *where* a shot is placed—intersect with one another and the other tools of rhythm: pacing and trajectory phrasing. Separating and identifying these things may have some value for understanding the processes of cutting rhythms. At the very least, all of these uses of the word "timing" can be turned into specific questions an editor can ask: "Which shot where? For how long? On which frame do I cut?" are all timing questions.

PACING

Pacing is created by the rates and amounts of movement in a single shot and by the rates and amounts of movement across a series of edited shots.

When Bordwell and Thompson describe "pace" in *Film Art*, they define it as "what musicians call tempo."[3] *The Grove Dictionary of Music and Musicians* tells us that:

> The system of musical tempo clearly has its origins in the functions of the human body and mind. It is related in particular to the speed of a normal heartbeat, between 60 and 80 beats per minute; on either side of this lie the sensations of "fast" and "slow" . . .[4]

So, pacing manipulates the audiences' sensations of fast and slow. For an editor, the word "pacing," actually refers to three things:

1. rate of cutting;

2. rate of movement or change within a shot;

3. rate of overall change.

Rate of Cutting

Pacing sometimes means the rate at which cuts occur, as in how often per second or minute or hour. This is not just another way of saying "duration of shots," although the two ideas do overlap.

Pacing in this sense can easily be seen when the rate of cutting occurs in patterns; e.g., accelerating the number of cuts per minute as a chase gets closer to its climax. (In this case the durations of the shots get shorter, and the two meanings overlap.) However, pacing, as in "rate at which cuts occur," is also a factor in the rhythm of film even when it is not patterned by design. For example, cutting frequently around a conversation may make the performances seem edgier or sharper. Here we are not looking at durations of shots directly, but at the content curve of movement within the shots and either cutting it very sharply, which creates a sense of the pace being quicker, or leaving it loose, with full arcs of movement intact, which makes the pace seem slower. Thus, the pacing, in the sense of the rate at which the cuts occur, manipulates the sensation of the movement of the conversation. Further, the rate at which cuts occur defines the rate at which new visual sensations are introduced—every cut is in itself a change, so lots of cuts make a faster rate of change.

Rate of Change or Movement Within a Shot

Pacing also refers to the juxtapositions of rates of movement or change within shots. If the rate of change within a shot is fast paced—for example, in one 5-second shot *the door opens—the vase falls over—the cook screams—and the burglar slips out,* and that shot is juxtaposed with another 5-second shot in which *the thief is cornered—he kicks the cop—he gets bitten by the dog and jumps over the wall*—the pacing of the sequence may be seen as very fast, even though the cuts are relatively infrequent. (Making one cut in 10 seconds is not a "fast" rate of cutting in contemporary cinema.)[5] If the editor chooses to present each of these events in its own shot, thereby making a cut every 3 seconds rather than one cut in 10 seconds, she would make the rate of change slow down—these events each shown in a single 3-second shot would take 24 seconds, not 10. The editor would have sped up the rate of cutting, but the overall effect would be of slowing the pacing.

However, it would not necessarily be correct to assume that the sensation of slowing the pace arises solely from a sequence taking more time. The actual reason the pacing could feel slower may arise if the full action of each movement is being revealed by putting in a 3-second shot of each "gesture." When it is possible to see the whole of an action—its beginning, middle, and end—and not just the height of its activity, a certainty about source and direction of movement replaces the uncertainty that makes one feel as though things are moving fast.

FIGURE 3.3
The rate of change within a single shot in any Marx Brothers movie, including this one, A Night at the Opera *(Sam Wood, 1935), is extraordinary. Even in this still image it is possible to see that at least four separate transactions are taking place at one time. Breaking these down into individual shots to "cut faster" would not only slow the pace but also lose the humor created by overlapping all of these unlikely events in one continuous time and space. [Photo credit: MGM; The Kobal Collection]*

Rate of Overall Change

Pacing also refers to movement of the overall film. A film's pacing may be the rate at which events move in the film or the rate at which movement of images or emotions occurs in the film. Each of the following three examples creates a fast pace through a different aspect of high concentration of movement overall.

1. A film with a series of moving camera shots traveling around a breathtaking array of characters, alluding to complex and fraught interpersonal relationships, has a high concentration of quick movement in visuals and emotions, which creates a sensation of

FIGURE 3.4

Robert Altman's 2001 film Gosford Park *feels fast paced because characters, camera, and emotions all move quickly, but the plot doesn't move quickly, and it is not cut especially fast. The furious rainfall, the pressing forward against the rain of the figures under the umbrella, and the alert focus of the two attendants on either side of the car all make this frame feel fast paced, but all that is happening is people getting into the car. [Photo credit: USA Films; The Kobal Collection]*

fast pacing. At the same time, it has only one plot event, such as "the house guests settle in." But this will feel like a fast-paced film even though there are few events, because the rate of physical and emotional movement is high (Fig. 3.4).

2. A film with rapid dialog, relatively infrequent cuts, not much camera movement, but a rapid series of events or changes in the character's fortunes can still be considered to have rapid pacing (Fig. 3.5).

3. A film with lots of cuts, timed to maximize the energy of the movement trajectory and the collision of the movements between shots, but with basically no movement of events or no

FIGURE 3.5
Cary Grant and Rosalind Russell in His Girl Friday *(Howard Hawks, 1940). With its rapid-fire dialog and quickly changing plot events,* His Girl Friday *is well known as a fast-paced film, even though there are almost no camera moves and, by today's standards, cuts are infrequent. [Photo credit: Columbia; The Kobal Collection]*

emotional change, as in a music video, may also be considered fast paced (Fig 3.6).

In each of these three films the high rate of overall movement or change and the consequent sense of fast pace are achieved through manipulation of a different aspect of pacing. The same three aspects of pacing could each be employed in the opposite manner to make a film's overall pace slower.

In general, all three of these uses of the word "pacing" interact with one another to determine a film's pace. Pacing is very important, especially for the creation of sensations of time, but rhythm also has other methods with which to shape time, energy, and movement.

FIGURE 3.6

Music videos do not need to have plot changes or character changes to feel fast paced; instead, they can have lots of cuts and/or lots of camera moves. In Adele's "Rolling in the Deep" (Sam Brown, 2010) the rate of cutting accelerates with the emotion in the song and the rate of movement in the images. The sharp collisions of movement won editor Art Jones an MTV editing award.

TRAJECTORY PHRASING

"Trajectory phrasing" is a term I made up to cover an area of editing rhythms that is not precisely covered by saying "timing" or "pacing."

Trajectory phrasing describes the manipulation of *energy* in the creation of rhythm. The word "trajectory" means "the path described by a body moving under the action of given forces."[6] So "trajectory" describes a combination of the direction of a movement and the energy that propels it. "Trajectory phrasing" then, is joining together movement trajectories in different shots to the shape the flow of energy between them.

The three operations that trajectory phrasing describes are:

1. linking or colliding trajectories (making smooth links or abrupt collisions of energy and direction);

2. selecting energy trajectories (choosing from among different energetic variations in different takes);

3. stress (creating emphasis points, or stress accents, by manipulation of the trajectory of movement).

These three operations will be broken down in a moment. But first the word "energy" itself requires some definition.

My use of the word "energy" draws on movement analysts Rudolf Laban and Irmgard Bartenieff's ideas about effort. Effort, as described in their in-depth study of movement, roughly translates as the *attitude and intention* behind movement that informs the way it is done.[7]

The kind of effort with which a person moves is what he or she means or intends with his or her movement. A punch means aggression, violence, forceful intentions, *if* its effort is aggressive, violent, and forceful. A punch can be playful; in other words, it may originate from a playful state of mind, and the effort that propels it will be entirely different. It may move along the same spatial pathway as an aggressive punch, be a similar speed, and have the same shape, but its effort, or energy, will tell us that it means something different. It can even be abstracted completely by changing its energy. A closed fist moving limply is not seen as a punch. It is an abstract movement, unless the narrative context explains the energy in some way. For example, a dying man may move his closed fist in a straight line quickly but limply to give his grandson a magic bean that he has hidden in his hand. We wouldn't see that as a punch. The energy has changed it completely, and the narrative context has explained the change.

Energy is inseparable from movement and made visible through it.[8] However, although the energy cannot be separated, as in extracted, from the movement, energy can be *described* separately from movement's temporal and spatial properties. The three examples of punches—the aggressive, the playful, and the limp movement in the shape of a punch—each describe a different trajectory and stress.

Although the spatial and temporal organization may be similar in all three, they each use a different energy, and therefore each has a different meaning.

Dance theorist Sandra Horton Fraleigh describes the way movement energy expresses intention:

> The dancer's movements are workings of her mind, will, intuitions and imagination . . . The audience perceives her dance through her movement as it conveys her intentions. In short, they see what she does and see the thought in it—not behind it or before it. If she moves softly they see softness, if she moves sharply, that is what they see.[9]

The same can be said for naturalistic movement of actors in a drama or characters in a documentary. For an editor, the implications of this are that she cannot just shape movement in time. She must also phrase its energy to make the rhythms of the film express the intentions of the film. Trajectory phrasing in film editing is the shaping of flows of movement energy and direction by choices of takes and cuts.

PRACTICAL EXERCISE

Time, Space, and Energy: Part 2

Using the same scenario set up in Part 1 of this exercise in the previous chapter, a third person now has a chance to direct the scene. The only direction he is allowed to give is of energy, but he has the whole of the expressive range of energy, or "effort," as described above, to work with. The actions of the performers have to be the same—sit and read, walk in, look up, etc., but the director may now use verbs that describe energy, e.g., "flirt" or "resist." Once again the emotion and the meaning of the scene will change. This illustrates the way an editor shapes the meaning of an exchange through the selection and juxtaposition of various takes with different energy qualities.

At this point in the exercise everyone will notice that time, space, and energy are really difficult to separate. In fact, they work cumulatively. You can manipulate time fairly discretely, but any manipulation of space will necessarily also change time because it will take longer to go from point A to point B if you have set point B farther away. Or the character will have to travel more quickly. Either way, longer (duration) or more quickly (speed), time is being manipulated, too. Energy cannot be expressed separately from time and space, and changing the instruction to the performers regarding their use of energy will necessarily change their use of time and space. "Flirting" might involve just a small shift of the eyes, whereas "resisting" might be a fast twist of the whole spine.

The editor receives material, shots, that already contain some fixed aspects of time, space, and energy. Her job is to arrange and juxtapose these aspects, using timing, pacing, and trajectory phrasing, into sequences of affective rhythm.

Linking or Colliding Trajectories

Should the connections be smooth or abrupt? This is one consideration in the shaping of trajectory phrasing.

In practice, this means looking at aspects of movement, such as screen direction and asking if they should link or collide. A smooth cut is one in which movement from right to left in one shot is *matched* with movement from right to left in the next shot. A cut in which movement from right to left is "collided" with movement from left to right, or simply *unmatched* in spatial organization and energy, is a little shock. In his ideas on 'collision', Eisenstein includes graphic directions, scales, volumes, masses, depths, shot size, darkness and lightness in his list of visual elements that can be collided.

Selecting Energy Trajectories

The phrasing of the movement energy is also a matter of selecting shots for the qualities of energy they contain and using the cuts to shape the flow of energy across shots.

In continuity style coverage, a cut may be a "match cut," a "match on action," or a collided cut, but it is not *just* a choice between linkage and collision; it also contains choices from among an array of *energy quality* possibilities.

For example, here is a scenario that will be cut in continuity style:

> a man and his wife sitting on the sofa have a small disagreement over a
> book they are reading together. She gets up and moves to the kitchen,
> he follows.

We will call the "getting up and moving to the kitchen" the movement trajectory of each character, and the two of them getting up and moving to the kitchen will be the movement trajectory of the scene.

Imagine that the coverage includes a shot of the woman moving with a degree of hesitancy and one of her moving with a greater degree of confidence. Same movement, different energy or attitude behind it. The coverage also includes shots of the man getting up with difficulty

FIGURE 3.7

Joel Grey in Cabaret *(Bob Fosse, 1972). In the film* Cabaret, *Editor David Bretherton often makes very hard cuts between scenes, slamming together the energy in images to make surprising connections between ideas and create a physical jolt or shock for the audience that underlines the film's themes and makes them palpable experiences of the motion and emotion of life in Berlin in the 1930s. [Photo credit: ABC/Allied Artists; The Kobal Collection]*

FIGURE 3.8

Kristen Scott Thomas and Ralph Fiennes in The English Patient *(Anthony Minghella, 1996). Editor Walter Murch favors smooth linkages of movement energies in* The English Patient, *which help him to underline the lyrical aspects of the film and the connectedness of the central characters to each other on a nonverbal level. [Photo credit: Tiger Moth/Miramax; The Kobal Collection; Phil Bray]* and other shots of him springing off the sofa. Any of these shots can be cut together to match (link smoothly) but the rhythm of the scene is shaped by the choices of movement energy. Is her move to the kitchen hesitant, whereas he springs off the sofa to follow her? Or is her move confident, whereas he moves with difficulty? Or perhaps her hesitation and his difficulty will be cut together to create the trajectory that best expresses the movement of emotions in the film.

These same principles apply in cutting of, for example, documentaries, in which there is no continuity style coverage. Cutting the movement energy of events, information, colors, textures, ideas, emotions, and so on is a process of shaping the flow of energy into a coherent, expressive rhythm.

Stress

"Stress" is emphasis created by the use of the energy in a shot as an accent. Choosing where to place the stresses or the accents is part of trajectory phrasing. Here is a definition of "stress" in poetry: "Accent in the sense of emphasis is the more general term, 'stress' is the more precise . . . stress can denote intensity as opposed to pitch or length."[10] And here is what *The New Grove Dictionary of Music and Musicians* has to

FIGURE 3.9
In this cut from the documentary Island Home Country *(Jeni Thornley, 2008), the raucous movement, colors, and framing of an Australia Day celebration picnic (a) collide with the flow and grace of the dolphins in the sea (b). Cutting these two shots together creates an idea through visual collision; in this case, the idea that colonization and nation building conflict with nature and First Nation peoples.*

USEFUL QUESTIONS

In a situation in which the flow of movement energy doesn't feel right an editor may be able to ask herself some questions about the trajectory phrasing she is creating. Examples of these questions may include: What are the flows of movement energy that are inherent in the shots available to work with? Where along the spectrum of matching versus colliding should these energies cut together? What is the "story" in terms of energy flow? (For example, after the little dispute on the sofa, is the wife confident and the husband struggling, vice versa, or some other configuration?) What point should be accented or stressed? Should it create stress by repetition, duration, or selection of energy? The answers to all of these questions will determine the trajectory phrasing that the editor designs.

say about the importance of "stress" in rhythm: "duration and stress—in other words constructions in time and gradations in strength—are the central determinants of rhythm, its constituent factors."[11]

Stress in movement is "gradations of strength" or intensity of energy. In a phrase of edited material, a 2-second shot may either be a 2-second close-up of a scream or a 2-second wide shot of a sigh. The shots are of equal duration, the rates of movement or change within them are comparable, but the stress (effort) they contain and the stress (emphasis) they create are different. Both the shot size and the energy being expended within the shot contribute to the energy accent it makes.

Trajectory phrasing is something spectators feel in a very immediate way. We feel the movement flows that are created across shots without conscious processing. Smoothness or abruptness, hesitancy or confidence are recognized immediately by our mirror neurons and kinaesthetic empathy (see Chapter 1). Our immediate feeling of a trajectory phrase is the result of many hours of intuitive work by the editor in which she cuts the flow of movement energy into one trajectory or another until her own mirror neurons and kinaesthetic empathy light up with the feeling of the "rightness" of the flow.

SUMMARY

Timing, pacing, and trajectory phrasing are the tools that an editor uses when cutting rhythms. Each of these three is actually a term covering at least three editing operations for shaping movement and energy over time. The creation of rhythm in film editing will generally rely on all of these tools and operations being employed simultaneously or in close alternation because:

> rhythm is not just a duration of time, accented by stresses. It is also the result of the interaction of effort combinations with variations in spatial patterns.[12]

To recap the story so far . . . Chapter 1 looks at what rhythm is and how to develop rhythmic intuition. Chapter 2 is about the choreographic phrasing of rhythm. Chapter 3 covers an editor's tools and operations for shaping a rhythm. Up next: Chapter 4 will look at the purpose of rhythm and why feeling it and shaping it matter.

ENDNOTES

1. Durr, W., Gerstenberg, W., and Harvey, J., "Rhythm," in *The New Grove Dictionary of Music and Musicians,* p. 805. The quote is from Jaeger, W., "Paideia," p. 174f.

2. Interested readers will also find expansive discussion of the idea of repetition as an expressive motif in *Film Editing: The Art of the Expressive* by Valerie Orpen.

3. Bordwell, D., and Thompson, K., *Film Art: An Introduction,* p. 197.

4. Durr, W., Gerstenberg, W., and Harvey, J., "Rhythm," in *The New Grove Dictionary of Music and Musicians,* p. 806.

5. In his book *Film Style and Technology: History and Analysis,* Barry Salt includes a study of average shot lengths in narrative drama films over time. David Bordwell picks up on his findings and develops them in an article published in *Film Quarterly* in 2002. Bordwell says, "In 1999 and 2000 the ASL (average shot length) of a typical film in any genre was likely to run three to six seconds." Bordwell, D., "Intensified continuity: visual style in contemporary American film—critical essay," in *Film Quarterly,* p. 16.

6. Stein, J., and Urdang, L., editors, *The Random House Dictionary of the English Language,* p. 1503.

7. For a thorough explication and contextualization of effort, see Bartenieff, I., with Lewis, D., *Body Movement: Coping with the Environment.*

8. "Physicists recognize the existence of a universal interaction of forces such that the separation of entities into discrete and autonomous units is called into question, and explorations of the microscopic constituents of matter suggest (*sic*) that there are no irreducible bodies in the world, simply 'modifications, perturbations, changes in tension or energy and nothing else' (1959, 337; 1911, 266), no things but only actions (1959, 705; 1913, 248) or movements (1959, 707; 1913, 249–250)." Bogue, R., *Deleuze on Cinema,* p. 16.

9. Fraleigh, S.H., *Dance and the Lived Body: A Descriptive Aesthetics,* p. 169.

10. Preminger, A., and Brogan, T.V.F., editors, *The New Princeton Encyclopedia of Poetry and Poetics,* p. 1068.

11. Durr, W., Gerstenberg, W., and Harvey, J., "Rhythm," in The New Grove Dictionary of Music and Musicians, p. 806.

12. Bartenieff, I., with Lewis, D., *Body Movement: Coping with the Environment,* p. 75.

CHAPTER 4

Tension, Release, and Synchronization

What is rhythm for? We know what it is made of (time, energy and movement—see Chapters 1 and 2). We know how it is shaped (timing, pacing and trajectory phrasing—see Chapter 3). But what is it for? Why does a film need it? This chapter suggests two reasons: we need it to create cycles of tension and release and we need it to synchronize the audience with the movement of the film.

Here's how it works: The editor shapes movement of events, movement of emotions, movement of images and sounds into rhythms that we follow empathetically. If she shapes them well we synchronize with them. We tense with the rise of tension, we let go with the release. Our minds, emotions, and bodies move with the rhythmic opening and closing of cognitive questions about events, the rhythmic rise and fall of emotions, the rhythmic patterns and punctuations of images and sounds.

Let's break it down.

TENSION AND RELEASE

Tension and Release in Events

Acclaimed film director John Sayles writes that movies depend on tension and release for their impact. "The audience is made to expect something, the event draws nearer and tension builds, then the thing happens and the tension is released."[1]

The story plants a question or expectation of some event happening and then makes the audience wait for it, anticipating the event—will it happen or won't it?—with rising tension. When the event happens (something the editor might have shaped to occur after a long time or a short time, a lot of energy or minimal energy) there is release of the tension. A short film may only have one of these events within it, a feature film (fiction or documentary) may have dozens. An episodic

FIGURE 4.1

The physical movement in this image from John Sayles's film Matewan *(1987) poses a question that creates tension, which is: Will the character catch up with the train? James Earl Jones's performance helps the story to create stakes—we empathize with the movement of his face and body and hope he will get on board, and fear he won't, and worry about what is at stake if he doesn't. The shaping of the rhythm of this sequence in editing would involve shaping the duration for which we are held in suspense about those questions and the timing, pacing, and energy of the way the answers unfold. [Photo credit: Red Dog/Cinecom; The Kobal Collection]* series may not only have dozens within a given episode, it may have an expectation or question about what will happen planted at the end of an episode so that the audience anticipates the next episode with growing tension (or downloads it straight away to relieve their tension!). Chapter 8 looks in detail at strategies for shaping cognitive questions and event rhythms.

Tension and Release in Emotion

Some fascinating discoveries are being made by neuroscientists about tension and release that people experience when we watch each other doing actions or experiencing emotions. Vittorio Gallese and other scientists working in his lab at University of Parma are testing people watching moving images and have put forward a theory they call "embodied simulation."[2] Embodied simulation picks up on mirror neuron theory and extends it. It suggests that not only do we mirror movements we see, we also *anticipate* mirroring movements when we see objects that we commonly associate with certain intentions and movements. Keys are a good example. When we see keys, we anticipate a grasping gesture. When we see an actor reach for their keys we empathize with the feeling because at the neurological level we imitate and thus embody the feeling.

Writing in 2012, Gallese and Guerra used the example of Hitchcock's *Notorious* (1946) to illustrate how embodied simulation creates an emotional cycle of tension and release. At the climax of the plot of *Notorious* Alicia (Ingrid Bergman) has to steal the key to Sebastian's (Claude Rains) wine cellar in order to prove his involvement in crime. Sebastian is in the next room. His keys are on his desk. At first the editor cuts between Alicia's eyes and a camera move that approaches the keys, implying that she is quite close to getting them. Our anticipation of grasping the keys is strenuously activated. Then the editor cuts to a shot that reveals she is quite far away from the keys and that her husband is between her and the keys. Our blood pressure spikes. Of course the spike occurs at a cognitive level when we realize that Alicia has to traverse the whole room to get to the keys. But that spike is enhanced by our embodied simulation—we don't just know it, we feel it. As we continue to anticipate grasping the keys mentally, our tension rises and rises about when Alicia will grasp them. We grasp for her, over and over, emotionally willing her to get there and grasp them and relieve our tension. Manipulation of the viewer's embodied simulation response is just beginning to be explored in cinematography and has not yet, at time of writing this edition, been explored as something an editor can play with, but it promises rich sources of understanding of how an editor can shape cycles of tension and release.

Grasping keys is not the only thing we mirror. When we watch people move, breathe, and feel we mirror them—feeling and breathing with them. Feelings may start out peaceful, and then grow stormy. The change raises tension. As we empathize with the movement of emotions, growing anger, for example, our own levels of tension are raised. When feelings settle, resolve, or even become the new normal for the characters, our tension is released.

The editor is in charge of modulating the performances—the time, energy, and movement of emotion—so that emotional cycles of tension and release are felt experiences woven through experiences, events and images. Emotional rhythm is the subject of Chapter 7.

Tension and Release in Image and Sound

Finally, there are cycles of tension and release in image and sound, and an editor shapes these into patterns, too. An audience is not consciously aware of these cycles, because they are constantly occurring, and sometimes very rapidly. For example if a punch is thrown in one shot a 'micro' tension is raised about whether and how it will connect. This tension is released in the next shot, so there is no time to think about whether it will connect, only to feel it. In other words this cycle occurs on a pre-cognitive level.

Rhythm's physical effect on the spectator is basically also an experience of emotional affect. Because "feelings," in the sense of emotions, are physical, too. Torben Kragh Grodal talks about this in his book *Moving Pictures: A New Theory of Film Genres, Feelings and Cognition.* Grodal reminds us that story gives us cues about how to feel, but the strength of feeling relies on how the images, sounds, and movement are shaped to impact on us physically. He says an important part of the experience of emotions relates to involuntary body reactions:

> These involuntary reactions are controlled by the autonomic nervous and endocrine systems, which regulate the viscera, the heart, stomach, lungs, liver and skin, and which play a major role in the constitution of emotions. The connection between "viscera states" and emotions has been known for centuries, because everybody experiences strong changes in the viscera when excited: tears, salivation, change of respiration, butterflies in the stomach, a pounding heart, blushing, sweating.[3]

In other words, emotions are, at least in part, *physical* experiences of movement in the body through rises and falls of intensity of activity. Grodal continues, "When a viewer chooses to watch a film, he thereby chooses to be cued into having constant *fluctuations* [my emphasis] of heartbeat, perspiration, adrenalin-secretion and so on."[4] Physical rhythm and its fluctuations in image and sound are looked at more closely in Chapter 6.

The editor is trying to create an appropriately felt rhythm of these fluctuations in the audience. The questions are: How long to keep the heart racing at one rate? When, how, and with what to slow it down? It is not just a matter of finding the right amount of time to build tension or hold off release of story information, it's a carving of the qualities of that time, also, through timing, pacing, and trajectory phrasing. A film's significance is not just "this happened and then that happened." A film's impact is in the *way* that this, then that, happened, including how fast or slow or bumpily or smoothly or forcefully or limply. As Theo van Leeuwen says:

rhythm plays a crucial role . . . in the *way* the story is told, in the game of revealing and withholding story information from the viewers to maximize both their active involvement in anticipating the events and their passive abandon to the story's events.[5]

So, whereas events, characters and images trigger specific emotions, expectations, and ideas, the rhythms of these modulate the rise and fall of the tension—the "resonance of bodily reactions"[6]—with which we follow them.

FIGURE 4.2

The 'auto-ethnographic' documentary Stories We Tell *(Sarah Polley, 2012) is structured as an investigation. In it, the filmmaker, Sarah Polley is trying to find out the truth about her father. Editor Mike Munn creates tension and release with the placement of events – as information is slowly released, tension builds about whether she will find the truth. Emotional tension and release play out as the characters struggle with their own feelings and experience some catharsis when the truth is revealed. The images and sounds engage us in the story physically, viscerally, revealing the textures of the story-world, the relationships and the deception. [Photo credit: National Film Board of Canada]*

PRACTICAL EXERCISE

Murderer in the Dark

Murderer in the Dark, sometimes called Murderer's Wink, is a game for experiencing tension and release. Gather together six or eight people to play; a classroom of between twelve and twenty is also an excellent amount. Everyone stands in a circle and closes their eyes. The game moderator walks all the way around the circle and, while walking, taps one person on the shoulder. That person is the murderer, and no one except the moderator and the murderer knows who he is. The murderer's objective is to "kill" everyone off without being discovered; his weapon is a wink. If the murderer catches the eye of another player and winks, that player has to count slowly to 5 while looking around the room and then "die"; the more theatrically, the better. To discover the murderer you have to see him wink at someone, but not at you.

The game is great fun to play, but the interesting part is the discussion afterward, which concerns time, the release of information, and tension. How much information do you have at the beginning of the game? You know there is a murderer but you don't know who—you are asking yourself questions: Who is the murderer? Will I be killed? When will someone be killed? With each death there is a shift both of tension and of information—you experience, in rapid succession, shock or surprise depending on how theatrically the death has been performed, then relief that it is not you, then escalating tension as the number of possible victims diminishes. So you could be next, and the tension, fleetingly released, begins to build again.

In working with rhythm, the editor is working with these devices to create tension. How long can a question go unanswered before interest is lost? If the murderer in your game is not bold and no one gets killed, the interest diminishes very quickly, because the tension of the questions "who" and "when" is answered by "no one" and "never"!

The release of information is not just a matter of timing, but also of energy—if a victim just shrugs and says, "I'm dead," there is very little impact. If he suddenly stands, shrieks, and falls writhing to the floor, there is, perhaps, overkill. Modulating the intensity or energy of a performance to release and rekindle tension is part of the editor's job, too.

The tension is a combination of these three things—timing, energy, and release of information. Tension is in the unanswered question; rhythm is the time, energy, and movement that modulate its build and release.

FIGURE 4.3
A classic wink: Bob Hope and Dorothy Lamour in Caught in the Draft *(David Butler, 1941). [Photo credit: Paramount; The Kobal Collection]*

By modulating tension and release, rhythm supports comprehension of a film. Rhythm refines the rides we take with a film—the rise and fall, the speed of the curves, the sense of balance or danger in the stability or suddenness of movement in the world of the film. It

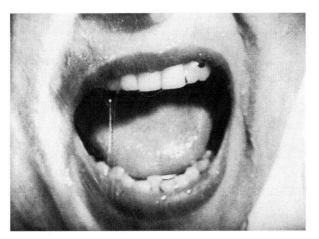

FIGURE 4.4
One of the reasons that the murder in the shower of Janet Leigh's character in Psycho *(1960) is so shocking is that it is so unexpected. Director Alfred Hitchcock, master of subverting our expectations, does not develop tension in the conventional ways, and so when the shower scene comes, our heart rates and other visceral responses jump very rapidly from a state of calm to a state of extreme activity. [Photo credit: Paramount; The Kobal Collection; Bud Fraker]*

doesn't matter if the film is a thriller or a romance, narrative or abstract; fact or fiction; the editor works with the "life of the object visibly recorded in the frame"[7] to determine the timing, pacing, and trajectory phrasing of its movement, and spectators' bodies respond to this rhythm.

SYNCHRONIZATION

Riding the rise and fall of tension and release when watching a movie, the audience's body rhythms and the rhythms of the film sync up. The "ride," rhythmically speaking, is the movement of the film composed in such a way as to influence the viewer's pulse, breath, and attention.

As discussed earlier, rhythm is part of our biology, and to survive we oscillate with the rhythms of our environment, our planet, and our solar system. Similarly, to survive socially, we coordinate our rhythms with those of other humans. For example, we meet the energy and pace of others in conversation, and we synchronize with them to have an effective transaction. If, at a gathering, everyone is talking in hushed tones and with terse gestures, we match these to understand and connect with the people. If those in the gathering are laughing uproariously and flinging their words and gestures freely, speaking in hushed tones and with terse gestures won't coordinate and will either cause those in the gathering to change or cause you to be left out. "As we act together we synchronize. The rhythms of our actions become as finely attuned to each other as the parts of different instruments in a musical performance."[8]

The implication of this social synchronization, for film spectatorship, is that the film becomes a rhythmical partner in a social exchange to which the spectator synchronizes. This physiological syncing function of rhythm in film is a significant source of affect. As philosopher Gilles Deleuze says in *Cinema 2: The Time Image*, "It is through the body . . . that cinema forms its alliance with the spirit, with thought."[9]

Deleuze goes on to suggest that cinema forms this alliance by making the body pass through a sort of "ceremony." This ceremony to which Deleuze refers is, I believe, a ceremony of synchronization. The film's rhythm synchronizes the body, influencing the spectator's physical and cognitive fluctuations to follow its own. My own description of this ceremony is of movies as a form of *meditation for the unquiet mind.*

Meditation is a practice that, through concentration, frequently on some rhythmically repetitive phrase or chant or breathing pattern, stills the fluctuations of the mind. The various objectives of this practice, from inner peace to complete enlightenment, are not what make it comparable with movies. What is comparable is the syncing or bonding that occurs through rhythmic connectivity in meditation. This aspect of meditation is imitated by the functioning of rhythm in film.

By shifting the spectator's physiological rhythms into sync with its own rhythms, film organizes the body's fluctuations into a single, focused, undistracted attention. The objectives of meditation can only be realized when "the fluctuations of the mind cease."[10] The objectives of rhythm in film are realized when the fluctuations of mind are subsumed into the fluctuations of tension and release in the film. Some of this work is done by story, structure, and performance, but some of it is done by shaping movement and energy over time to create the cycles of tension and release to which the spectator's mind and body synchronize.

CASE STUDY IN TENSION, RELEASE, AND SYNCHRONIZATION: *BROADCAST NEWS*

There are hundreds of sequences that could be chosen to illustrate the movement of tension and release in films. I have chosen this sequence from *Broadcast News* (James L. Brooks, 1987), not just because it works so well, but because it is a scene about the rhythm of the editing process. In it, there is a brief moment in which the synchronization that happens between the director and the uncut material is dramatized, revealing and illustrating the activation of mirror neurons and kinaesthetic empathy. The other especially useful aspect of this sequence for talking about shaping movement into cycles of tension and release is its overtly physical expressions of emotion and events. The director, James L. Brooks, takes delight in shaping the physical expressions of rhythm to draw us, physically and psychologically, into the tensions of the situation.

The plot of *Broadcast News* is about the shift in the culture of television news coverage from serious journalism to entertainment. It is told through the stories of three central characters: Jane Craig (Holly Hunter), a producer who believes passionately in journalistic integrity; Tom Grunick (William Hurt), a handsome, airheaded news anchor who performs well but doesn't really understand what he's saying; and Aaron Altman (Albert Brooks), an intellectual reporter who is too earnest and can't compete with the smooth, self-confident Tom, even though he's a better reporter.

FIGURE 4.5

Richard Marks, editor of Broadcast News *(James L. Brooks, 1987), cuts to this scene in the middle of Jane Craig's (Holly Hunter) phone conversation and edit. She is multitasking, talking rapidly into the phone, watching the rushes, and barking orders at the online editor (Christian Clemenson) all at once, which immediately establishes the base pulse and energy of the scene—this is as calm as things are going to get. [Photo credit: Americent Films, American Entertainment Partners L:P, Gracie Films]*

At the beginning of an early sequence in the film, there is a tight cut to Jane Craig, the producer, in the edit suite, working to a deadline, commanding her online editor, Bobby (Christian Clemenson), to run the story they are editing one more time (Fig. 4.5). He protests mildly and she overruns him with overlapping dialog and a much more forceful tone. Immediately, with the timing of these first cuts and the energy of the exchange, a tension is created. Most particularly it is Holly Hunter's portrayal of Jane's physical tension that is driving the scene. Her tone, speed, and attack express a furious will to keep control, overlaid on an edge of panic. The editor of *Broadcast News,* the extraordinary Richard Marks, cuts between Jane and Bobby in such a way as to highlight, extend, and physically impress this tension upon us as we experience the flow of the story. Marks cuts back to Jane as she grabs her water bottle and drinks abruptly, and to Bobby as he stabs the keys of his console with a rapid-fire staccato. Even though

FIGURE 4.6

In (a) Holly Hunter is speaking the same line as the character in the news story she is cutting (b; character on the left). She imitates his cadence and says the words with him, essentially singing along with him to immerse herself fully in his intent and the rhythm that expresses it. She has raised her pen in a gesture like a conductor's and waves it sharply at Bobby, the online editor, to indicate where she wants him to cut in to the shot.

they are both just doing their jobs and nothing too dramatic is happening, we experience these punctuations and emphasis points as a rhythmic volley that lifts the energy and attention.

At this point in the scene, Holly Hunter's character, Jane, actually enacts the synchronization that takes place between the material and the people working on it in the editing suite. As the voice in the videotape she is editing says a line, Jane says the line, too, aloud, mimicking the videotaped character's intonation and intent (Fig. 4.6a). Holly Hunter perfectly plays out the way that Jane, as the person cutting the film, would mirror the video image, embodying it physically, as a quick and direct way of giving herself the physical feeling of the uncut material. This physical imitation of the material is like blinking or breathing with it, or as will be discussed later, "singing" with it. As the timing, pacing, and energy of the material inhabit the body of the person cutting the film, she has a direct physical feeling of where to cut. She knows what the phrasing should be because she can feel it, in her body. This moment gives a succinct insight into the action that directors and editors do over and over again in shaping the rhythm of a film; whether they are shaping it at their leisure or under the bone-crushing pressure of a broadcast news production, they physically imbibe the rhythms they see and hear, and shape them to feel right in response to the feelings they have for them in their own bodies.

As the scene in *Broadcast News* progresses, more characters enter the tiny cutting suite, each bringing with them a contributing rhythm. First is Tom Grunick, who, as played by William Hurt, is a placid, accommodating presence. His rhythmic function is as a "rest." Shots of him, bemused and observing quietly, are dropped in between shots of other characters to give us breath, a contrast, and a bit of distance from the escalating tension. The entrance of Blair Litton, played by the inimitable Joan Cusack, brings with it the question at the heart of the tension of the sequence. Everything that happens for the rest of this sequence, both rhythmically and narratively, refers back to this question. Blair says, or rather insists, urgently, "We don't have enough time!" (Fig. 4.7), thus planting the most classic, oft-used, and reliable tension creator in motion pictures: the time pressure. Will they make it on time? It is important to note that time pressure is not just a

FIGURE 4.7
Holly Hunter and Joan Cusack play their characters' relationships and intentions, the subtext of the scene, physically. Holly Hunter is shutting her eyes to try to shut out Joan Cusack's manic intrusion, with the realities of time, on her vision for the piece, while Cusack thrusts her energy and anxiety forward at Hunter with every muscle and intonation.

narrative device; it is, of course, a rhythmic device, because time is a key element of rhythm. The time pressure almost acts as another character or voice in the rhythmic composition being constructed here, because each character's rhythm is played against it. Jane's tight, terse gestures get tighter and terser, for example. And when Bobby makes a little mistake, it triggers a major movement into another gear.

By the time this little mistake occurs, much has happened: new narration has been recorded, new relationship tensions have been revealed, we've cut away and come back to the edit suite, and we're down to 2 minutes before the story is due to air. Bobby fumbles (offscreen), says "whoops," and everyone shifts (Figs. 4.8a and 4.8b). The actors move into position like a string quartet or a corps du ballet,

FIGURE 4.8

(a) When Bobby says "whoops," all of the characters assembled in the edit suite in Broadcast News *reveal their panic about the time pressure they are under. They move into position (b) and start a rhythmic chant that has the function of probably driving poor Bobby, the online editor, crazy, and of raising the spectators' heart rates and blood pressure as we get caught up in the rhythm the characters create.*

and the director, James L. Brooks, begins to have some fun with the tensions and rhythms he has set up. Holly Hunter's character, Jane, the producer, takes the lead—her voice is the strongest and she has the most to lose here. She starts chanting, "Bobby, Bobby, Bobby, Bobby," at a rate and consistency designed to move our heart rates up a couple of notches. Her friend Aaron, the intellectual reporter who has come in to support her, plays the viola to her first violin. He punctuates her chant with low moans and a steady rocking. Jane's adversary in this scene, the hysterical timekeeper played by Joan Cusack, takes up the counter-melody with a steady stream of high-pitched squeals or grunts as though she is under torture of some kind, and William Hurt's character Tom, the cello in this quartet, grinds his teeth steadily, his eyebrows working contrapuntally to the hysteria around him. This is a staged bit of physically and aurally expressed rhythmic tension, and it gets me every time. I know it is coming, and yet when the rhythm begins, I still sync up to it. The rhythm acts on my body, and my conscious knowledge of its purpose, direction, and outcome is irrelevant to its physiological effect on me as a rhythm.

The moment ends abruptly with three shots: (cut) Bobby pops the tape out of the machine, (cut) hands it to Blair, and (cut) Tom says "GO!"

But the release is minimal—the tension of the little rhythm ballet described above is capped off with the punctuating three cuts and the word "GO," but the tension of the scene's big question—Will they make it in time?—is not resolved; in fact it is rekindled with the force of Tom's "GO!" And so ensues a beautifully cut madcap physical comedy sequence as Joan Cusack's character, Blair, all flying hair, flopping limbs, and flinging exclamations, dashes from the cutting room to the newsroom (Fig. 4.10). Every possible visual and physical obstacle, encounter, and energy in this sequence is shaped by the editor, Richard Marks, to have maximum impact and inspire the gravest and funniest kinaesthetic empathy in the spectator. We *feel* every one of the great Joan Cusack's galumphing moves in our own

FIGURE 4.9

Three shots in less than 2½ seconds conclude this part of the Broadcast News *sequence. In (a) Bobby pulls the desperately needed tape from the machine; he passes it to Blair in (b), nearly knocking Tom out with it; and in (c) William Hurt, as Tom, uses his energy to throw the tape and Blair into a headlong hurtling trajectory toward the newsroom with one word: "GO!"*

FIGURE 4.10
Broadcast News *Editor Richard Marks cuts together three shots to make a dazzling trajectory of Joan Cusack's move as she dodges a file cabinet drawer in her mad dash to the newsroom with the tape that is due to go straight to air in 15 seconds.*

body, and although it feels as though it is happening to us, it isn't; it is happening to her, and is therefore madly funny.

I find it interesting that my students consistently find this sequence both tension-filled and humorous, even watching it twice in a row. The first time I screen it, I just let them watch and laugh. The second time, I break it down into all of the points articulated above, but, piece by piece, they still find it funny, and they are still filled with tension. I attribute this phenomenon to the power of rhythm over information. As we mirror and empathize with the movement of images and sounds, emotions and events on the screen, our hearts, pulses, breaths, and bodies get caught up with these movements even though we cognitively know where they will lead. If the film's movements are directed and cut so that we feel with them, then we synchronize to them, and their rhythms move us through cycles of tension and release.

SUMMARY

The function of rhythm in film is to create cycles of tension and release, which the spectator "rides" physiologically, emotionally, and cognitively. The ride is felt as variations on the pulse of a temporal world that is created in the process of editing the rhythms of the film. By syncing the spectator's rhythms to the film, rhythm functions in a way that is comparable to meditation; it provides a "restriction of the fluctuations of consciousness."[11] This "meditation for the unquiet mind" is not a path to enlightenment, but it activates a physiological focusing effect similar to that of meditation to carry the spectator along on the ride of the rhythms of the film.

This chapter on tension, release, and synchronization also connects the findings of the first three chapters to propose specific ways that the editor's various intuitions, processes, and tools shape the spectator's experience. The ideas about mirror neurons and kinaesthetic empathy, about the choreographic shaping of pulses and phrases, and about the timing, pacing, and trajectory phrasing of rhythm have been looked at in the light of their impact on the spectator's experience of rhythm in film. The result of this discussion can be summarized in an aphorism frequently repeated by filmmakers: *The editor is the film's first audience.* The movement that the editor shapes into rhythm must first affect the editor in order to become the cycles of tension and release and the synchronizing force that move the spectator.

The conclusion at the end of the first four chapters of this book is that rhythm in film editing is shaped by editors through an intuitive knowledge of the rhythms of the world and of their own bodies as informed by their kinaesthetic empathy and mirror neurons. The same physiological rhythm detectors are, of course, present in the spectators, who imbibe the edited/shaped rhythms of the film physiologically. The editor's knowledge and experience of rhythm are gathered through participation in movement, so movement is the material that is choreographically manipulated to have the desired effects on the spectator. One could say that rhythm in film editing is this shaped movement or, more precisely:

> **Rhythm in film editing is time, energy, and movement shaped by timing, pacing, and trajectory phrasing for the purpose of creating cycles of tension and release.**

ENDNOTES

1. Sayles, J., *Thinking in Pictures: The Making of the Movie "Matewan"*, pp. 114–115.
2. For more on embodied simulation, see: Gallese, V. "Intentional attunement: A neurophysiological perspective on social cognition" and Gallese, V. and Guerra, M., "Embodying movies: Embodied simulation and film studies."
3. Grodal, T.K., *Moving Pictures: A New Theory of Film Genres, Feelings and Cognition*, p. 42.
4. Ibid.
5. Van Leeuwen, T., *Introducing Social Semiotics*, p. 186.
6. Ibid.
7. Tarkovsky, A., *Sculpting in Time*, p. 119.
8. Van Leeuwen, T., *Introducing Social Semiotics*, p. 182.
9. Deleuze, G., *Cinema 2: The Time Image*, p. 189.
10. Gannon, S., and Life, D., *Jivamukti Yoga*, p. 26.
11. Feuerstein, G., *The Yoga-Sutras of Pata ñ jali: A New Translation and Commentary*, p. 26.

CHAPTER 5

Physical, Emotional, and Event Rhythms

The next few chapters of this book breaks rhythm down into different types: physical rhythm, which is what we will call patterns of image and sound; emotional rhythm which is the shaping of rise and fall of emotions in the characters and in the spectators; and event rhythm, which is sometimes also called movement of plot, movement of story, or even "structure."

As discussed in Chapter 1, the movements of actors, on however large (whole body) or small (blink) a scale, are the expression of their internal rhythms and emotions. Leisurely strolling and frenetic running have different rhythms, their timing and energy have different feelings and different meanings in the context of a character's story. But the movement available to an editor to shape into patterns is not limited to the human body. Movements in the world of the film are shaped into rhythms, too. Water, for example: rushing, trickling, boiling, and freezing water all contain different qualities of time, space, and energy, and these, when shaped into the rhythmic composition of a film, extend their movement feeling across the images and the sense of rhythm in the film's world.

Movement as a material from which edited rhythms are shaped is not limited to movement of images. It includes movement of sound, emotion, ideas, and stories. As Linda Aronson, author of *Scriptwriting Updated*, writes:

> In fact everything about film—about *moving pictures*—is connected with time and movement in time, that is to say action, in every sense. Film

consists of movement in all ways, physical, emotional and spiritual. In screenwriting, story is movement and our characters move through their own mental landscapes.[1]

Aronson makes distinctions between different kinds of movement, when she refers, for example, to "physical, emotional, and spiritual" movement. Making distinctions between these kinds of movement creates the possibility of articulating subtly different approaches to the shaping of each kind of rhythm. Below, I define and describe three kinds of movement that editors work with and look at some possible approaches to them.

THREE KINDS OF MOVEMENT

One experience the spectator has of movement is the sensory experience of physical movement, the movement of images and sound. In this kind of experience, there is kinaesthetic empathy with the rise and fall of the energy of the physical movement by itself. Does movement flow freely or is it restricted? Is it flailing or lyrical? Curving or direct? Each of these qualities expresses a different feeling, a different character or a different world. Following along with the arcs and flows of movement is a kind of ride in and of itself, in which the contraction and expansion of dynamics in time, space, and energy are a physical experience. Shaped into patterns, the movement of image and sound become physical rhythms (Fig. 5.1).

The next sort of rhythm is barely separable from the first, and in many cases will have precisely the same source, but is experienced slightly differently. It is the experience of the trajectory of the *emotions* in relation to the trajectory of the movement. Performances and juxtapositions convey emotions and provoke emotions. The editor's attention when cutting psychological exchanges is not so much on the motion of the images as on the movement of the emotions. The editor is still shaping the physical movement (that's all she has to work with), but she shapes it with her focus on how it conveys emotion, not

FIGURE 5.1

Bernadette Walong in No Surrender *(Richard James Allen, 2002). Dance films and scenes are driven by physical rhythm. The physical movement is the meaning. [Photo credit: The Physical TV Company/ Dominika Ferenz]*

on how it conveys pattern or spectacle. The movement patterns created by an editor *could* be understood as physical experiences, because the emotions are being physically expressed, but in fact, the editor is watching for and creating a pattern of the dynamics of emotions seen on the screen. The term I will use for the rhythms an editor shapes from movement experienced as emotional movement is emotional rhythm (Fig. 5.2).

The third kind of movement is the movement of *events*. An event is the release of new information or change of direction for characters as they pursue their goals. Each significant change in a story or structure is an event. Some events are big and have repercussions for the whole plot; others are minor and only change the direction of the plot a bit. In some films events occur rapidly, even dizzyingly; in other films there may be little change over the course of the whole, and the story

FIGURE 5.2

In En Kongelig Affære (A Royal Affair) *(Nikolaj Arcel, 2012) Princess Caroline's (Alicia Vikander) physical movement is restrained by her corsets, her position, her husband, and her time period. But, pushing against all of these physical restraints, her emotional life is turbulent and drives the film's rhythms. [Photo credit: Zentropa Entertainments, Danmarks Radio (DR), Trollhättan Film AB]* may consist of just one substantial event. In either case, an event is a perceptible change at the level of story or structure. It is what happens in a story as distinct from the emotional exchanges (which may, of course, be the source of story changes) and image flow (which expresses and reveals the events). Event rhythm is the shaping of time, energy, and movement of events over the course of the story or structure as a whole (Fig. 5.3).

These three types of rhythm—physical rhythm, emotional rhythm, and event rhythm—are cumulative. The physical rhythm sets up a kinaesthetic empathy. The emotional rhythm relies on emotionally expressive physical movement. And the event rhythm relies on both the physical and the emotional to communicate its world, ideas, and story.

FIGURE 5.3
Bruce Willis in Live Free or Die Hard (Len Wiseman, 2007). Almost everything in this action-packed film is an event that changes the course of the plot or story. The actors are not known for the emotional strength of their performances, but that's not the point of this sort of film, in which the thrills for the spectator come not only from the fireworks of the visuals but also from the rapid-fire change of events. [Photo credit: 20th Century Fox; The Kobal Collection; Frank Masi]

All three kinds of rhythm are ultimately just strands of one rhythm—that of the edited film—but making distinctions does have practical uses for the editing process. Distinguishing between kinds of rhythm allows us to identify more precisely where a problem may lie or where attention needs to be focused to make a rhythm work. It gives us something specific to look at and describe in our consultations about the progress of an edit, as opposed to trying to look at what has often been called "invisible."

Distinguishing between the kinds of movement an editor is shaping is useful for the judging of editing, too. It is a way of describing what we know or mean when we say something feels right.

When the Australian Screen Editors Guild was trying to start up its annual editing awards, there was a lot of discussion about the difficulties of judging editing and the lack of shared language for describing good editing. We wanted to institute awards to give editors the credit they deserve, but the question of how to judge the editing almost sank the process. The distinction between the movement of

---

australian | screen | editors

Australian Screen Editors Guild Awards Judging Criteria

(Judges assign a score from 1 to 10 for each criterion; the highest score out of 50 wins.)

1   Movement of story

Is the story clear? On a scale of 1 to 10, how well organized is the flow of information or plot events to convey the film's intentions?

2   Movement of emotion

Is the film compelling? How well shaped are the performances and interactions in the film to convey feeling and provoke emotional responses?

3   Movement of images

Are the film's images shaped effectively? From cut to cut and over a sequence or series of cuts, how well has the editor shaped the flow of images to create a visually engaging experience?

4   Style

Whether obvious or unobtrusive, has the editor established and sustained an approach to cutting that is appropriate to the production and supports the ideas and themes?

5   Structure and rhythm aggregate

This criterion addresses the integration of the other four, story, emotion, image flow, and style, into a whole that is well paced, timed, and organized to convey a compelling experience.

events, of emotions, and of physical images and sounds proved very useful to me in putting forward a set of judging criteria for the awards. The guild steering committee adopted these criteria, and I am reprinting them here as an example of how the distinctions between kinds of movement and rhythm can be helpful in judging the whole.

To elaborate on how an editor shapes physical, emotional, and event movement, the next three chapters will each focus on a particular type of rhythm. Chapters 6 and 7 each have a case study to demonstrate the practical applications and outcomes of focusing on a particular strand

GOOD EDITING IS *NOT* INVISIBLE

People often say that good editing is invisible; that if it's good, it lets you sink into the story so that you don't see the edits. But good editing is not invisible. True, you don't see the edits, but you *do* see the editing. In fact, saying "editing is invisible" is like saying films or videos are invisible.

So what do you see? You see movement. Movement shaped by editing.

You see physical movement. Watching the visual images is one level of seeing a film or video, and the flow, the pattern, or the movement from one image to another and over a sequence is created in editing.

You see (and hear!) emotion. Performances and interactions convey emotions and provoke emotions. Just like the movement of images, there are lots of ways that these can be spun in the editing suite. The flow of emotion doesn't shape itself, and when you experience it, you are experiencing editing.

All of these images and emotions are governed by structure or the movement of events. What happens? How is information released? The flow of the story is also shaped in editing. You definitely don't see structure when you see a good film, but if you experience a good story, one that moves along in a way appropriate to its subject matter, that doesn't confuse or bore, then you've seen the editing.

I propose that editors stop perpetrating the myth that good editing is invisible. Instead, when someone says good editing is invisible, editors can say, "Well, you can see movement, can't you? Editing shapes the movement that you see." If the images fall into a compelling visual pattern, if the emotions engage, if the story makes sense and keeps moving, the editing has shaped these three kinds of movement.

It would be easier, of course, not to argue. But this is not just a theoretical issue for editors; it's practical, political, and cultural. If we keep letting the myth that good editing is invisible slide by, it's an easy step from there to not knowing the difference between good editing and not-so-good editing, and an even easier step from there to just having the director or producer cut it himself.

When we say that good editing *is* visible, we can say how a good editor's talents are vitally important to the success of a production. A good editor has a talent for shaping movement. And this talent is distinct from the talents required for directing, producing, or shooting. It is a sensitivity to the movement of shots, performances, and story; a facility for shaping the flow of movement for an audience; and a creativity with combining the movement of images, emotions, and events laterally, to come up with something that is much more than any one of those things on its own.

of rhythm, and Chapter 8 has case studies focused on bringing all three types of rhythm back together to look at rhythm as a whole as "indispensable in fusing together the meanings expressed . . ."[2]

ENDNOTES

1. Aronson, L., *Scriptwriting Updated: New and Conventional Ways of Writing for the Screen,* p. 40.

2. Van Leeuwen, *Introducing Social Semiotics,* p. 182.

CHAPTER 6

Physical Rhythm

In the late 1920s Soviet filmmaker Dziga Vertov made a strong argument, in words and through his films, for editing being a means of showing the truth of the movement of the world:

> To edit; to wrest, through the camera, whatever is most typical, most useful, from life; to organize the film pieces wrested from life into a meaningful rhythmic visual order, a meaningful visual phrase, an essence of "I see."[1]

If one is concerned with physical rhythm, one is concerned, as Vertov proclaims above, with "meaningful rhythmic visual order," not as a means to something else but as a revelation in and of itself.

"Physical rhythm" is the rhythm created by the editor when she prioritizes the flow of the visible and audible physical movement in the film over other types of movement (such as emotional interactions of characters or larger patterns of events in stories). As we will see when looking at emotional rhythm and event rhythm, both of these types of rhythm crafting also rely on the shaping of the visible and audible, but physical rhythm is made when the visible and audible movement and energy are the primary concern of the sequence, the initiating rhythm.

In physical rhythm, movement patterns create meaning directly. Dance scenes, fight scenes, chase scenes, and action scenes are usually examples of this in narrative film. In abstract films, physical rhythm is often the only kind of rhythm being shaped, as these films are made exclusively of abstract flows of color, line, shape, etc. In physical scenes and abstract films, form and content are one: the spectator is watching the movement patterns, and the movement patterns are the meaning and metaphor.

Shaping physical rhythm means shaping the flow of physical movement's size, speed, force, direction, and other visible or audible elements across cuts. Cutting choices might be around whether to link or collide arcs of movement, and how to modulate the rise and fall of energy, the rate and concentration of movement, the pulses and cycles of tension and release in the flow of image and sounds.

When shaping physical rhythms, editors intuitively use a range of techniques and approaches. I have given names to four of these approaches, and described them below.

RECHOREOGRAPHING

Directors block or choreograph scenes and sequences to express meaning and convey intentions. But once on camera, blocking and

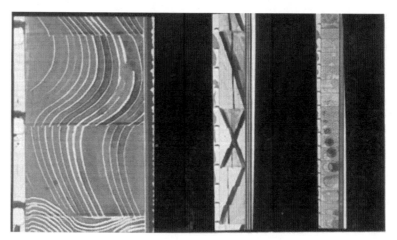

FIGURE 6.1
Frames from Len Lye's Colour Box *(1935). New Zealand filmmaker and "motion artist" Len Lye scratched lines and patterns directly onto the film—he was not using the movement of light, color, and shape to represent anything but the movement of light, color, and shape. Lye's short, abstract "ballets" are compelling for their surprising and humorous patterns and crafting of physical rhythm.*

choreography changes. It might be fantastically dynamic or it might be flat and un-dynamic from certain angles. It might take longer than is needed or it might be too quick. The framing might flatten performance. The performances themselves may not have all been equally dynamic. All of these variables come down to one problem: live movement does not simply transfer to the screen, it changes when it is filmed. So the editor may have to rechoreograph the movement in order to return its expressive intentions.

One method of doing this is to redesign the movement phrases using shots that allow one character or image to finish another's move. In other words, have a movement impulse start in one shot and then continue or complete its trajectory in the next shot. For example, a soldier shoots an arrow in one shot, and in another shot, the arrow plunges into the enemy's body. Or a wave crests in one shot and crashes in the next. Rechoreographing allows the editor to use the most dynamic bits of each shot and also to lengthen or contract the arc of the movement to make the most effective use of its energy, speed, and direction. The screen can flatten three-dimensional physical movement and rob it of expressive energy, but this technique returns the fullness of that expressive energy.

FIGURE 6.2

Battle scenes such as this one from Lord of the Rings, Return of the King *(Peter Jackson, 2003) may be choreographed in real life to unfold in real time, but they are rechoreographed in editing to make the most dynamic use of movement, energy, and time. In shot (a) the editor, Jamie Selkirk, has chosen to show us the peak of the movement curve as a warrior is slain. We don't see him fall to the ground, though; instead the editor cuts to a complementary movement in shot (b) that picks up the arc of the first shot's movement trajectory and shifts it in another direction, moving our eye to another action in the battle. [Photo credit: New Line Cinema, WingNut Films]*

PHYSICAL STORYTELLING

This method involves asking the question: What is a particular movement communicating in emotional or narrative terms? When cutting a dance scene or a fight scene, for example, ask yourself or the director: Where are we now in the movement's "story"? Where have we come from? The answers guide the direction of the editing. If the fight starts between equally matched opponents, you may start by looking for shots in which their movement energy in the frame is equally strong. If one fighter then gets the advantage, it is important to know where in the movement story that happens, on this punch or that fall, or this jab or that stumble; otherwise, you risk emphasizing the wrong energy for telling the physical story. It is possible to shape the movement of time and energy in physical rhythm to tell innumerable different physical stories, and it is often the case that the editor changes the story or how it unfolds, because particular shots have more impact, beauty, or energy and so the physical story she cuts unfolds differently from that which may originally have been intended. This is an excellent way of working, and is very common, but not the only way. It can also be creatively stimulating to get the director to tell you the movement's story. Either knowing the director's version of the story in movement quality/energy terms, or building a version of the physical story based on what the material is asking for, informs decisions about how long to stay with things, how quickly to build or to establish them, and where their development is leading.

DANCING EDITS

As discussed in Chapter 2, editing is a form of choreography. An edit is a way of limiting or shaping the flow of movement, creating a smooth connection or a shock. The edit is the join in movement arcs or the accent that creates a phrase. To "dance the edits" means to use the edit point as an expressive element of the physical action. This approach uses the cut as an element in the dynamic of the sequence. In this

FIGURE 6.3

Editor Thelma Schoonmaker and Director Martin Scorsese had a different physical story for each of the many fight scenes in Raging Bull *(1980), and each is cut accordingly, to be a pure physical expression of what is going on narratively and dramatically. [Photo credit: United Artists; The Kobal Collection]*

FIGURE 6.4

Audiences sometimes complain that in dance films like Chicago *(Rob Marshall, 2001), the editing is too fast or there are too many close-ups, so that they can't "see the choreography." No one would ever say this about a fight scene or a chase scene. That's because the choreography of these cinematic scenes is always created in the editing, and has been since the earliest days of cinema. Fred Astaire would not let directors edit his dance scenes because the entire rhythmic composition within them was created by him and his dancing partner. Without in any way diminishing the greatness of Fred Astaire, it is possible to say that cinema has other things to offer in an experience of physical movement than just recording the dancer's moves. In contemporary dance film, it is not that you are missing the "dance" by seeing only one dancer or one body part or by seeing a rapid hit–hit–hit of cuts. This is a screen dance, whose ultimate choreographic form is created with the cuts. What you see in the moves, the shots, and the cuts is, cumulatively, the action or the dance, not a version of the action all cut up. In these four shots from* Chicago, *Editor Martin Walsh makes a dance by editing together four moves into a rhythmically coherent phrase. [Photo credit: Miramax, The Producer's Circle, Storyline Entertainment]*

approach, the movement phrases, experiences, and actions are created with the cuts, which are themselves part of the action, part of the storytelling, part of the dance.

SINGING THE RHYTHM

During the cutting process, movement trajectories shaped by cuts can "sound" in the editor's head. This phenomenon draws on a kind of synesthesia that I think a lot of editors have. As the editor Tom Haneke says, "I hear spaces."[2] This may also be one reason editing is so often compared with music. The movements "sound" in editors' heads (bodies), with their timing, pacing, and trajectory phrasing making a kind of song. It is very hard to vocalize this song, and I'm not much of a singer. So when I say "sing," I often mean just tuning my awareness to the song in my head. I sing my cuts, too, not just the movements in a given shot, but the phrases that I make with edits, listening to breath, intensities, tensions, and releases of the flow of energy, time, space, and movement to see if I've hit a false note. It is not just because my background is in dance that I also "dance" as I cut. I have heard other editors speak of this phenomenon, too, wherein they notice their head, shoulders, eyebrows, blinks, or breaths moving sympathetically with the movement phrases being cut together, tracking their rise and fall of energy, and noting their punctuation points with a short sharp nod.[3] Singing the rhythm is an embodied manifestation of thinking rhythmically as described in Chapter 1. It is tuning one's own physical rhythms to the rhythms being perceived in the rushes, and it is a process at work in every single rhythmic decision I make.

In sum, when creating physical rhythm, editors often contend with the movement patterns visible in the raw material by *rechoreographing*. They find out the intentions of the director or the story and practice *physical storytelling*. They exploit the possibilities for using a cut as a form of movement, for example, as a link or a collision, with *dancing edits*. And editors tap directly into their own innate rhythms by *singing the rhythm*.

What follows is a brief analysis of the ways in which I used rechoreographing, physical storytelling, and dancing edits to cut a dance scene in the Physical TV Company production of *Thursday's Fictions* (Richard James Allen, 2006). As noted above, singing the rhythm is happening all the time.

CASE STUDY: "NOW" SCENE FROM *THURSDAY'S FICTIONS*

Physical TV Company productions are stories told by the body. Dance and storytelling are integrated, and there are moments when the whole story is carried by the physical. The final dance scene in *Thursday's Fictions* is one of these moments.

The dance scene at the end of *Thursday's Fictions* is a roughly 12-minute sustained movement sequence. Because this particular dance scene was always intended to be realized on the screen and not on the stage, its problems and possibilities are similar to those presented by many physical scenes: the movement has exciting moments, but its overall shape must be constructed in editing to give it direction, flow, cycles of tension and release, and a rhythm to which the spectator can synchronize. This particular scene had some inherent shape, as would, for example, a choreographed fight scene or sex scene, but the editing challenge was not to realize that precise shape, but rather to find the rhythm that expressed its intention.

At the beginning of the sequence (Fig. 6.5), the character Wednesday (Richard James Allen) has just asserted himself forcefully to save the trunk full of dances from Saturday (Emma Canalese, voiced by Mêmé Thorne). Shaken, and barely recovered from his exertion, he opens the trunk, thinking the dances will come flooding out.

But the trunk is empty (Fig. 6.6).

Stunned, Wednesday moves tentatively out of his safe, warmly lit corner, into the cavernous, gray room where all of the furniture left over from his father's life is scattered about, covered in drop cloths (Fig. 6.7).

The dance sequence begins when Wednesday starts to uncover the furniture and realizes that under each cloth is not a piece of furniture but a dancer, frozen and lifeless (Fig. 6.8).

FIGURE 6.5
Wednesday (Richard James Allen) shouts Saturday (Emma Canalese) out of his house. [Photo credit: The Physical TV Company; Simon Chapman]

FIGURE 6.6
Wednesday opens the trunk. [Photo credit: The Physical TV Company; Simon Chapman]

FIGURE 6.7
Drop cloth-covered furnishings in Wednesday's house. [Photo credit: The Physical TV Company; Simon Chapman]

FIGURE 6.8
Wednesday pulls drop cloths from the frozen, lifeless dancers. [Photo credit: The Physical TV Company; Simon Chapman]

The movement journey of the scene is from frozen lifelessness to floating freedom. It does not move in a straight line; its trajectory moves forward in three waves, and each of these waves needed a rhythmic cycle of tension and release within the cycle of the whole dance.

The dancing starts with Wednesday doing an "unfreezing" solo (Fig. 6.9).

The *physical storytelling* in Wednesday's opening solo, after all of the drop sheets are off, is that, like the dancers but in his own way, Wednesday is frozen, too. He reels and catches himself and then performs a series of gestures that move from a Frankenstein-like circling of his arms to a flowing, generous hand gesture. In the cut, I worked to create the feeling that sometimes Wednesday was moving and sometimes he was being moved by the energy and atmosphere around him. There is a 70-second tracking shot that leaves his movement and returns to it, de-emphasizing the effect of his movement and stressing the stillness in the room and the dancers. This long tracking shot is beautiful, and beauty is one of the reasons the dances need to live.

FIGURE 6.9
Wednesday moves creakily, unfreezing. [Photo credit: The Physical TV Company; Simon Chapman]

But it is dead beauty. The long time that it goes on for creates desperation for changes, dynamic variations, and movement. Getting the audience to want and value these things seemed like a good idea because these things are about to be served to them in spades. Coming out of the tracking shot, the stress and trajectory connections of the cuts are the start of the character's physical transformation. The cuts here obey the rules of continuity cutting, but just barely, so they feel magical, and this begins to lead to the next bit of physical storytelling in the dance.

What wakes the dancers from their frozen, lifeless state? In the script Wednesday's warming warms them. His feeling stirs theirs. When he starts to move more fluidly, his energy spreads around the room and awakens the dancers' movement energy. But, in rough cut screenings, this bit of story wasn't coming across because the screen flattened the movement energy. So we *rechoreographed*. I found and cut in shots that could be juxtaposed to look as though one movement caused the next. This was a matter of gauging the timing and trajectory phrasing of the juxtapositions. I rechoregraphed the order of movements and used select parts of the gestures rather than whole gestures to create the impression that Wednesday's movements stirred the dancers back to life.

For example: Wednesday throwing his body creates a current of air that stirs the dancers' skirts, then their hands, then their breath. We did this to make the connection physically visible. His movement trajectory stirs them (Fig. 6.10).

Then the dancers start their movement journey by breathing. The question here was how much breathing is needed to make that point? In the original choreography you could see the whole room come alive in just three long, visible inhalations and exhalations. (The movement exaggerates and shapes the in and out of the breath.) I thought at first I needed to go around the room to each dancer and see her take her breath, to show the breaths of each dancer awakening.

FIGURE 6.10
Wednesday also throws one of the drop cloths he has removed to try to stir the air around the dancers.
[Photo credit: The Physical TV Company; Simon Chapman]

(We have to stay close to feel breath—moving to a wide shot to show them all breathing just reads as bland.) But once we had the "stirring/waking" working better, we found we needed far fewer breaths—in fact, it was now back to the original three. Inhale in one shot, exhale in the next—I rechoreographed so that the dancers finished one another's breaths.

In the next moments the dancers come shuddering to life in a sequence that stops and starts haltingly. The same problem occurs as with the breaths—when you see the whole room live, you see that only three dancers are moving, and it looks like a little spike that shudders to a stop. The whole group has not yet coordinated, but the little spikes spark once, twice, three times around the room. But if we go out to the wide shot to see the three moving dancers isolated in a still room, their spike has no spark. The solution here was in rechoreographing to get the feeling intended. Instead of a whole room going still for 1 second, we ended up prolonging the stillnesses by cutting around the room on the dancers so that the beginning of each

FIGURE 6.11
Dancers Terri Herlings and Linda Ridgway begin to catch the spark of life and disperse it around the room. [Photo credit: The Physical TV Company; Simon Chapman]

movement spike, coming out of stillness, can be seen. The movement story is that the spikes spark around until, by the third one, everyone takes off (Fig. 6.11).

A sequence follows in which the dancers' energy is a bit frenetic, all over the place (Fig. 6.12). The physical storytelling is that they are coming to life awkwardly, struggling to break the ice and to get coordinated. To make this visible onscreen, we use a lot of *dancing edits.* We have gestures colliding, only peaks of energy being used, no full movement arcs until they stop.

In the next sequence, high-energy twists, leaps, spins, and dives are cut together with respect for screen direction and energy, not real time (rechoreographing). This montage of individual gestures travels first from screen right to screen left (Fig. 6.13a), then back from left to right (Fig. 6.13b), as the dance did. In the live dance this happens three times. In the cut it occurs only once, but the dancing edits create far greater intensity of juxtaposed movements. The composition of a

FIGURE 6.12
The dancers' moves and energy go wild. [Photo credit: The Physical TV Company; Simon Chapman]

FIGURE 6.13
Leaps and twists cut together to create a flow. [Photo credit: The Physical TV Company; Simon Chapman]

series of short stabs, each one triggering the next, makes the same feeling as was on stage but through a different approach.

As pioneering dance film maker Amy Greenfield says:

> Filmdance energy is produced through editing as well as the camera. Movements can be shortened, interrupted, and put together in such a way as to heighten the perception of energy. An extreme example of such an energy is obtained by interrupting movement at its climax.[4]

At 11½ minutes into the scene comes the penultimate sequence of the dance (Fig. 6.14). Called the "tribal" sequence, it is designed to emphasize the peak of unity and power of the group, as it reaches the climax of the dance's story. The dancers have come fully to life. They have explored different configurations of fractured movements; of solos, duets, and trios; and now they finally come together in a unison of powerful downward stomps and elongated stretches. The visual

FIGURE 6.14
Unison energy for the first time in the dance. [Photo credit: The Physical TV Company; Simon Chapman]

rhythm is complicated by the fact that the whole group starts the beat and keeps the beat, but individuals split off to dance in counterpoint and then return. Given the complexities of the physical rhythms and their importance to the physical story, I sang this one out loud as I cut, making sure I knew where the downbeat was on each cycle of stomping, stretching, and circling. I stretched the beat sometimes, which worked better visually but created difficulties for the composer. The downbeat then became a discussion point between myself; the director/choreographer, Richard James Allen; and the composer, Michael Yezerski. Michael was eventually able to find a continuous and urgent rhythmic pattern through this climactic section.

The physical storytelling of the last section, known as the final float, is that the dancers, their beauty, breath, life, energy, and movement are all dissolving into one another (Fig. 6.15). The final digital effect returns the dancers to their state of light, but out of the trunk, where they can shine.

FIGURE 6.15

Dancers dissolve into one another—an editing device functioning narratively. [Photo credit: The Physical TV Company; Simon Chapman]

FIGURE 6.16

Dance becoming light. [Photo credit: The Physical TV Company; Simon Chapman/Mark Woszczalski]

MUSIC, SOUND, AND PHYSICAL RHYTHM

Dances in musicals are cut using the music to which they were choreographed, but the final 12-minute dance scene of *Thursday's Fictions* was choreographed in silence, with the dancers creating a strongly rhythmical bond between themselves to keep in time. It was done this way on purpose. One of the core principles of Physical TV Company productions is that rhythm in the final film is created in the edit suite. The composers I work with don't like temp music because it boxes them into a corner when the director gets attached to it. I don't like it because it defeats the point of the whole exercise. If you cut according to some external rhythm, what happens to the rhythms inherent in the movement? And what happens to the rhythms the editor sees, imagines, or dreams of bringing into being by the choreography of cuts? They get no opportunity to exist, never mind be brought to life.

Some physical scenes will very often benefit from the use of temp music, particularly if they have no choreographed shape and the editor has to invent the structure of the rhythm. In this case editors may use some music to help them find a first cut or direction, but they are wary of letting the music impose too much of itself on the images and will strip the music out periodically to check that the visual flow has integrity without the music.

Much more important than temp music for physical scenes are temp sound effects. Much of the rise and fall of emphasis and energy in an action, fight, or chase sequence is carried on the sound. So, the editor is wise to have a cache of punches, whooshes, thuds, and crashes handy to indicate the punctuation marks she intends to have in the phrasing of the movement of image and sound through the scene.

SUMMARY

Working with the physical movement of dance in *Thursday's Fictions* gave me the opportunity to work directly on shaping physical rhythms. In this case, rhythmically complete phrases of movement were devised by the choreographer, but the timing, pacing, and trajectory phrasing of any movement are always somewhat altered when movement is framed and captured by a camera. Therefore, the editor's job is to re-create not the precise choreography, but the *feeling* of the original choreography. The same is generally true of most scenes in which physical rhythms dominate. Chases and fights, for example, must have their rhythms created in editing to *feel* like chases and fights. This involves shaping the relative timing, pacing, and trajectory phrasing of movement. I have named the processes I use to accomplish the shaping of physical rhythm: rechoreographing, physical storytelling, dancing edits, and singing the rhythm. Each of these is a name for a method of activating my intuitive rhythmic thinking in service of the choreographic shaping of physical rhythm. To some extent, because the visible and audible movement of a film is the material the editor uses to shape any rhythms, these same processes occur in the cutting of emotional and event rhythms, too.

The next chapter will look at emotional rhythm and articulate some ideas about seeing and shaping the movement of emotions in the physical movement of performers.

ENDNOTES

1. Vertov, D., *Kino-Eye: The Writings of Dziga Vertov*, pp. xxv–xxvi.
2. Tom Haneke, quoted in Oldham, G., *First Cut: Conversations with Film Editors,* p. 44.
3. In the documentary about editors and their processes, *The Cutting Edge: The Magic of Movie Editing* (Wendy Apple, 2004), there is a sequence in which Walter Murch demonstrates his version of singing the edits. He says he edits standing up to feel "sprung" and able to "hit the cut with my knees bent . . . this allows me to internalize the rhythms, the visual rhythms of what is happening."
4. Greenfield, A., "Filmdance: Space, time and energy," in the *Filmdance Catalogue*, p. 6.

CHAPTER 7

Emotional Rhythm

This chapter is about shaping emotional exchanges onscreen and emotional responses of audiences. It is about the timing, pacing, and trajectory phrasing of movement of emotions. Practically speaking, this means letting the edit be guided by the performance. "Performance guides the cutting" is something editors say a lot, and it is a good starting place for looking at the principles of crafting emotional rhythms.

In *In the Blink of an Eye* Walter Murch writes about being guided by one particular movement in performances: the blink. He says an editor can look at when the actor blinks to see the rise and fall of the character's emotional dynamic:

> our rates and rhythms of blinking refer directly to the rhythm and
> sequence of our inner emotions and thoughts . . . those rates
> and rhythms are insights into our inner selves and, therefore, as
> characteristic of each of us as our signatures.[1]

But the blink is just one of a huge range of visible movements of emotion. The performers' faces and bodies make a dance of emotions—of impulses and responses fluctuating over their bodies. Their pauses, hesitations, shifts of position, glances, swallows, twitches, smiles, sobs, sighs, startles, shivers, affirmations, denials, and so on are all contractions and releases of feeling, all energetic motions written all over the screen. Similarly, the rise and fall of intonation, the pauses and stress points, are the movement of emotion and intention through sound.

FIGURE 7.1

Documentary generally uses non-actors, but the same rule applies: people convey emotions through intentional movements. In the documentary Thin Blue Line *by Errol Morris, (1988) this character, Randall Adams, who is on death row for killing a police officer in Houston, conveys his innocence and sincerity to the audience through his movement and intonation, his upright posture and direct gaze to the camera, as much as his words. He was, as a result of this documentary, acquitted of the crime. [Photo credit: American Playhouse/Channel 4; The Kobal Collection]*

In cutting emotional rhythm, a performance is given to the editor and the editor has to work with its rhythm and make choices about it. The choices might range from respecting it completely to disrupting it entirely and creating a new rhythm. There is a lot of room for rhythmic creativity and decision making along the spectrum between these two poles. One consideration is the strength of the performance—a strong performance is more likely to be used and to be respected. It will shape the emotional rhythm by putting emphasis on the emotions it conveys. But this can raise another consideration in cutting emotional rhythm: Which emotion is being conveyed, for how long, and at what level of strength or intensity? A performance may be strong by itself, but is it what is needed in the story at that moment? Does it meet the energy of the other performances or does it overwhelm them or take them in another direction? An editor can select different takes, or different timings of takes to alter the energy of a performance pretty radically, so that a scene can end up playing out onscreen as it was written or it may end up being quite different in tone, pace, and even content to the original script.

Given that performances and scenes are often covered in more than one take and from more than one angle, there are interesting problems for an editor to grapple with in shaping the emotional rhythm. Most of these problems can be summed up with three questions:

- Which shot?

- Where?

- For how long?

Which Shot?

When looking at different takes of performances in order to choose "which shot" the editor looks for moments of authenticity in the performance, moments where the framing or light has caught the actor just right to emphasize their qualities of feeling or intention, moments where an expression has crossed their faces and revealed subtext, and especially moments where their energy or intention throws an emotional opening, question, or challenge to the other performer.

Where?

When deciding where to place a shot an editor may start at the beginning of a scene and add, shot by shot, to the unfolding of the emotional exchange. Or she may start with the shot that she has decided is really at the heart of the scene, the one everything else needs to lead to, and build outwards. Cutting toward a shot in this way means finding shots that build to it logically in other performances, shots that throw the openings or questions or challenges needed to set up or reveal the heart of the scene. Ether way, deciding where a shot goes is a creative process that decides the timing of the emotional exchange, its pace, and its phrasing or emphasis.

For How Long?

This question of choosing the precise duration of a shot can come later in the process, once a scene's logic and flow has been roughly put into place. Trimming frames off of shots can make cuts smoother or more abrupt by eliding or colliding movements with the edits. Trimming can also focus attention on the key aspect of a performance, the key glance or shrug or other emotion driven move that tells the story. The important thing here is to cut on the frame that gives the strongest impression of the emotion being thrown from one performer to the next. This is because, with lots of takes and shots to choose from, you are looking for the strongest feeling of cause and effect, you are trying to create the feeling that one actor's emotional throw is caught by the other actor and has an impact on how they, in turn, feel and express their feelings.

In editing, the decisions about "which shot, where, and for how long" are decisions about how to throw the emotional energy from one shot to another. I use an improvisation exercise called Throwing the Energy as a metaphor for what an editor is doing when shaping emotional rhythm. Here is a description of how it works, and later, some instructions for playing it yourself, which is recommended— better to experience something physically than to just read about it!

In the Throwing the Energy game, the first person pretends he has a ball of energy in his hands. The ball is invisible, but he articulates its outlines by shaping and moving his hands around it. He plays with it for a while, letting it travel through all parts of his body, and as he does, we get to see what kind of energy he imagines it to be. If it is fierce, compressed energy, the moves that shape it are tight and force-ful. If it is easygoing, playful energy the moves that shape the invisible energy are relaxed and light. Once he has played with the energy for a while, he throws the energy ball to the next person, and this is where it gets really interesting. The first person may throw the energy in a hard fast direct move. If he does, than the next person catches it, *as it was thrown*. If the first person slams the ball of energy at the second person's head, the second person will instinctively reel as though hit. If the first person dribbles drops of energy into the second person's palm, the second person will crouch around the drops protectively, gathering them before they slither away. In other words, the kind of energy the first person throws, combined with the force, speed, and direction of his throw, equal the kind of energy that the next person receives.

Why does it matter how one person throws the invisible ball of emotionally laden energy and how the next person catches it? Because throwing the energy is what an editor is doing with cuts.

An editor chooses the first shot's duration and frame to throw a certain kind of energy. This shot is then juxtaposed with another shot. The second shot receives the energy the first shot throws. The editor is

FIGURE 7.2

One of the earliest things children learn is to respond to emotional energy. As infants, although we cannot understand words, we still understand the energy with which they are spoken. For example, we shrink from anger or embrace delight, because the energy communicates the emotion on a nonverbal level. In this sequence from Down Time Jaz *(Karen Pearlman, 2002), I used the children's innate capacity to respond to energy qualities in movement and got the child performers to dance very convincingly by playing the Throwing the Energy game with them. [Photo credit: The Physical TV Company; Dominika Ferenz]* creating an impression of cause and effect, an impression that the energy and action in the first shot causes the responsive motion seen in the next shot.

Because the energy thrown creates a cause-and-effect relationship with the energy of the next shot, the editor has begun to shape a trajectory phrase of emotional energy. For example, if a character smiles gratefully in one shot (the gratitude being the energy or intention that propels the movement of the smile), and another character shrugs awkwardly in the next shot, the gratitude appears to have caused the awkwardness. The timing, pacing, and trajectory phrasing of this exchange are a little piece of emotional rhythm built from the rhythm of the performances.

PRACTICAL EXERCISE

Playing the Throwing the Energy Game

Playing the Throwing the Energy game with editing or film-making students gives them a very immediate experience of how this concept works in the filmmaking process.

Get together a group of five or more people; a small classroom of ten or twelve students is ideal. Start the game off by pretending you have a ball of energy in your hands. Shape your hands around the ball, shift it from one hand to the other, and then toss it, as you might toss a tennis ball to someone else in the room. The person you throw it to will catch it. And not only will he catch it, but he will raise his hands to catch it in the air along the trajectory in which it was thrown. I have seen students raise both hands overhead and stumble backward five steps to catch a wildly thrown pitch that is sailing overhead. I have even seen students duck when they think they will be hit by the energy and then turn around and run to the spot where it would have fallen, had it been a real ball, and retrieve the invisible, imaginary substance, the energy that was thrown.

When everyone playing has had a chance to throw and catch the energy, there are two things to be discussed.

1. Everyone catches the energy the way it was thrown. This is what makes the game such a useful metaphor for what an editor does. She throws the energy from one shot to the next. She chooses the shots, their placement, their duration, and the frames to make an emotional arc from one shot to the next, so that it appears that the emotional energy thrown in one shot is the energy that is caught, or responded to, in the next shot.

2. The next thing to point out is that the energy is invisible. This always gets a laugh, because of course everyone knows the energy is invisible. But the interesting thing is that, *even though it is invisible, everyone watches it.* No one's eyes stay on the person who has thrown the energy, all eyes *always* follow the invisible ball to the next person. And this is exactly what the editor is doing to create emotional rhythm. She is catching your eye with the emotional energy and then throwing it to the next shot with exactly the right timing to keep you watching the invisible movement of energy as it travels between the performers.

In the Throwing the Energy game, we watch the energy course through the players, changing and expressing their intentions. This is also what we are watching when we watch a character's emotion move. We are watching, on a much more minute level, the play of emotional energy in his body, how slowly he smiles, how awkwardly he shrugs. These are the expressions of emotion in movement. Seeing the emotional energy work its way through an acting performance is more subtle than seeing energy in an energy game, but there are some specific things that actors do in creating their performances, which, if an editor knows to watch for them, can help her shape the energy and arcs of emotional rhythm.

PREPARE, ACTION, REST

One useful idea about actors' movement comes from the Russian theater director Vsevolod Meyerhold, who was a direct influence on the seminal Soviet director, editor, and teacher Sergei Eisenstein. Meyerhold's influence on Eisenstein had a significant influence on the development of editing and film form. One of his ideas is that every movement has three phases: a preparation, an action, and a recovery.[2]

For the editor of emotional rhythm this idea of "preparation, action, recovery" is a way of seeing a trajectory through an actor's movement. It implies a phrasing in every complete action that can be marked off, with a conceptual grease pencil, as a possible place for a cut. If an editor can watch an actor picking up a cup of tea (or throwing a bomb) and see these three phases of movement, then the editor can ask herself: What do I need from this movement to throw the emotional energy to the next character or event? Do I need just the preparation? Is it enough for the audience to know that the first character does pick up the tea, and it is the way he goes for the tea that causes the other character's disapproving glance? Or do I need to see it all the way through to the first character's obvious enjoyment of the tea, and that becomes what causes the disapproving glance? By watching for the prepare, action, recovery arc of a given movement, whether by a professional actor or by a social actor in a documentary, editors can find an optimal point to cut in the trajectory of the emotional energy to convey the force and quality of emotion required by the scene.

Two very different concepts that are also helpful to editors in training their eyes to see emotions move come from Stanislavski's "method."

THE ACTOR'S ACTIONS

One important concept Stanislavski introduced to the training of actors is the idea of "actions." An action, in actors' terms, is the actor's psychological intention spelled out as a verb. The reason for making his intentions into verbs is to give the actor something to do rather than to be: doing is active, being is passive. Most importantly, for the editor, the action, being a verb, implies movement of thoughts or feelings.

Actions in this sense make the text or the subtext into emotional movement. If an actor has the line, "May I have some cake?" his subtext may or may not be the same as the text. He may be saying the words that ask for cake, but the subtext is asking not for cake, rather, it is asking for affection.

Actors will try to make their actions as active and emotionally accurate to their subtext as possible. "To ask" is one possible action, but depending on what the actor thinks is his real objective in the scene, "to ask" might turn into "to plead," "to manipulate," "to distract," "to deceive," "to declare love for" . . . Whereas some of these may seem outlandish with reference to a simple piece of cake, it is important to remember that unless all the character really wants is cake, he could be asking for any number of things—love, time, respite, engagement, or forgiveness, for example. His objective is what he really wants; his action is what he is doing to get what he wants. His action is the energy that propels his movement.

An editor can look at the actor's movement (including the aural movement of the voices rather than the words) and see what an actor is doing *subtextually*. If the editor can see the action, for example, pleading, behind the words, then she can discern a point at which the action has reached its optimal energetic point for the throw. The editor can perceive the action as a movement phrase, see where its cadences, breaths, stress points, etc., are, and make the cut at the exact point at which she wants to throw the energy to the next actor, for precisely the impact she wants it to have.

If we look at an actor's action as what he is *really* doing, then we can explain why cuts that don't match perfectly in continuity still work. When the emotional energy is being shaped, we don't notice little continuity errors or mismatches because we are not watching the character reach for cake; we are watching him reach for affection. Our attention is not on the movement patterns in and of themselves, it is on their emotional meaning. If the cut throws the emotion well, then our eye follows the emotion, not the cake. The emotional movement is visible, as Murch tells us, in the rate and quality of blinks and it is also visible in the breath, the tilt of the head, the purse of the lips, the raise of an eyebrow, etc. All of these movements, especially seen in close-up or medium close-up, are effective ways of throwing the emotion. So, if an actor reaches for cake with one hand and then picks it up with the other, this continuity gaffe will go unnoticed if the actor is truthfully inhabiting the body of the character. If the actor is playing his action and throws his emotion to the other character with movement—such as a hopeful raise of his eyes—then, as his eyes lift up, the editor sees the emotion move and cuts to the other character. Does the other character reassure or turn away from that hopeful pleading? The editor has thrown the movement of the emotional energy and opened the questions, "How will it be caught?" and "What will be the effect this emotional cause has?"

Throwing the emotion well is not just a case of deciding on the cadence of the emotion being thrown but how it is going to be received. If we go back to the Throwing the Energy game, the players receive the energy as it is thrown, so what they are reacting to is not just the energy but where it is directed. If it slams at their head, they don't shake it off their fingers. Film actors are not improvising; even if they were on set, now that they're on filmstrips, they are not any longer. So, the editor can look both at the available range of re-actions and at the available range of throwing actions before choosing exactly where to cut. The editor's job is to shape the movement of the emotion into a *feeling* of cause and effect, a feeling of throw and catch. It is the actor's performance that draws our "eye-trace"[3] to the emotional movement; it is the editor's cut that determines the trajectory of the throw.

PRACTICAL EXERCISE

Goals and Actions

To understand how actions work, it is helpful to have an experience yourself of what you are doing to achieve your goals at any given moment. You could ask your self questions about your actions and goals in almost any scenario, but we'll use a classroom as an example.

Ask yourself: why are you in class today, what did you come here for? It is likely that you will come up with a fairly small range of answers that might include knowledge, skills, and to see your friends, but will almost definitely include the answer "to pass the class or to get a good grade."

Once a goal such as "gain knowledge" or "get a good grade" has been established, then ask yourself: What will you do to get what you want? The answers will vary, from showing up to staying awake, paying attention and asking questions, making comments that make you look smarter than the other students, bringing an apple for the teacher, or doing the readings or helping shift the tables into position, and so on.

At this point you discover that you easily identify your "actions"—what you will do to get what you want. If you try cracking jokes to get a good mark, you will keep doing that if it gets a smile from the teacher and stop doing it if it gets a frown. So your goals and actions create a cause-and-effect chain in life. The effect you get will determine whether you continue using an action or change actions and try something else to achieve your goals.

Or you may change your goals. If you switch to cracking jokes to make your friends laugh and to irritate the teacher, then your action will have changed based on the change in goals, and a new cause-and-effect chain will have been set in motion.

Armed with this immediate, embodied knowledge of how you perform actions to achieve goals, you can begin to see what actions the characters are doing when they play actions to achieve their goals.

BEATS

The Stanislavski method has another word that can be very useful for editors in shaping emotional rhythm: "beats." There are a number of possible interpretations of this idea, but for our purposes we will say that the beat is the point at which an actor changes or modifies his action.

For example, if a character named Joe wants affection but asks for cake, his girlfriend might say, "Help yourself." But if his girlfriend is withholding affection and her action is "to ignore," then Joe, having failed to achieve his objective (getting affection) with his first action, will then shift his action to any number of other actions such as "to demand," "to inspire," or "to insist." The change of action, or change of what Joe is doing to achieve his objective, from asking to demanding is called a beat. There may be any number of beats in a scene until objectives are achieved (Joe gets affection) or thwarted (his girlfriend breaks up with him). Keep in mind that, in the real world of a documentary or in a well-crafted drama, the other person, the girlfriend in this case, will also have objectives. She will have actions she is doing to achieve her objectives, and beats as she changes her action to accomplish her goals. The emotional energy is thrown between the two characters, back and forth. If Joe throws his request for affection gently, by asking, and the girlfriend throws back a block by ignoring, then the change of Joe's action to demanding is caused by the emotional energy his girlfriend threw. This is a cause-and-effect chain. Asking causes ignoring, ignoring causes demanding, and so on. Emotion moves back and forth, like a tennis ball in play. But it is the editor who shapes the rhythm of the game. She shapes it by choosing the shots for the energy they contain, placing the shots to make a dynamic and credible emotional arc, and trimming the shots to the frames on which the energy is optimally thrown and caught.

What is important for the editor is that a beat gives her the chance to see the end of one emotional energy trajectory and the rise of another.

The energy of the actor's movement will change according to the actor's intention, and editors who sensitize themselves to these changes can see beats as little movement phrases. For example, if Joe's action is to ask, his eyes will move directly, and he is likely to blink at the end of his request, throwing it to his girlfriend with a simple and direct energetic motion. If his girlfriend throws back hostility by ignoring him, Joe will have a beat, a responsive shift of his action to this new emotional development. Possibly that beat can be seen as he looks away, blinks a few times, maybe bites his lip or sighs, possibly not. Either way, the beat will occur as he shifts into his new action, in this case to demand, and his eye, breath, head, and face movement will change again. The editor uses all of these moves as potential cutting points, because they are the movement from which she will shape the rhythms that the audience experiences as the *meaning* in the actors' exchange.

In sum, editors throw the emotional energy of one shot to the next by choosing which shot, where, and for how long. When the throw is caught and the response is thrown back, the editor has shaped a cause-and-effect chain. To shape the cause and-effect chain effectively, the editor watches for the movement of emotion across faces, gestures, and sound. The ability to see a preparation, action, recovery arc, and an actor's actions and beats gives editors the ability to see emotional energy move and ways of cutting emotional movement into rhythms.

KEEPING EMOTIONAL ENERGY MOVING

To paraphrase Woody Allen from the end of *Annie Hall*, an emotional exchange is like a shark—it has to keep moving forward or it dies. For an editor this means: you can't repeat an emotional moment without killing it. In a drama, one way of keeping emotion in motion is by keeping the characters moving toward their objectives.

Ask yourself:

1. What does this character want? These are their *Objectives*

2. What will they do to get it? These are their *Actions*.

Actors do actions to achieve objectives, but if the action doesn't work they move on, they change tactics—this is called a *"beat."*

Ask yourself:

1. Where are the *beats*?

An actor's beat provides you with a cutting point.

Here's an example:

In this two hander the woman wants to go, and the man wants her to stay.

Objectives: Her objective is to get away, his objective is to keep her there.

What will each of them do to get what they want?

His *Actions*: To ask, to cajole, to demand, to plead, to beg.

Her *Actions*: To dodge, to tease, to dismiss, to resist, to reject.

Tip: You can see all of this going on in the way they speak— intonation, force, speed, and the movement of bodies— posture, gesture, movement energy. Watch and listen to the way they move and you are watching and listening to the movement of emotion.

He asks. Cut. She dodges. Cut back to him – what does he do when she dodges? He has a *beat*, he changes his *action*, asking didn't work, so he tries cajoling, and so on.

Your job as an editor is to keep the emotions MOVING. If he asks, she dodges, and he asks again (repeats), the scene dies. He asks, she dodges, he cajoles—now the scene is in motion he is changing because her actions have an effect on him. He makes another choice, she makes another choice, we cut the emotion moving between them escalating/diminishing, winning/losing, causing/effecting to keep the emotion in motion.

What do you do?

1. Select the shots where they execute their *actions* most effectively.

2. Pit these against the counter actions of the other characters.

3. Cut back to the first character to find out what they do next to achieve their objective.

   Beware:

   Don't cut back to them doing the same thing or the emotion stops in its tracks.

   Don't cut back to them just feeling something, like feeling sad because their action didn't work (unless it is the end of the scene).

4. Cut back to them *doing* something and the emotion stays in motion.

CASE STUDY: *THE HOURS*

What follows is a case study on the cutting of a scene from *The Hours* (Stephen Daldry, 2004), a drama scene in which the emotional rhythm is shaped from the energy thrown between two characters as each tries to achieve her objectives.

There are, of course, thousands of scenes that could demonstrate the principles involved in shaping emotional rhythm. I chose this scene from *The Hours* in the first instance because of the brilliance of Toni Collette's performance as Kitty, the neighbor who comes to call on one of the central characters of the film, Laura, played by Julianne Moore.

Toni Collette has an astonishing capacity to reveal the layered symphony of emotion moving through her character's soul through the movement of her face, head, and body. But her performance in this scene had to be balanced against the elegant performance by Julianne Moore, whose character is tentative and uncertain compared to Toni Collette's brassy extroverted Kitty. The editor, Peter Boyle, does an extremely effective job of balancing the two performances, shaping Toni Colette's to just the right amount of expressive activity and providing respite from the intensity of her energy with well-measured interjections of the restrained Julianne Moore.

This scene, with its surprising climax, is played almost entirely on subtext, and the richness of that subtext is experienced in the emotional arcs shaped by the editor. Boyle has been guided by the performances, but also shaped them to give balance between them and continually renew the questions of how each character's utterances will affect the other. If, for example, Kitty confesses, what does Laura do? If Laura probes, what does Kitty do? These questions, as discussed in Chapter 2, are not consciously asked. They are created and understood immediately by the movement that expresses emotion, movement that we experience directly through our mirror neurons and our kinaesthetic empathy. The shape, rate, and intensity of emotional movement, and the tension and release of the emotional questions are in the hands of the editor.

This scene between Kitty and Laura is complex and traverses, in the course of the 5 minutes it takes to play out, an escalating series of character objectives, actions, and beats. It starts with Kitty coming in on Laura at a vulnerable moment, when Laura is cursing her own incompetence at baking; her cake has turned out lumpy and lopsided. Kitty's objective at the beginning seems to be to boost her own confidence, to compare herself to her neighbor and come up favorably. Laura just wants to appear to be a proper homemaker or, on a more basic level, to survive, to keep her head above water in this competition.

Kitty notices that Laura has baked a cake and walks over to inspect it. Cut to Laura getting coffee spoons from the drawer as though she

FIGURE 7.3

The emotional rhythms of this scene from The Hours *(Stephen Daldry, 2004) are beautifully modulated by editor Peter Boyle. In this exchange he balances Laura's (Julianne Moore's) discomfort, visible in her tense shoulders and back, with Kitty's (Toni Collette's) friendly mocking to give the exchange a bit of sharpness but not draw blood. [Photo credit: Paramount Pictures, Miramax, Scott Rudin Productions]*

wishes she could just crawl into the drawer and hide (Fig. 7.3a). We see just enough of her tension to know she feels Kitty's inspection keenly and then cut back to see just enough of Kitty's tinkling, mocking laugh to know that her good humor is laced with scorn (Fig. 7.3b). Too much of Laura's anxiety in this exchange would make her look hopelessly neurotic. Too much of Kitty's mocking would make her look cruel. The balance that Boyle has achieved in the time spent on each of them and the timing of cuts onto their gestures gives the relationship complexity—there is friendliness, helpfulness, good cheer, and irony at the same time there is neurosis, mocking, and gloating.

Once Kitty is seated at Laura's table with a cup of coffee, there is a series of shot–reverse shot cuts of the two women in conversation. This is a very common configuration for a two-handed scene, and the emotional rhythm is shaped by choosing when to cut from one character to the next. In this case Kitty's flirty self-confidence bounces energetically against Laura's quiet, self-effacing comments and inquiries. Until Laura says something that Kitty doesn't really understand (Fig. 7.4a) and Kitty reacts, first defensively (Fig. 7.4b) and then by withdrawing her attention from Laura and looking around the house irritated and bored. When Kitty's eye lights on a book Laura has left on the counter top, there is a cut to a wide two-shot. Cutting out

FIGURE 7.4
After some chit-chat, Laura throws an idea toward Kitty that she doesn't really understand (a) and Kitty reacts by closing off her charm and openness (b).

of a shot–reverse shot sequence and into a wide two-shot is usually a signal that the emotional objective of a scene has either been achieved or thwarted. In this case Kitty's objectives have been achieved—she is confirmed as commanding and vivacious—and Laura's have been thwarted—she has lost Kitty's approval by her clumsy introspection. Up until now, we have been watching the emotions being thrown between the two, watching first one character, and then the other, receive the emotional energy and bat it back. When the emotional question has been resolved, cutting to a two-shot gives the audience a more objective view of the state of play. The two-shot serves as a punctuation point, closing one question and opening another.

In the wide two-shot, a book, *Mrs Dalloway* by Virginia Woolf, is in the foreground, in focus, and the two characters are out of focus in the background (Fig. 7.5a). The cinematographer shifts the focal point from the foreground to the background in the middle of Kitty saying the line, "Oh, you're reading a book." This line is an accusation. If the subtext were written as text it might read, "That's a very strange thing to do; no wonder you're so strange." Kitty gets up, covering her distaste for books with a teasing inquiry and swinging her hips in a mix of officiousness and flirtatiousness as she goes to pick up the book, asking, "What's this one about?" (Fig. 7.5b). Laura, left in

FIGURE 7.5

Editor Peter Boyle comes in on this two-shot as a way of changing the subject and tone of the scene. The shot starts with the book in focus and Kitty's attention on it, out of focus and in the background. Then the focus shifts to Kitty, who takes charge of the dynamic of the conversation once more and sashays over to have a look at the book.

the background of the wide shot that Kitty now dominates completely, starts to explain, haltingly.

The spatial dynamic and performances create tension—is Laura going to manage to stumble through an explanation or dissolve tongue-tied in the path of Kitty's effusive handling of the conversation? Laura manages. She looks inward and draws on the strength she's gotten from the book to say, "Well, it's about this woman who's incredibly, well, she's a hostess and she's incredibly confident . . ." Here Boyle cuts to a reverse shot of Kitty in time to see Kitty's expression change from boredom and distaste to apparent interest and delight as the key character in the book is described as "confident" and "giving a party." Seeing Kitty shift from boredom to engagement is important because it aligns Kitty with the confident character in the book.

Boyle then cuts back to Laura, who gently delivers a blow to Kitty, a velvet-covered hammer that cracks Kitty's façade. We are on Laura, who looks more glowing and energetic than she has yet in the scene; when she delivers the blow. She says, ostensibly about the main character in the book, but clearly also about Kitty, "Because she's confident, everyone thinks she's going to be fine. But she isn't" (Fig. 7.6a). This is an emotional throw to Kitty, and Boyle cuts to her to let us watch the whole arc of her receiving and responding to the emotional energy. Toni Collette, as Kitty, speaks volumes with her facial

FIGURE 7.6
Laura is gently cracking open Kitty's façade by describing the plot of the book, Mrs Dalloway. *She throws her energy gently but confidently, and it hits its mark, making Kitty slow down and reflect.*

expressions, even the way she flips through the pages of the book, by slowing down and absorbing the impact of this blow to her façade (Fig.7.6b). She closes the book with a degree of deliberateness that delivers subtext something along the lines of: "I don't want to be like this character anymore, but I can't just dismiss her."

Laura's action now is to expose Kitty; Kitty's is to keep control. This moment is sustained by the cutting. Kitty closes the book; cut back to Laura, watching; back to Kitty as she puts the book down; back to Laura, who quietly says "So"; back to Kitty, who gathers herself together and tries for a perky smile but breaks it off to look away. This series of five shots sustains the moment rather than being a series of throws and catches of emotional energy. Nothing changes between the two characters. It is as though the moment is holding its breath. They are both holding the energy, filled with the question of how Kitty will deal with this sudden revelation about who she really is.

Holding the moment in this way is a very delicate operation and needs to be done fluidly and lightly. All too often one sees a strong emotional scene become heavy-handed by sitting too long on the emotionally laden shots with no change or variation. But Boyle's handling of this moment is both fluid and light. He cuts very fast: all five shots in under 15 seconds. But because the characters are both concentrating intently, the very fast cutting does not draw attention to itself. In fact, if ever cutting could be called invisible, this is it. We see the movement between the two characters as though it is utterly "natural," when, of course, it is anything but. The sense that it is natural comes from the perfectly judged timing of the cuts. It feels as though, if we were standing in the room with them, we would look from one character to the other at exactly this rate, to see what would happen. I believe that this is an example of the editor's internal body rhythms at work in shaping the emotional arc of the scene. He is watching and cutting to coincide with the way the question sits in his own body, as though he has placed himself in that room as our proxy, watching and wondering, moving from one shot to the next, on behalf of us, quietly—without disturbing the energy of the scene, but quickly, so that we don't miss a beat.

The scene now moves through another series of beats: Laura has watched Kitty trying not to be like the woman in the book, the one who seems fine but isn't. Now Laura probes and Kitty confesses that she is also not fine. In the exchange that follows, there is a series of escalating revelations by Kitty about her fears and feelings of inadequacy. The cutting comes back to a shot–reverse shot pattern, and Boyle makes a series of very effective choices about where to place the cuts. As Kitty speaks, her sentences are punctuated with bright, fake smiles. Boyle uses these smiles as throws and catches of the emotional energy. He leaves a shot as Kitty begins to smile and pull her façade up (Fig. 7.7a) and cuts to Laura listening or nodding (Fig. 7.7b). Then he comes back to Kitty as the smile disappears (Fig. 7.7c) and she speaks the truth once more. Starting to smile throws the energy to Laura; Kitty is begging for reassurance. Laura's sympathetic nods throw the energy back to Kitty, and Boyle cuts back just in time for us to see the last few frames of Kitty's smile disappearing as Laura's probing sends her deeper into her pain.

The emotion escalates and Laura stands up, coming into Kitty's shot to hug and comfort her so that once again we are in a two-shot, when the objectives of the scene are achieved.

FIGURE 7.7

At the end of shot (a) Kitty starts to smile again. She is moving away from her pain by putting on a happy face, but Boyle doesn't let her get away with it. Instead he cuts to Laura, nodding gravely (b), and doesn't come back to Kitty until he can come in on the shot just as her smile starts to fade (c)

Laura kisses Kitty tenderly, lovingly, on the mouth. Kitty returns the kiss willingly. Laura has achieved her real objective; she has expressed her true desire, her love, her forbidden sexual longings. Kitty has also achieved her real objective, to get respite from her pretense, to be loved for who she is, not for the act she puts on.

But the scene doesn't end there. Kitty at first seems to accept what has occurred; she says to Laura, "You're sweet," and then Boyle cuts in a long close-up on Laura so that we can see the dawning of revelation on her face. The time spent on Laura's reaction also gives Kitty time to pull herself together. It is a long beat for each of them as they adjust their objectives and actions to respond to what has just happened, with Laura moving toward her feeling and Kitty turning sharply away from what has passed between them.

Kitty interrupts Laura's reverie, and Boyle gives us just enough time on Laura to see her respond to the interruption before cutting back to Kitty so we can see her grabbing the energy back from Laura and changing the subject completely. Now Boyle uses Toni Collette's performance differently than when her character was on the back foot, needing help. Each of the succeeding shots of Kitty shows the complete preparation, action, and recovery of each smile and gesture. Kitty's bright forced smiles and gestures are barriers deliberately thrown up between her and Laura, rejections of Laura, and denial of any need to be comforted. So the scene ends at the door, where it started, the relationship apparently unchanged. Kitty is confident, swinging her hips, click-clacking along in her high heels; Laura is disheveled, teary, and vulnerable. But as an audience we witnessed everything changing between them, because the scene was cut on subtext and emotional movement, and we are utterly changed by the intensity of the emotional ride we have just been on.

SUMMARY

In the cutting of emotional rhythms, editors make decisions about the extent to which they manipulate and alter a performance or leave its rhythms intact. The strength of the performance and the relative importance of various emotional moments in the story are considerations in the editor's decision-making process. In shaping the emotional movement the editor throws the energy or intention of one performance across a cut to create the feeling of a cause-and-effect relationship in the movement of emotions. If an editor can see the performers prepare, action, rest movement arcs, or their actions and beats, the editor can use these physical movements as guides for phrasing the emotional movement, finding the best cutting points, and shaping its rhythm across an exchange.

ENDNOTES

1. Murch, W., *In the Blink of an Eye,* 1992, p. 62.
2. Schmidt, P., "Introduction," in *Meyerhold at Work,* p. xiii.
3. Murch, W., *In the Blink of an Eye,* 1992, p. 62.

CHAPTER 8

Event Rhythm

A film's event rhythm is the rhythm of its structure. The shaping of the event rhythm is the creation (in documentary) or realization (in scripted fiction) of structure. So first let's talk about structure.

What is structure?

Structure is the strategic organization of the events in a narrative to create a coherent and compelling experience of story and ideas.

An architectural metaphor for structure is well worn but still useful, as long as we keep in mind it is a metaphor, not a prescription. A film's structure may have logic, flow, and coherence, just as a building's structure does, but a film's structure does not need to stand still and hold up a roof. Rather, it needs to move. The event rhythm is the flow of structure in motion. It is the movement of story.

The way that film's structures and event rhythms can move has become increasingly diverse. Distribution channels for alternatives to the three-act structure of the Hollywood blockbuster, or the five-act structure of free-to-air television have made it possible for refreshing variations such as the ten "act" structure of *Holy Motors* (Leos Carax, 2012), to reach international audiences. Netflix offers complex serial structures in chapters rather than episodes. Subscribers got the whole structure of, for example *House of Cards* (Beau Willimon, series creator, 2013–2015), at one time, just as we would if we bought a novel. Structures of material made for online distribution are wide-open spaces for creativity of content makers and curators. The "building codes" of broadcasters and studios don't apply. These screen experiences still have structures and event rhythms, but we can think of these as more like Frank Gehry's architecture, with curves and flows that stimulate the mind rather than the inexorable march of a pre-fab functional box where the hero moves toward his goal in prescribed increments.

FIRST SCENES

As a metaphor for editing a structure, architecture is useful because it is easy to visualize. The size, shape, and order of rooms are analogous to events and the expectations they create. If you go through the front door of an office building and find yourself in a grand marbled foyer that it takes 30 paces to cross, you have a sense of the building, its rhythms, and the ways it will shape experience. If you open the front door of a brick house and find a small, cluttered living room with wood beams and a fireplace, a different expectation is created. If you open the front door of a house and find yourself in a bathroom, or a prison, or a portal into John Malkovich's brain, expectations are confounded and you prepare yourself for a different kind of experience altogether.

Similarly, in shaping of a film's event rhythm the editor sets up expectations and begins a pattern with their choice of opening shots and scenes. For example, James Bond films will invariably open onto explosions because the James Bond franchise is designed to meet expectations that are formed before even entering the cinema. The explosions in the opening sequence will "rhyme," in a sense, with the explosions at the film's climax. In this way, the structure is rhythmically, if predictably, fulfilled. Conversely, Alfonso Cuarón's *Gravity* (2013) sets us up with expectations of a sci-fi/action thriller with a high stakes opening sequence in space, spiced with light banter from well known Hollywood star George Clooney. We think that this will set the rhythm for the film, but expectations are subverted. *Gravity* uses the rhythmic conventions of an action movie in the first sequence as a cladding to cover what is at heart the introspective story of a single mother with regrets. The climactic sequence of *Gravity* (spoiler alert) when the character must rescue herself does rhyme with the disaster/action feeling of the first scenes, but not by repetition of the rhythm. Instead the film has aligned us intimately with the character's breath and fear, so that although the ultimate rescue action is small scale compared to the opening, it *feels* bigger and higher stakes than the opening. The rhythm that opens the film has developed, modulated. and focused on the fate of one woman. As in all films the first scene or "room" of these films creates expectations, from there the editor, working with the writer and director, meets, develops, changes, exceeds, or subverts expectations with the rhythms and events that follow.

The important point for editors to consider, or rather to tune to, is the rhythmic pattern suggested by the first scene. Will its qualities of time and movement become a motif in the film? Will this motif form a rhythmic structure repeating and developing throughout the film? First scenes are surprisingly malleable and there are examples of first scenes being altered by editors

- to clarify stakes sooner and set up a pattern of tension and release more effectively;

- to alter the time structures of films and give them more complexity;

- to introduce characters differently and align audiences more clearly;

- or to set up visual style with shots that may have originally been intended to go elsewhere but which have the qualities the editor wants to use to paint the whole experience to come.

First scenes, as will be discussed in the two cases studies in this chapter, set up the event rhythms of films, create expectations, and set the pulses of audiences to synchronize with the movement of the story. But editing first scenes can be like writing introductions: sometimes best to write them after you know how the rest of the essay will unfold.

> Recommended: editor Jacob T. Swinney has cut together a fascinating and thought provoking study called *First and Final Frames*, which places first and last shots in 55 films side by side. *First and Final Frames* can, at time of writing, be found online at: https://vimeo.com/122378469

DRAMATIC QUESTIONS

A dramatic question is a question with something at stake and an action implied.

A film built around dramatic action often has a dramatic question being raised soon after the story-world is established. Once we know where we are and who we care about in the story, the plots will get us to ask: Will something in particular happen? Will someone get what they need? Will the problems resolve? Plots are then designed to complicate, escalate, and ultimately resolve these questions, and the editor's job is to parse events out so that the plots do their job—they give us some resolution, but also keep us asking.

Dramatic questions raise tension by making us worry about the stakes and the actions they imply. The tension of these questions is the energy that propels the viewer's interest forward. The editor can arrange or re-arrange events to create or heighten dramatic questions and thus shape the rise and fall of tension and release. One tool the editor uses for this is timing (in the sense of when she puts events in relation to each other). She can shift the timing of events around the sequence to shape the plot so that questions are posed by events and resolved in a satisfying flow.

Editors can also employ the tool of the ellipsis. Will someone do something? Cut out the bit of the scene where a character answers the question by saying "yes I will do it" and jump straight to the scene of

FIGURE 8.1

In this sequence from Episode 2, Season 3, of The West Wing *(series creator Aaron Sorkin, 1999 to 2006), flashing lights, moving cameras, emotional tensions, competing points of focus, and multiple agendas crowd the frames of eleven shots (with only one setup repeating) as they race by in under 30 seconds. But there's only one question that has been asked and answered: Will the President run for re-election? The series makers sustain our attention on that question while reminding us of all the stakes and keeping the question in motion, like a fast-moving soccer ball, around the array of stakeholders. The editor, Bill Johnson, A.C.E., organizes the motion of that ball in play, revealing the President in close-up only when he reveals his answer. As soon as the first question closes, a new one is launched. Yes, the President will run, but will he win? This question structures the events of the whole of Season 3. Using this kind of classical patterning,* The West Wing *sets up stakes and the effective action of individual characters on their journey. This is quintessentially American storytelling, with a quintessentially American subject. The question is clear, the answer is clear and the time taken in between question and answer escalates tension. [Photo credit: John Wells Productions, Warner Bros. Television]*

them doing it. This creative ellipsis on the part of the editor activates the viewer's mind in piecing together the cause-and-effect chain, and this activation has an energizing effect.

Soviet film director and theorist Vsevolod Pudovkin articulated this principle as early as 1929. His notion of "transference of interest of the intent spectator" applies as the events in a film pulse between posing questions and answering them, between creating tension and releasing it:

> If the scenarist can effect in even rhythm the transference of interest of the intent spectator, if he can so construct the elements of increasing interest that the question "What is happening at the other place?" arises and at the same moment the spectator is transferred whither he wishes to go, then the editing thus created can really excite the spectator.[1]

Since 1929, the methods and rates of assimilation of information by audiences may have changed. Certainly, according to studies done by Barry Salt and by David Bordwell, the average shot lengths in films have been cut in half.[2] However, the practice of creating the question in the spectator's mind and then simultaneously resolving that question and creating it anew is still salient to the creation of event rhythm.

FIGURE 8.2

The West Wing *finished in 2006 and the American version of* House of Cards *(Beau Willimon, 2013–2015) began in 2013. Much changed in the intervening years, including the shift from free-to-air television (with its constraints on the structuring of events around ad breaks) to streaming services which allow for more complex rhythms to match the complexity of characters, storylines, and audience expectations. In watching* House of Cards *we seem to be able to hope the central character, played by Kevin Spacey, overcomes his obstacles and achieves his goals at the same time we fear he will. Getting audiences to like and hate him at the same time is no mean feat on the part of the writers, directors, and performers. The editor's role in this complexity may come about when the order or emphasis on events has to be manipulated so that not too much of one quality overshadows the other. [Photo credit: Media Rights Capitol, Panic Pictures (II), Trigger Street Productions]*

WORKING WITH DRAMATIC QUESTIONS

A dramatic question is a question that *implies an action* and *has something at stake.*

What does this have to do with editing?

Usually it is the writer's job to create these questions in a story, but sometimes an editor has to help them along. The editor is responsible for shaping the audience experience of dramatic questions—when they are raised and when they are resolved, how much emphasis is given to them.

Here are three tips for shaping and sustaining dramatic questions:

1. *Make Sure You Know What Your Dramatic Questions Are*

   Talk to the writer and/or director and agree on the dramatic questions. Speak them out loud, even write them down and post them on your edit suite's wall.

   A dramatic question almost always starts with the word: *"will."* Will someone *do* something, *say* something or *get* something.

   For example: "Does Joe like Liz" is not a dramatic question. "Will Joe hook up with Liz?" is a dramatic question because an action is implied (Joe hooking up with Liz, or not) and something is at stake: the relationship. If you know what your dramatic questions are then you can choose shots and shape sequences that follow the characters as they pursue their goals, and heighten our tension—our hope and fear—about what is at stake. If

you don't know what your dramatic questions are, it is easy to get distracted, and put in unnecessary stuff.

2. *Don't Answer Dramatic Questions Without Raising New Ones*

   (Unless it is the end of the story.) In order to keep us wondering what happens next we need to know what action is implied and what is at stake. If Joe hooks up with Liz and they live happily ever after it had better be the end of the movie. If Joe hooks up with Liz but is then offered a job overseas we have a new question: "Will Joe choose the job or the relationship?" Action implied? Choosing. Stakes? Career and relationship.

3. *If Your Script Answers Questions Without Raising New Ones, Try Using Ellipsis*

   If you have a scene in a bar where the question is "Will Joe hook up with Liz" and at the end of the scene they leave the bar in each other's arms, we know the answer. That's fine, unless the next scene is one of them in bed together, and there is no new question. Try cutting off the end of the bar scene so we don't know the answer. That way, seeing them in bed is a revelation, not a repetition. You may even be able to insert other scenes in between, keep us wondering about Joe and Liz while you raise a new question in another part of the story. Then, when you answer your first question, you have a second one open and in play.

STRUCTURES AS EVENT PATTERNS

Not all structures work by raising and resolving dramatic questions. Other kinds of questions may be at work in engaging an audience's interest and getting them to stay with a film. For example, questions of how will something unfold, what is the nature of something, who is right or wrong, why are things so? These questions do not necessarily have anything at stake or imply an action, but they do create opportunities for fascinating films and event rhythms. Here are just a few examples of structures without dramatic questions, but with huge creative opportunities for editing:

Life: in the film *Boyhood* (2014) Richard Linklater structured a fiction film around the actual growing and a changing of real people over 12 years, returning each year to film another event. While this happens more often in documentary, it is a revelation in fiction to use a real life to show the actual inherent structure of a human experience. Here the editor Sandra Adair's decisions were not about dramatic questions, but about emphasis and relationship of scenes over time.

Argument: films can be structured around points to be made. In argument structure the first question is: are we presenting both sides or just lining up the evidence to prove one point? In Michael Hanneke's *Caché* (aka *Hidden*, 2005) an argument seems to be being made about the French involvement in colonization and repression of Algiers, but there is ambiguity in the unfolding of events that forces the viewer to leave with questions rather than answers. Conversely, in a Michael Moore documentary, there is no ambiguity about perspective: evidence is lined up so pointedly that there is no room for debate.

List: in this structure one thing follows another within a bounded category. The 2008 film *Pockets*, by James Lees, is a "list" film.[3] It presents a series of people who tell us what they have in their pockets. In just under 3 minutes the juxtapositions of people's words, tone, expressions, faces, and the contents of their pockets creates a compendium of experiences, a metaphor of human diversity and connectedness. The editor William Bridges' decisions would have been about: order of characters; duration of shots to weave a dynamic fabric of these experiences; and making juxtapositions to give rise to reflections and metaphors.

Braids (in Multi-Strand Narratives): The braid structure is just one of many available for integrating multiple narratives in a single story. The braid structure involves juxtaposing the elements of three different story or idea lines so that as each one unfolds it reveals further, or comments on something about the others. In *"...the dancer from the dance"* (Pearlman, 2014) three documentary stories are braided together in order to reveal a diversity of ideas, practices, and experiences of life lived in dance. Complex narrative television has created a renaissance of multi-strand narratives and a full dissection of their diverse structures is probably its own complete book, waiting to be written.

Musical or mathematical: This kind of structure foregrounds pattern and may even explicitly name the film for the pattern, e.g., *32 Short Films about Glenn Gould* (Francois Girard, 1993) Unlike a simple list, however, the pattern of repetition of motifs, emphases, durations is an intrinsic part of the structure and may create an experience which is non-narrative, abstract, and direct address to the senses rather than the cognitive processes. The editing of music videos will often overtly reveal their musical structure or patterning around chorus and verse.

Portrait: a person may be the structuring principle of a film. A fictional or documentary portrait will reveal a person's themes and perspective, their empathies, metaphors, memories, and plans in such a way that does not necessarily take an audience on a journey through the experience but rather places these expressions of a life in such a way as to reveal the person or community. Sally Potter's 1992 adaptation of Virginia Wolff's *Orlando* functions in this way, as does the underlying text. Erroll Morris' *The Fog of War: 11 Lessons from the Life of Robert S. Mcnamara* (2003) is just one example of many portraits that can be found in documentary. In each of these films a character is juxtaposed with events, times, and places and each juxtaposition creates a new understanding of the character and of the culture.

There are as many other types of structure as there may be organizing principles. The key to differentiating a structure from "just anything, anytime" is the notion of organizing. Structure requires boundaries for its foundations—what will be included and excluded—and it requires

FIGURE 8.3

Holy Motors *(Leos Carax, 2012) is a series of seemingly discreet events. Each event or "act" is preceded by a ride in a car and a change of clothes by the character Oscar (Denis Lavant) as he goes on his way to carry out the work of his next "appointment." This structure could be compared to a string of different shaped beads interspersed with square stones. There is alternation between the beads and stones, the beads themselves are each distinctive. The pattern is dynamic and holds interest while continually subverting or changing expectations. [Photo credit: Pierre Grise Productions, Théo Films, Pandora Filmproduktion, Arte France Cinéma, WDR / Arte]*

support beams—the rhythmic revelation of plots, images, emotions or ideas to create a coherent experience of events over time.

ENERGY, PACE, AND TIMING

The flow of energy in one scene or sequence can be "thrown" to the next one so that events feel as though they are in response to one another, and the chain of the whole holds together. If events are given too much emphasis by being too long or over accentuated they may feel disproportionate to the events that follow them. Similarly, if they whip by too quickly, they may not have the impact needed to make what follows them feel related. The useful question for an editor here is: What is this scene, sequence, or event about? This may at first seem obvious, but the answer is not always so obvious and needs to be considered not just in relation to itself, but in relation to events that preceded and that follow. A scene may appear to be about a car crash, for example, but really be about rebuilding trust between two characters. If the event is cut only for the text and not for the subtext, then events later on, where the trust is at stake, will lose their links in the cause-and-effect chain.

Sometimes scripts are overwritten because things that are in black-and-white print don't have the same energy, impact, or information that is present in sound and moving image. One of my first editing teachers, Sara Bennett, tells a story that neatly sums this up. She had a job where there were ten pages of script setting up a character's social and economic status. There were scenes in his office, scenes at a restaurant, scenes at home, none of which contained events that really mattered to the plot, they were just there to set up the character's status. Onscreen, the ten pages were cut down to one shot of the character in his suit slamming the door of his Mercedes and walking into his beautiful suburban home. One shot said it all.

Directors may easily have the same thing happen when shaping a performance. When the performance is in little bits being shot over hours, days, or weeks, it may be hard to tell when an emotional moment has been stated. Once the editor starts shaping these moments into sequences, though, she can see when an emotional event has already occurred. Leaving in moments in the unfolding of an event that are emotional repeats will dull the impact and break the momentum of the audience attention or interest in what happens next.

Shaping event rhythm relies on knowing when and how audiences know enough about one event and are ready for the next. If a film engages the interest of a particular audience, but that audience stops caring "what happens next," then the event rhythm has been misjudged. The editor, in this case, can ask herself: Is there a problem with energy, timing or pace of a particular event? It may not always be the point at which the audience loses interest that has to be changed. In fact it is often something before that point, something that has given too much away, gone on for too long, dragged too much in its energy, been a distraction, or in some other way stolen the impact of the later event.

CREATING STRUCTURE AND RHYTHM SIMULTANEOUSLY

Before digital editing systems, editors were taught to cut "structure first, then rhythm." Editors working on actual celluloid strips of film had to take care not to mangle the work print by excessive handling. So they would make assemblies of all of the good takes laid end to end, then, choices would be made about which take to use. The selected takes would be roughly cut into a structure so that the editor and director would then be able to view the structure and the order of the shots that would convey them. Later, in the transition from the rough-cut to the fine-cut stage the rhythm of emotional exchanges would be refined, images and sounds would be trimmed to flow well. Because cutting on celluloid required a linear progression from rough structure to refined cutting the idea of structure became separated from the idea of rhythm.

But editors don't have to worry about mangling celluloid any more. So we start thinking about structure and rhythm at the same time, and these two things have been re-integrated. We can manipulate the precise timing, pacing, and trajectory phrasing of shots and cuts right from the start of a process, so structures have rhythms right from the start, and these rhythms are how we experience the movement of story.

This has changed the expectations that directors and producers bring to the first screening of a cut. If we go back to the architectural metaphor, we can say that in the pre-digital era producers and directors might expect to see bare foundations first with pillars and beams exposed. Their eyes were trained to understand how a structure would evolve into an experience. But this training of the eye is rare now, so editors cut everything at once—structural foundations and support beams are rarely seen without the rhythms of emotional interchanges, images, and sounds being somewhat polished.

It is now very unusual to make an assembly and rough-cut of structure without an articulated rhythm. Instead, the first presentation of a structure will have been given some rhythmic consideration at the level of the individual cut, the scene, the sequence, and the whole. Then, the process is to refine, adjust, or completely change structure *and* the rhythm of the structure simultaneously. In the contemporary process, the shaping of rhythm is part of the shaping of structure. Throughout the cutting process, from the first cut forward, events are restructured and rhythms are refined simultaneously.

USING KINAESTHETIC ANTIPATHY

One pitfall that needs to be avoided when cutting structure and rhythm simultaneously is becoming attached to lovely individual cuts or moments and trying to keep them in the film even if they do not really have a place in the structure. To avoid this, I have developed a particularly useful awareness of kinaesthetic empathy, which is actually a skill at pinpointing my kinaesthetic antipathy.

During cutting processes I am, as most editors are, under pressure, working long hours, and juggling schedules, expectations, deadlines, technology, egos, and so on. When I find, at certain points in the process, that I am getting very tired, I usually just imbibe more tea and M&M's and chalk it up to the wear and tear of daily life. Soon, however, I begin to realize that, although I'm tired, I'm not always tired *in the same way* in the edit suite. I begin to tune my awareness to the particular kinaesthetic experience of watching the film and find that I can observe myself "taking the ride" and pinpoint quite precise moments of ennui, particular moments when I stop physically attending to the trajectory of the film's movement and tune out. Once I realize that my tiredness is being triggered at precise points, I am able to use this pinpointed kinaesthetic antipathy to ask myself questions, such as: What is the information being conveyed in this passage? How is it being conveyed? When has it been assimilated? When am I ready to know what happens next? This is a way of looking at the visually lovely material and polished cuts and asking myself if I am being seduced by beauty that worked well on its own but actually doesn't work in the structure.

REAL EVENTS V. FICTIONAL EVENTS

Cutting documentary and cutting scripted drama diverge somewhat in their processes for shaping event rhythm.

Using the architectural metaphor for structure and applying it to documentary we can say that an editor is often a documentary's architect. The foundations may have been planned through a written treatment, but in documentary the foundations of a structure are more malleable than in fiction. Life gives plans a battering when shooting many kinds of documentary. This doesn't mean documentaries don't have foundational structure that guide decisions about approach to shooting, and what is included and excluded, what characters get followed, events get observed, questions get asked. But the characters, events, and questions may not behave as expected and the foundational structure of documentary is often, therefore, determined in editing. The editor watches material and decides what its support beams are—what characters and events will be emphasized and what relationship they will be placed in within the structure. In this way, the placement of support beams—the characters and events—into relationships with different frequency and emphasis determines the foundations *and* the rhythm of the structure simultaneously.

Working with scripted fiction, on the other hand, it might be most useful for editors to think of themselves as creative engineers rather than architects. An editor's function in scripted fiction is not to design the structure, but to make it work, which may mean making adjustment to its design, and may just mean making its scenes strong and arranging them in an order that sustains interest and reveals ideas.

In fiction, foundational structures are usually set in scripting and if the shooting follows the script, a radical change to these foundations is tricky to accomplish. It can be done. *Mullholland Drive* (David Lynch, 2001) apparently started out as a TV series and was structurally redesigned from foundation upward when the funding fell through.

Another example, as editor Ralph Rosenblum writes in his memoir *When the Shooting Stops*, is *Annie Hall* (Woody Allen, 1977). Apparently *Annie Hall* didn't really have a foundational structure. It was a series of events without a plan that Rosenblum turned into a poignant and culturally resonant love story by giving it structure. In these cases the editor shaped the foundations and then gave that shape a rhythm through decisions about where to place the support beams of events.

But these are exceptions. Usually in fiction a structure is designed before shooting, and the editor re-shapes it and realizes it by making decisions within the foundations that are set by the story-world. An editor can't turn a marble foyer into a cosy cottage, but she can decide if you enter the marble foyer and cross it with 30 echoing footsteps first or if you enter the film by hearing a ping! and stepping straight into the elevator at the back of the foyer, and thus set completely different expectations for your film.

REINTEGRATING RHYTHMS

In most productions, physical, emotional, and event rhythms are all three at work, all the time, to create the movement and energy of the film. The physical moves emotions, the emotional moves events, and the events move visually and aurally. In this way, the rhythm of the film is experienced as a whole, greater than the sum of its parts.

Delineating distinctions between kinds of rhythm is useful as a method for understanding aspects of the whole. Separating physical, emotional, and event rhythms is a way of talking about strands of rhythm that may all be present in any two shots. One place where the distinctions can be useful is when an editor needs to know what dominates the movie she is cutting: What kind of movie is it? What kind of sequence or scene or cut? What are its priorities? The questions that each kind of rhythm poses can be asked of the raw material. The answers will point clearly to the film's priorities. But the awareness that at any given point all three kinds of rhythm may be present will be helpful in making the cut that much more subtle and articulate in its rhythms.

A film is like a living body in that it has physical movement, emotional movement, and changes in circumstances or events all occurring, balancing and working in a cause-and-effect relationship with one another almost all of the time. The editor, who shapes the film's rhythms by using knowledge of the rhythms of the world and the rhythms of her own body, knows that there is not much life in a film without all three rhythms counterpointing, energizing, and shaping each other. To shape rhythms with a balance of physical movement, emotions, and events, intuitive editors draw on their own internal balancing act of physical, emotional, and event rhythms.

The shaping of event rhythm takes into account physical and emotional rhythm and weaves them into an integrated, rhythmic structure. Accomplished storytellers will set up these rhythmic patterns from the outset. The openings of their films establish the rhythm to be developed, the feeling of the story that will unfold. The following case studies focus on the beginnings of two films and how they set up the films' overall event rhythm. From the openings, we can tell that each film has a radically different rhythm even though they are both stories of Italian mobsters in America. Each one's patterns of time, movement, and energy are established in the first minutes and then developed and woven over the whole of the structure to convey the story rhythmically.

CASE STUDY: *THE GODFATHER* (FRANCIS FORD COPPOLA, 1972)

The core rhythm of *The Godfather* is stated in the first shot, established in the first scene, developed in the first sequence, and consistently maintained as a storytelling element conveying the themes and attitudes of the film. There is another countering rhythm in the film that is set up in the second scene and appears at intervals throughout the film until, 2½ hours later, in one of the most famous scenes in editing history, the two rhythmic qualities are intercut to bring the film to a climactic and complete realization.

The first shot of the film is a 2½ minute pull back from the face of a middle-aged Italian man, Bonasera (Salvatore Corsitto), telling a harrowing story of his daughter's abuse at the hands of callous young American boys. The shot slowly reveals the silhouette of the Godfather (Marlon Brando), who is listening. The physical movement of time and energy in this shot starts out being concentrated in Bonasera's face and eyes as he states his beliefs (beliefs that set up one of the central tensions of the film, the tension between the new life and ways of America and those of Sicily, the old country). But as the frame widens out and pulls away from Bonasera's face, the darkness around him becomes more engulfing, his expressions less visible, his stature and energy diminishes, until the silhouette of the Godfather fills a third or more of the frame. The stillness creates physical tension by holding the question of who will disturb this physical space and energy with movement and how.

The emotional rhythm in this shot is in the tension between the movement of Bonasera's voice, his cadence of outrage, counterpointed by the movement of the camera away from him, pulling back evenly, dispassionately. It is as though Bonasera is throwing his emotional energy into a growing void. This handling of emotion is also thematic for *The Godfather*. The shaping of the time, movement, and energy of emotion in this shot speaks directly to the spectator about how emotion is handled in this world: the outrages and blood feuds are kept at a distance, handled deliberately; they are "just business," not personal (Fig. 8.4).

The first scene of *The Godfather* is an event that will be repeated four more times in the first sequence: someone will come into the Godfather's office and ask him for a favor, which, on this day of his

FIGURE 8.4
Amid somber colors and stately movements Bonasera whispers his request into the Godfather's (Marlon Brando's) ear. [Photo credit: Paramount; The Kobal Collection]

daughter's wedding, he cannot refuse. Each time the supplicant achieves his objective, but so does the Godfather, who makes a business of placing others under obligation to him. The rhythm of this first scene—stately, controlled, sustained, void of any physical or emotional violence—establishes one of the two initiating rhythms that work in counterpoint to each other to make the overall event rhythm of the film.

FIGURE 8.5

Al Martino and Talia Shire in the raucous movement of bright colors and sounds in the wedding party scene of The Godfather *(Francis Ford Coppola, 1972). [Photo credit: Paramount; The Kobal Collection]*

The other rhythmic quality of the film is established in the second scene, the scene of the Godfather's daughter's wedding party (Fig. 8.5). This buoyant party is filled with effusive gestures, bright colors, crowded, busy frames, and movement in all directions. The brightly jagged physical movement of people, voices, patterns of leaves and dresses, and songs are the meaning, just as, later in the film, the bright, jagged movement of extreme violence will carry the meaning of the physical energy that disrupts and punctuates the dispassionate rhythm of the other transactions.

The first and second scenes of *The Godfather* establish the pattern that the event rhythm of the film will have: grave deliberation occasionally jarred by energetic outbursts. In the climactic scene, known as the Baptism Scene, the two qualities are brought together. The stately, composed shots of a Catholic baptism in a cavernous church, a holy place of exalted worship, are intercut with the sudden, shocking brutal murders of five of the Godfather's enemies. By pulling the sound of the liturgy and the church music across the shots of the murders, the editors William Reynolds, A.C.E., and Peter Zinner, A.C.E., impress the stately, sanctifying sounds of the family's beliefs across the images of the horror they are committing. By timing the cuts to convey the clear culpability and knowledge the Godfather has of the violence he is perpetrating, and slicing through the peaceful baptism with countering thrusts of the ferocious energy of vengeance, the editors create a masterful dance back and forth that encapsulates the meaning of the film: the clash is what shapes the character of a man destined to be a powerful "Godfather."

In *The Godfather*, as in all great films, physical, emotional, and event rhythms are integrated. Together they are the shape of time, movement, and energy that express the meaning of the film. In *The Godfather* the shaping of the rhythm creates our understanding, at an immediate, visceral level, of the grave and ceremonial world in which honor and family sanctify, contextualize, even justify the chaotic and jarring acts of extreme violence that both disrupt and fuel it.

CASE STUDY: *GOODFELLAS* (MARTIN SCORSESE, 1990)

The two driving forces that structure the events of the entire film *Goodfellas* are set up in the first scene: a murder and a lifelong desire. The first is the murder. A guy in a trunk is stabbed and shot. We don't know who he is or why he is being killed so cold-bloodedly until an hour or so later, and we don't know the consequences of that murder until yet another hour after that. By organizing the story events in this way, to play out at intervals over the whole film, the writers, Nicholas Pileggi and Martin Scorsese, and the editor, Thelma Schoonmaker, create a story arc that functions the way that pillars might function in a building, supporting the roof at regular intervals but not cluttering the space between them. They also start off the film with a blast of physical activity and an insight into the emotions of this story.

When the guy in the trunk is well and truly dead, having been stabbed nine times and then shot four times, the narrator and central character of the story, Henry Hill (Ray Liotta), steps forward to close the trunk as his voice-over tells us, "As far back as I can remember, I always wanted to be a gangster." This introduces the film's other through-line of events: the story of Henry Hill's life and his rise and fall in the underworld. The voice-over is ironic. The killing is ignominious; there is nothing great or even courageous about it. Is this what young Henry, even from childhood, aspired to? Henry's statement is punctuated by another irony: a freeze-frame on him looking detached but slightly dazed (Fig. 8.6). Freeze-frames are a convention often used in cheaply produced dramas. In soap operas they hang in the air, directing the audience to sustain the emotion and recognize the importance of an event. But in *Goodfellas*, the freeze-frames emphasize the ignominious.

FIGURE 8.6

In Goodfellas *the first introduction to the protagonist Henry Hill is as a slightly dazed man, buffeted by events, but also complicit in them, as he helps out with a routine murder and stays on track with his lifelong ambition to be a gangster. [Photo credit: Warner Bros.]*

They place weight and significance by stilling the constant motion and creating an accent. But the accent is almost random, resting on off-key compositions, occurring mid-action rather than at the climax or resolution, offering us a chance to examine something in detail in such a way as to actually undercut its potential importance. They freeze emotion and action and let us look at it dispassionately, make our own judgments about the lives it is framing: Are they fast, fun, and sexy, or meaningless, immoral, and nasty? Or both?

The film's first freeze-frame, accompanied by the raucous trumpet of an upbeat jazz song, plays with the conventional use of the freeze-frame, using its implication that this is a significant moment, to place emphasis on the ordinariness of Henry closing the trunk and the coolness of being a thug. It indicates that anything could be significant in this world, and the insignificant, the closing of the trunk, can be given as much weight and emphasis as murder.

The details of this scene are important because they set up the physical and emotional cadences that are repeated in macro by the rhythm of events throughout the film.

In *Goodfellas* murder is not more or less important than pasta. The film is not about the Godfather or the boss of a Mafia gang, who is the still center of the whirlwind of death and life around him. It is about the guys who do the boss's bidding, the guys who are in the vortex, flailing, swinging, drinking, laughing, cooking, killing, and never ratting on their friends. These guys are in constant motion, and the weight and gravity of events in their lives are not measured by the same standards as the weight and seriousness of events in other people's lives. This lack of moral compass is a central theme of the film, which is expressed (as it is in all great films) as much through the form of the telling as through the information being told.

The rhythm of *Goodfellas* is characterized by fluid and continuous motion and the ironic counterweighting of events in life with events of crime and death. Some of the most startling, momentous scenes of the film are of ordinary events, such as entering a club by the back door or telling a funny story around the dinner table. These events are accented in the unfolding of the film by the physical or emotional movement within them.

The scene in which Henry and his girlfriend (Lorraine Bracco) enter the Copacabana (a popular and exclusive nightclub in New York in the 1960s) through the back way is told entirely in one dizzying, sweeping glorious steadicam shot, which, through its intricately choreographed time, movement, and energy, synchronizes us with the girlfriend. We share her physical experience of being dazzled and swept up in the glamour of the back-alley life.

The scene in which Henry's friend Tommy (Joe Pesci) tells a funny story and then lashes out at Henry for laughing is filled with an extraordinary tension and fear about Tommy's paranoia and ability to turn on his friends. Nothing much happens in this scene; it turns out Tommy was just teasing Henry. But the emotional tension it creates colors the rest of Tommy's story so that, later, when Tommy casually shoots a waiter and kills him, there is very little fuss—it's just Tommy being Tommy.

The event rhythms in *Goodfellas* build to a cataclysmic sequence in which humor, motion, trivia, and passion bang into each other across hard cuts of stinging rock-and-roll music, perpetual cocaine-induced manic movement, and the basso continuo of paranoia, embodied in a helicopter buzzing overhead, following Henry through his harried day.

The sequence starts with a title card announcing the date and time: May 11, 1980, 6:55 AM. Rock-and-roll slides in under the title. There's a cut to a close-up of cocaine being inhaled, guns being dropped into a paper bag, and on the next shot the lead guitar kicks in as Henry exits his quiet, brick-fronted suburban home, wiping the traces of coke from his nose. The combination of music, camera moves, and cuts that follow in the next four shots set up the whirlwind ride that's coming over the next 10 minutes:

- close-up of paper bag full of guns thrown into the trunk, fast pan up to Henry's squinting up at the sky;

- cut to helicopter flying between the trees;

- cut back to a quick pan past Henry, glimpse the bag, the trunk slams down;

- wide shot tracks in on Henry as he hurries into the car;

- jump cut, he's driving and smoking.

Then in comes the relatively laconic voice-over, counterpointing the wildly erratic movement of the cuts, and adding a layer of irony. "I was going to be busy all day . . ." Henry explains he has to sell guns, pick up his brother, deal drugs, and cook the pasta sauce.

The time of day appears on the screen at irregular points in the recount of Henry's day; it has an objective, distanced quality, as though labeling the evidence as in a police report, but so erratically it would mock any jury's desire for an orderly, clear, evidentiary report of the events leading to Henry's arrest. And what exactly is relevant as Henry hurtles toward his demise?

8:05 AM: Gun sale unsuccessful, Henry hatches a new plan and narrowly avoids a car accident. The series of preposterously repeating cuts from his foot on the brakes to his face as he screeches to a halt is entirely in subjective time—this is what it feels like to Henry, not necessarily the facts of what really happened.

8:45 AM: He picks up his brother, gets forced into having a checkup, the doctor is jovial, but Henry is sweating. He pops a calming Valium but the rock-and-roll is screaming. Voice-over: "Now my plan was . . ."

11:30 AM: Henry has yet another new plan; he's creating dinner and a sense of order, but at least one of these isn't going so well.

About 4 minutes into the sequence, 12:30, 1:30, and 3:30 all appear in 30 seconds of screen time, highlighting the sense that time is erratic, careening past wildly and then sticking on a detail. Music cuts in and out suddenly but exultantly, emphasizing the energy and anarchy of the movement through the day. The hard-driving rock-and-roll gives flow, direction, and energy to an action and then deserts it abruptly, only to slam in at another moment, another screech of tires or hit of cocaine.

Two minutes later, it's 6:30 and Henry is running out of the house again. "I told my brother to keep an eye on the stove. All day long the poor guy's been watching helicopters and tomato sauce. See, I had to get over to Sandy's, mix the stuff once, and then get back to the gravy." The "stuff," of course, is the cocaine, not the sauce, but even though one can get you arrested and thrown in jail for life and the other cannot, they both have to be stirred.

Fifteen seconds later, it's 8:30 PM, more coke, a complicated love affair, and back in time for dinner, which, suddenly (at 10:45 PM, the onscreen time tells us) is ending. Henry doesn't look happy; nothing's amounted to much, the family is annoying to be with, and he has to get on the road to get rid of the coke. Leaving the house, Henry is arrested.

This climactic sequence, as with the baptism scene in *The Godfather*, brings together the rhythms of the whole film and their meanings to create a sense that Henry's destiny is defined by the way he lives, and the rhythms of his life have spun out of his control. These rhythms have sucked us in, too, so we feel with them how fun it is to be constantly in motion, fleeting, dodging, ducking, and sliding over precipices to land on our feet. We're with Henry on his wild ride, exulting in the spin and whirl as long as it stays in motion, reflecting only when we're forced to see the consequences, the debris left in the dust by the tornado of this kind of life.

SUMMARY

Physical rhythm creates tension by posing the question of win or lose, catch or escape, or, at an even more subliminal level, by creating a pattern that the spectator participates in and wants to see fulfilled. Emotional rhythm creates tension or questions at the level of every cut. Each throw of a character's emotional energy, each emotional maneuver he tries, is a question being asked: What will be the response or the emotional effect of this action? Event rhythm is working at the level of the scene, the sequence, or the whole film. Each scene is a question in a drama: Will the character achieve his objective or be thwarted? It is actually impossible to separate the experience of event rhythm from the experiences of physical and emotional rhythm because the three kinds of rhythm are cumulative. Event rhythm is the flow of both the physical and the emotional through scenes, sequences, and structures that release information in a way that supports and conveys the sensations and emotions of the film.

ENDNOTES

1. Pudovkin, V., "Film technique," reprinted in *Film Theory and Criticism*, p. 87.
2. See Bordwell, D., "Intensified continuity: Visual style in contemporary American film—Critical essay," *Film Quarterly*, p. 16.
3. Available at https://vimeo.com/14216866.

CHAPTER 9

Style

The word "style" in editing refers to the combination of a few different choices. It's a tricky word in that it can be quite amorphous, but it is one that comes up a lot in the discussions between directors, producers, cinematographers, and editors. In these conversations about editing style, it is useful to break down the possibilities available, what they are, and what effects they create, so that everyone has a common vocabulary.

Editing style is generally determined by the director when they work with all of the collaborators on a production. When directors and cinematographers make a shot list, they are, to some extent determining editing style. When decisions are made about production design, sound, music, and digital effects these will all have an impact on editing style, because the editor is the collaborator in charge of bringing these materials together.

In this chapter I propose two intersecting ways of discussing and analyzing editing style.

The first is a spectrum running from thematic montage to continuity cutting (Fig. 9.1).

Thematic Montage ◄————————————► Continuity Cutting

FIGURE 9.1

Collision

Linkage

FIGURE 9.2

The second range of choices editors and directors make runs along a spectrum from what I will call collision to linkage (Fig. 9.2).

"Collision" and "linkage," are words borrowed respectively from Eisenstein and his contemporary, Pudovkin. They were the subject of heated debate and much animosity between these two key figures in the development of film in the Soviet Union in the 1920s. Eisenstein and Pudovkin each approached editing and ideas about film form differently, but the passage of time has softened the ideological distinctions between these two approaches to such a degree that we can now consider them as points along a spectrum of choices about style.

I will first discuss montage and continuity cutting, and then I will briefly outline some of the key ideas behind collision and linkage before I bring them all together to look at some case studies of their possible combinations.

THEMATIC MONTAGE

"Montage" is the word the French use for editing; it would literally translate into English as "assemblage" or "assembly." The implications of montage in French are both technical and creative. Technically, the editing is assemblage of pieces into a whole. Creatively, montage is assembling of images and sounds into relations that generate rhythms, ideas, and experiences of a whole.

My use of the word montage, however, is going to be slightly different from the French usage, which refers to the whole of editing operations. Instead I will draw on the common understanding of the term among English-speaking editors, who use "montage" to mean a particular kind of editing. We use it to mean bringing together images and sounds that are unrelated in time or space. In other words, we actually mean "thematic montage." Images that are unrelated in time and space brought together to create an impression, an idea, or an effect.

Films such as *Koyaanisqatsi* (Godfrey Reggio, 1982) and *Baraka* (Godfrey Reggio, 1992) are examples of thematic montage in this sense. They are constructed from a wide range of images collected at different times and from all over the world. When cut together in a thematic montage, they create ideas about cultures and civilizations. There is no narration that explicitly states the themes, but the power of thematic montage is such that the ideas arise vividly in our minds. We make connections between the images and derive a clear meaning from their overall composition.

It is quite unusual to have entire feature films constructed in this way; more typically, there will be thematic montage sequences within a feature film. Often thematic montage, or assembly of images unrelated in time and space, may be used in realist narrative feature films as a device for suggesting the inner, subjective mental state of a character who is hallucinating, dreaming, on drugs, or so overcome with emotion or sensation that he is outside of ordinary time and space.

This sense of montage as the close juxtaposition of disconnected images is a mainstay of advertisements, music videos, and title sequences that summarize and introduce the themes of the whole film. In these contexts, thematic montage is a technique that allows audiences to surmise a message through their very powerful experience of making associations—an experience that is carefully modulated and shaped by rhythm.

CONTINUITY CUTTING

Continuity cutting is the cutting up of something that *could* unfold in real time and space into shots that will be put back together to create the *impression* of the events they contain unfolding in real time and space. The important question about using continuity cutting is: Why would you do it? Why shoot something that could simply be done in one shot, in real time and space, and cut it into many shots that may have to be taken at many different times and in different configurations of the space, so that you can then put them back together to create the impression of one time and place?

One answer, of course, is rhythm. What the multiple shots provide an editor with is a much finer degree of control over the shaping of time, energy, and movement. Each shot and take of a scene that could have unfolded in real time and space will contain its own unique potential for contributing to rhythm. Performances will have different uses of time: faster or slower, shorter or longer. Shots will have different uses of space: close-ups, two-shots, wide shots, or other configurations. They will also each contain their own movement—movement of camera, characters, or composition, and the near-infinite range of energies with which these kinds of movement can be executed.

So, for the purposes of this discussion, thematic montage is the association of things unrelated in time and space, and continuity cutting is the cutting up of things that could have unfolded in a single continuous time and space. These two approaches are being placed at either end of a spectrum, and the style of an edit may fall at one end or the other of that spectrum, but may also fall in the area between the two edges of the spectrum.

POINTS ALONG THE SPECTRUM FROM THEMATIC MONTAGE TO CONTINUITY CUTTING

One editing operation that is somewhere between thematic montage and continuity cutting is "temporal ellipsis." Using temporal ellipses simply means cutting out bits of time, along the lines of the well-worn aphorism "drama is life with the boring bits cut out." Although that does not really describe the whole of what drama is, it is useful to a

FIGURE 9.3

Humphrey Bogart as Rick and Ingrid Bergman as Elsa in a romantic moment, one of many from a sequence of elided romantic moments in a flashback of Rick and Elsa's early days together in Casablanca *(Michael Curtiz, 1942). [Photo credit: Warner Bros; The Kobal Collection]*

writer or an editor, each of whom can cut out time between events to highlight special moments to sustain the tension of an open question or simply to make the story move along faster, more rhythmically, or without irrelevancies.

A classic example of a sequence that relies on temporal ellipses to tell the story of a whole relationship in just a few minutes is the thematic montage sequence in *Casablanca* (Michael Curtiz, 1942), which tells the back-story of the two main characters when they were young and in love, in Paris at the start of the war. There are images of Rick (Humphrey Bogart) and Elsa (Ingrid Bergman) laughing and walking in the streets of Paris, on a boat on the Seine, in a restaurant, and so on. These images are not exactly unrelated in time and space; in theory they could have been shot continuously, but then this section of the film would have been several days long and jam-packed with irrelevancies. So there is strong reference to continuous time and space, pushing this sequence away from the pure end of the spectrum that we are calling thematic montage. However, although they could have been shot continuously and then cut up, they do not *actually* present continuous time and space. The ellipses are there precisely for the purpose of showing time elapsing and to give rise to the impression of love deepening over time. This impression is something we surmise from the association of images. Therefore, it is also not pure continuity cutting. The temporal ellipses within this sequence fall somewhere on the spectrum between thematic montage and continuity cutting. The choice to make the sequence a somewhat discontinuous association of images and to make it also refer strongly to a continuous unfolding of time and space is a style choice.

Temporal ellipsis *between* scenes is another point on the spectrum between thematic montage and continuity cutting. There are very few examples of feature films, documentaries, or television series in which the duration of the film is the same as the duration of the story. So almost every film has a montage of distinct times and spaces. A film may have scenes within it that are absolutely continuous in time and space; for example, Jim Jarmusch's 1984 film *Stranger Than Paradise*, in which every scene is covered in one long shot. But these completely continuous scenes nonetheless form a montage when they are cut together into the whole time and space of the story. Most films are less extreme than this example and use continuity cutting inside of scenes and then cut these scenes together into a montage in which we surmise the connection between the scenes and the passage of time in the story. The cuts between the scenes can be more or less extreme: they may be cuts between leaving the house and arriving at the office as in *Mad Men* (Matthew Weiner, 2007–2015). Or they may be cuts that collapse nearly 15 years into 1/24 of a second, as in *Citizen Kane*, when the edit between Thatcher wishing Kane a "Merry Christmas" at the age of 10 jumps to a shot of him saying "and a Happy New Year" on Kane's 25th birthday. These two examples illustrate the use of the same technique—temporal ellipses between scenes—with radically different styles, *Mad Men* using a style much closer on the spectrum to continuity cutting, whereas the *Citizen Kane* example would have to be placed closer to thematic montage.

What is the purpose of distinguishing between thematic montage and continuity cutting? We can use this knowledge, that the editing of a film will sit somewhere on the spectrum from the association of images that are completely unrelated in time and space to the shaping of images to give the impression of continuous time and space, to discuss style. We can ask: What is this project's approach to time and space? Is it different from one scene to the next? Is there a thematic montage sequence within it, and is that thematic montage a wild hallucination or simply a way of running quickly through a series of events? Do the transitions between scenes just cut out the boring bits? Or are they extreme statements about the passage of time?

But the range of choices from thematic montage to continuity cutting is just one style guide or spectrum. The other style spectrum concerns flow of images and could be described as the range from collision to linkage. We'll look at the spectrum from collision to linkage next, before examining how the two sets of ideas come together to describe editing style and the rhythms in stylistic choices.

COLLISION

Collision is a term borrowed from the great Soviet filmmaker and theorist Sergei Eisenstein, whose ideas and films have had inestimable influence over the development of cinema and in shifting editing from being a means of stitching things together to being an art.

One aspect of Eisenstein's use of the word "collision" is neatly summed up by Louis Giannetti in his book *Understanding Movies*:

> Eisenstein criticized the concept of linked shots for being mechanical and inorganic. He believed that editing ought to be dialectical: the conflict of two shots (thesis and antithesis) produces a wholly new idea (synthesis). Thus, in film terms, the conflict between shot A and shot B is not AB (Kuleshov and Pudovkin) but a qualitatively new factor—C. Transitions between shots should not be flowing, as Pudovkin suggested, but sharp, jolting, even violent. For Eisenstein editing produces harsh collisions, not subtle linkages. A smooth transition, he claimed, was an opportunity lost.[1]

The dialectical ideology behind this notion of collision has, for better or worse, not really survived into the twenty-first century as common parlance among editors and filmmakers. In Eisenstein's terms, collision made the world go round. Change was the result of two opposing forces colliding together, and the energy and explosion of their clash propelled the world's metamorphosis from one system to the next. This idea extends into editing and film form for Eisenstein. He puts together remarkable collisions of various forces within his shots and films to propel ideas and emotions forward.

I often ask my students, by comparison, "What makes the world go round?" and, as I usually teach in developed, democratic, capitalist countries, the students consistently, invariably, and without exception reply, "Money." What they mean is that money is the agent of change, money is the force that can influence the turn of events. It is not, therefore, surprising that collision as a force in editing has been assimilated into editing style as just one way of cutting. It is used to suit the subject matter, and the rhythm of the production at hand. Collision is part of style, not a means of inciting revolution, because the purpose of most productions made in these countries is not to incite revolution but to engage, enlighten, uplift, inform, or entertain a target market.

Eisenstein's aesthetic development of the notion of collision has nonetheless exerted great influence over the development of editing possibilities, and his explanations remain valid and useful ways of describing a way of cutting at one end of the spectrum of stylistic choices available to an editor. Eisenstein's idea of montage is collision of independent shots. And "the degree of incongruence determines the intensity of the impression and determines that tension which becomes the real element of authentic rhythm."[2]

But what does collision or incongruity actually mean for us in terms of how images and sounds are joined? Eisenstein identifies every aspect of image and sound, including light, movement, shape, direction, tone, shot size, focal length, contrast, dimensions, durations, speeds, performances, symbols, and so on, as possible "attractions" to the eye. Each of these is something that might draw our attention in a shot. So a collision is the juxtaposition of differences between these elements rather than, as we shall see in linkage, a juxtaposition of their similarities.

A collision might therefore be a cut that juxtaposes light and dark, close-up and wide shot, movement left to right with right to left, stillness with activity, religion with politics, and so on. Each of these is a little shock, a little challenge to smoothness. Even now, when these juxtapositions are so common in our world, it still takes the eye and the mind a bit of time or effort to connect and make sense of things that conflict in these ways. Making this effort engages the audience more actively in putting together the images and surmising the ideas of the film. It is harder work to make these associations connect; it requires a more active viewer. By energizing the audience, collision energizes the film. Sequences or films that use collision as a style may therefore feel more energetic, vibrant, angular, or aggressive.

Collisions of these kinds are routinely used in action scenes, fight scenes, chase scenes, music videos, and ads in which the energy of the production needs to be upbeat and active, even aggressive, to convey its meanings. It is tempting to say that any scene driven by physical rhythm relies on this kind of cutting, and scenes driven by emotional rhythm do not, but this is not the case. Dance scenes, for example, frequently make use of smooth, "uncollided" cutting, whereas conversations may use surprising juxtapositions of frame size, performance, character movement, or other collided elements to make a point or an emotional impact.

It is also tempting to say that collision is the same as thematic montage, but as we shall see in the examples below, this is not the case. Thematic montage, in my definition, may be the bringing together of things that are unrelated in time and space, but it is not always a bringing together by collision; sometimes it is a comparison of similarities that gives a thematic montage its driving force.

Collision, then, is about difference, and difference is, according to Eisenstein, what allows us to perceive rhythm in events, in images, in music or sound. If all was the same there would be no rhythm, just a continuous hum in a custard-colored world. Eisenstein's emphasis on collision shifts editing from being a job of connecting shots to being an art of making ideas out of juxtapositions and creating rhythms out of contrasting images.

LINKAGE

Eisenstein's less well known but deeply influential contemporary, filmmaker and theorist Vsevolod Pudovkin, put forward a different idea about the function of editing. His notion of linkage is, I propose, less well known because it has, in fact, been more widely assimilated. It has seeped into the culture of editing and filmmaking to such an extent that it is normalized. I have often heard students call smoothly linked editing "normal" cutting or explain that they are going to shoot "normal" shots to make a smoothly linked film. But linkage, like any technique of artistic construction, is, of course, not normal or natural. It has behind it an ideology and an aesthetic purpose, which define its usage and its usefulness.

Pudovkin saw editing as a means by which the filmmaker could "see through the confusion of history and psychology and create a smooth train of images which would lead toward an overall event."[3] For him, the aim of a smooth linkage was to create a clear and comprehensible image of the world, one that cuts out irrelevancies and focuses the viewer on the significant moments, exchanges, and events. Linkage, to paraphrase Pudovkin, guides the spectator psychologically. Pudovkin's intention, it could be said, was not so much to incite or ignite the audience as to immerse, influence, and convince it. To achieve this, he put forward ideas about film being built up, constructed, brick by brick. Any brick that stands out, draws attention to itself, is of an excessively irregular shape, size, or movement disrupts the flow of the construction and therefore disrupts the audience's immersion in the film.

This view of editing is normalized in the Hollywood continuity system (which began being used even before Pudovkin's articulation of the ideology of linkage). In classical continuity editing, shots are often designed and juxtaposed with the ideal of smoothness of transition, the least possible disruption of the viewer's sense of the flow of time in continuous space.

But not always. It is possible to have continuity cutting with collision. Linkage is not the same as continuity cutting. Linkage is often used with continuity cutting, but, as we shall see in the examples below, the spectrum from collision to linkage is different from the spectrum between thematic montage and continuity cutting, and some continuity cutting employs collision very effectively.

So continuity cutting is a technique, and I am using the term "linkage" to describe a style within that technique. It might be more appropriate to use smoothness than linkage, because linkage could describe something that is abruptly linked, but I have chosen to use the word linkage for this aspect of style to remind us of the purpose behind the style: to create a smooth train of images. With linkage, we are at no time shocked out of the world of the story or characters; we are smoothly guided by the film's construction to empathy with characters and easy agreement with ideas it contains.

Smooth linkage of shots involves the opposite approach to collision. Rather than colliding light and dark together, lighting values from shot to shot are similar. The same is true for shot sizes that don't jump from wide to close, but link smoothly from wide to mid to close. Movements right to left link smoothly with other movements right to left, rather than colliding with movements left to right. Match cutting, or matching on action, is a key operation in making smooth linkages of shots. An unmatched cut from one part of a movement to another is a jump, or distortion of a movement's continuousness in time or space, and therefore a little shock or collision. This aspect of smoothly linking movement shape and direction is the cornerstone of an "invisible" editing style in which movement flow appears to be smooth and continuous. However, as discussed in Chapter 5, editing, even editing style that emphasizes linkage, is not invisible. What we see is movement flow, smooth or collided, shaped by editing.

POINTS ALONG THE SPECTRUM FROM COLLISION TO LINKAGE

Is difference or similarity emphasized by a cut? Is the intention to engage the viewers energetically with a series of little shocks or to guide them seamlessly into empathy and understanding with a series of linkages? These are choices along the spectrum from collision to linkage. This spectrum offers a range, a playing space, for the shaping of each of the elements of rhythm: time, energy, and movement.

Time can be collided or linked in shots. Speed of movement can be connected with similar or different speed. Duration of shot can be connected with similar or different duration. Collisions can be created even when connecting similar uses of time by choosing to cut before the peak of a movement arc. Cutting quickly, before a spectator can assimilate the full content curve of an image, creates a collision somewhere on the spectrum between pure collision and pure linkage. It unsettles the viewer and activates tension about what is unseen in a shot that has flashed by.

Energy qualities can also be collided or linked. Energy qualities, which are visible or audible in movement, color, light, tone, intentions, proximities, and so on, can be collided with their opposite, or matched with their like, from cut to cut or in patterns across any number of cuts.

Movement, as discussed above, can also be collided or linked. Shaping patterns of colliding or linking movement is one way of shaping the moment-to-moment rhythm and the overall rhythm of a film.

STYLE CASE STUDIES

As noted above, it is tempting to associate thematic montage with collision and linkage with continuity cutting, because it would seem that thematic montage is a tendency to collide together things unrelated in time and space, and continuity cutting has as its goal the smooth creation of the impression of continuous time and space.

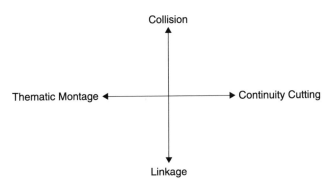

FIGURE 9.4

But in fact it is only when we separate and articulate these two ranges of possibilities for cutting that we can describe a full range of cutting style choices.

Each of the following four case studies pairs up a different combination of approaches, and the result is four distinctive styles.

Psycho—Continuity Cutting and Collision

One of the best known scenes in editing history, the shower scene in which Norman Bates (Anthony Perkins) stabs Marion Crane (Janet Leigh) to death in *Psycho* (Alfred Hitchcock, 1960), is an example at the extreme edge of both spectra (Fig. 9.5). The scene could have been shot continuously in one take. The action could simply have unfolded in real time and space, but it was cut up into (many!) individual shots for the purpose of controlling rhythm and affect very precisely.

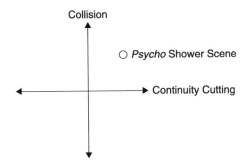

FIGURE 9.5

FIGURE 9.6
Anthony Perkins as Norman Bates collides with his victim in the continuity cutting of the shower scene in
Psycho *(Alfred Hitchcock, 1960). [Photo credit: Paramount; The Kobal Collection]*

The scene is also a very strong example of collision. The shots are designed to collide in as many aspects as is possible, especially screen direction and symbolic value. The butcher knife is sharp and dark, the skin of the victim is soft and white. The water pours from the shower head in dramatically angular directions, emphasized by tight close-ups. Janet Leigh's movements by contrast are soft and circular, often masked by the filter of the shower curtain that diffuses light and form. And of course there is the music, by Bernard Herrmann, with its abrupt bursts of screaming strings, sharply staccato against the quiet that fills the space before and after the deed is done.

There are dozens of camera setups in this scene, and each of these is specifically designed to create a collision, a change, a difference from one to the next. By covering the scene in this way, Hitchcock gives the scene an energy of rapid, violent change, which does away with the need for explicit images. We never see the knife actually pierce the body; instead, we feel the tearing, stabbing qualities as we experience the extremes of collision between shots, their content, durations, shapes, sizes, angles, and symbols.

Apocalypse Now—Thematic Montage and Linkage

Francis Ford Coppola's *Apocalypse Now* (1979) is well known to have had a chaotic shoot riddled with problems ranging from a coup d'état in the country where they were shooting to the lead suffering a heart attack, an uncooperative star in a small but key role, the monsoons of the jungle, and simply scope and ambition beyond its budget. Once shooting had finally finished and cutting was in full swing, the editors found they did not have a satisfactory opening for the film. So they created one.

The opening sequence of *Apocalypse Now* is a smoothly linked thematic montage (Fig. 9.7). It blends together long shots of a jungle, which at first appears peaceful and untroubled and then is slowly enveloped in the distinctive yellow smoke of napalm, with the close-up of a face (Martin Sheen as Captain Willard), upside down on the screen, eyes wandering restlessly (Fig. 9.8). It links the sounds of helicopter blades whirring with the image of a ceiling fan spinning, with the upside-down face, a gun, a domestic snapshot, a whiskey bottle, and the war machines flying over the jungle.

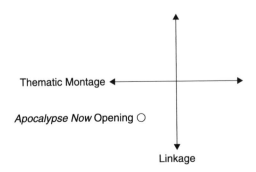

FIGURE 9.7

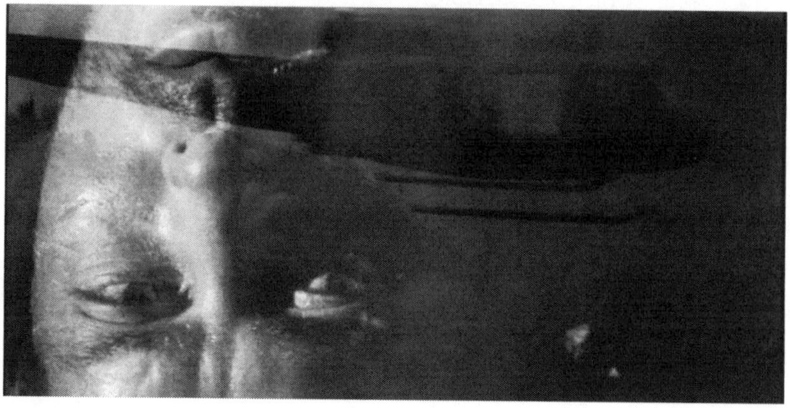

FIGURE 9.8
The thematic montage at the opening of Apocalypse Now *(Francis Ford Coppola, 1979) links Captain Willard's (Martin Sheen) mind with the machines of war. [Photo credit: Zoetrope/United Artists]*

Linking all of these diverse images together and smoothly associating, even blending them into a single idea, is done by use of music and dissolves. The music, "The End" by The Doors, is much more than a quilt backing holding all of the pieces together. Its long continuous organ tones provide linkage, through tonal similarity, from one image to the next. And the lyrics, also a low-pitched dirge-like drone, tell an aspect of the story in their words and their delivery. "This is the end," warns lead singer, Jim Morrison, both a peaceful oblivion to be longed for and a moment filled with dread. The music is part of the thematic montage. It was built into the edit as images were being associated. It associates America, rock-and-roll, and hedonism with the jungles and war of Southeast Asia, connecting them via smooth linkage with the central image of Willard's head.

The connection of all images, sounds, and music through the mind of Willard is made visible through dissolves. A dissolve blends images together, softening their differences and linking their similarities. The longer it goes on, the softer it is, and these dissolves are very long. By dissolving together the image of Willard's head (upside down and therefore already somewhat out of kilter with the world) with the images and sounds of battle and home, these things are smoothly, seamlessly linked to give rise to the impression that the man's mind is whirring, spinning in circles with images of peace and war. The opening of *Apocalypse Now* sets up the character, his inner problems and his environmental problems, by using both linkage and thematic montage to create an overlapping image of a chaotically integrated internal and external world.

Breaker Morant—Continuity Cutting and Linkage

The continuity cutting and linkage in *Breaker Morant* (Bruce Beresford, 1979) does precisely what this smooth, unobtrusive style is designed to do: uses editing to subtly shape and modulate the story, cutting for dramatic purposes, emotional emphasis, and clarity rather than shock or association (Fig. 9.9).

The film is a flashback narrative, with the story in the present unfolding in a military court in South Africa during the Boer War and the flashbacks showing the stories the various witnesses and defendants are recounting. As it is a flashback narrative, there are substantial and very effective jumps in spatial and temporal continuity between scenes. But within the scenes, the continuity cutting is seamless and supports the story subtly, with well-judged cuts heightening tension by shaping time and emphasis.

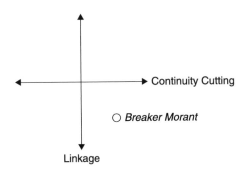

FIGURE 9.9

The coverage is spare in this beautifully directed, designed, and shot film, and this contributes to the sense of linkage. By repeating setups, similarity is enhanced and difference lessened. During the interrogation of the first witness, a repetitive pattern of shots is established. Each new setup is only one gradation of shot size up or down from the previous, and each is used at least twice before the introduction of a new shot. Until the first bombshell in the witness's testimony is dropped. Suddenly, the pattern of cutting changes and three new setups are seen in rapid succession. The moment settles down, and the editor (William Anderson) returns to a back-and-forth pattern of repeating shots until the next new damning revelation in the testimony, and again the pattern of repeating setups is broken and new angles are revealed.

All cuts, needless to say, are beautifully aligned to the principles of cutting emotional rhythm as described in Chapter 7, with the characters throwing the energy of their glances, sighs, questions, or lies from one to the other, motivating the cuts to show us reactions and actions in a revealing rhythm and steadily increasing pace. The linkage and continuity cutting function in seamless unity to create the impression of a continuous time and space with all ten people in the room intently focused on the same thing. The cutting lets us be swayed, just as the defendants and judges are, by the body language of the witness. It clearly reveals attitudes of all by cutting to reaction shots that are as responsive to subtext as they are to text (Fig. 9.10).

The coup de grâce is the timing. The British in the room hold themselves as though they are the very poles holding up the empire, and the edits on them are as clipped and neat as their moustaches. The Australians exchange uneasy glances and muttered comments framed and cut to reveal messy relationships and tensions. Their lawyer (Jack Thompson) makes a substantial piece of business out of shuffling papers noisily, and the editor extends the duration of each shot on him to include the maximum arc of each bumbling action so that

FIGURE 9.10

Edward Woodward and Jack Thompson play two Australians involved in a British court martial in Breaker Morant *(Bruce Beresford, 1979). This courtroom scene links images of the soldiers and officers, and their different cultures, under pressure in the continuous time and space of the interrogation.*
[Photo credit: S. Australia Film Corp/Australian Film Commission; The Kobal Collection]

when he finally does score a point, the contrast of the quick short shot on him in victory underlines the change.

Most importantly, two moments, each after a sharply targeted question and before the damning answer, are extended to create suspense. These moments are extended by a series of short close shots. At these two moments it is as though the whole courtroom has held its breath. Although the cuts are quick, nobody moves. The stillness minimizes collision and maximizes the tension.

Requiem for a Dream—Thematic Montage and Collision

Requiem for a Dream (Darren Aronofsky, 2000) makes use of thematic montage and collision to convey the themes of the film in a visceral way (Fig. 9.11). The style synchronizes our physical experience of movement and energy with the protagonists' and sucks us down into the vortices of their stories.

Early on in *Requiem for a Dream* there is a quick, splashy, and stylish collided thematic montage of cocaine use on the part of the protagonists (Harry Goldfarb, played by Jared Leto, and Marion Silver, played by Jennifer Connelly). The flashy and upbeat sound effects dance around the pristine framing of quirky shots of powder, money, pupils dilating, and bubbles splashing happily through the bloodstream. The sequence is so quick, the sound design such a funky music, that drug use looks fun and playful. It's a bit alarming, but the collisions of these tangentially related images are more like percussion than concussion,

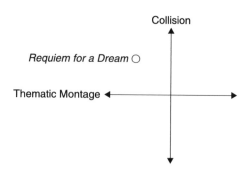

FIGURE 9.11

and they have a rhythmic effect that is analogous to drugs themselves. Seeing and hearing these sequences is a bit of a buzz, a wake up, an aesthetic treat that makes you look forward to the next one.

And for a while these thematic montages keep coming, but they grow a bit more harrowing and a bit more manic each time, soon mixing in Harry's mother's (Ellen Burstyn) growing addiction to diet pills and her subsequent hallucinations with the happy bubbling of heroin. As the film continues, the viewer experiences a kind of longing to return to the vibrant, surprising, upbeat little collisions of the early drug use. But instead, like the characters, we find ourselves increasingly bogged down in drug-induced hallucinatory nightmares. We stop getting the fun of using and start to experience the consequences. Thematic montage images still collide, but they are longer, more loosely framed, and altogether messier, until the final sequence (Fig. 9.12) in which

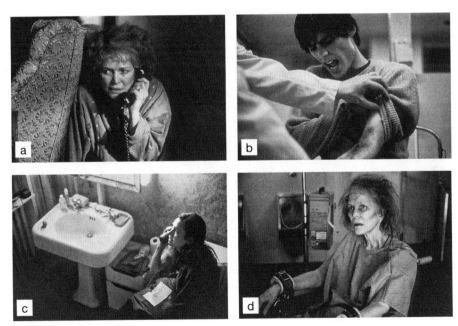

FIGURE 9.12
Ellen Burstyn, Jared Leto, and Jennifer Connelly in a colliding thematic montage of each of their downward spirals in Requiem for a Dream *(Darren Aronofsky, 2000). [Photo credit: Artisan Pictures; The Kobal Collection; John Baer]*

the worst horrors imaginable befall each of the characters. This last thematic montage sequence is neither quick nor pretty; it's not percussive or seductive. Instead, there is a relentless collision of images of pornographic rape, amputation, and electric shock therapy, each shot a sharp and painful degradation, all cut together in an almost unbearable expression of the cumulative disintegration of life, human connection, and hope. This sequence mirrors the first sequence of drug use by being a collided thematic montage, but it takes our pleasure in that stylish rat-a-tat of images and sounds and twists it into despair, thus using form and style to create the meanings of the film itself.

CONTEMPORARY STYLE: AFTER THE NEW WAVE

For this style rubric to have the flexibility needed to be useful in the long term, it must work when applied to contemporary cutting. It must therefore contend with some of the unique arrangements and derangements of time, energy, and movement in film editing, from Jean-Luc Goddard's *A bout de soufflé* (*Breathless*) (1960) onward.

Flying in the face of strict Hollywood style continuity cutting Jean-Luc Goddard opened a floodgate of new editing possibilities with the jump cuts in *A bout de soufflé*. Goddard's intentions, like those of his forbears, the Soviet montage theorists Eisenstein and Pudovkin, were political. Fed up with the hegemony of the Hollywood style and its messages about orderly social behavior, the jump cuts "warn viewers that they are watching a film and to beware of being manipulated."[4] The idea of reminding viewers of this fact was indeed revolutionary. It took the most effective form of propaganda available at the time and rendered it toothless. Unless audiences are allowed the luxury of slipping into the story unobstructed, they are unlikely to be convinced of its message.

But whether these jump cuts succeeded in their purpose of disconnecting viewers from their unreflective engagement with story or not is debatable. They may have at the time, but now they have become part of style, or as Ken Dancyger, author of *The Technique of Film and Video Editing*, says, "The jump cut has simply become another editing device accepted by the viewing audience."[5] Even Cecile Decugis, the editor of *A bout de souffle*, reminds us that, "As Cocteau said, 'all the revolutionary ideas in art become conformist after 20 years.'"[6] Jump cuts can indeed appear in the most mainstream of Hollywood films now. When Goddard shoots an action in a continuous time and space and then cuts a chunk out of the middle so that a continuous action jumps *out* of ordinary time and space, he turns continuity cutting into thematic montage, or at least shoves the continuity cutting down toward the other end of the spectrum. The action was continuous in time and space when it was shot; in other words, it was covered as continuity cutting and then cut to be discontinuous montage. One could also say it was probably shot as linkage but then cut into collision. By dropping frames from within continuous shots, *A bout de souffle* is broken into discontinuous pieces, and those pieces are then re-associated without continuous flow so as to give rise to a new idea or understanding. Breaking temporal and spatial continuity creates what could be thought of as a jagged edge to each bit of action, which collides with the next bit's equally jagged, torn, continuity.

The question then is, stylistically speaking, why do such a thing? What is the purpose of discontinuous continuity and jaggedly collided linkage in a contemporary film (given that it is not the same as Goddard's original purpose)? I propose two possible answers: first, it's cool. It is cool to put in jump cuts in the same way that all harmless rule breaking is cool. Cool is defined in reaction to the establishment, though. Therefore, it is cool to put in jump cuts if they fly in the face of the rules of continuity cutting, but only until such time as jump cutting has been assimilated into those rules, which I believe it has been.

The other reason to use a jump cut style is to present a state of extreme subjectivity. As with thematic montage, a jump cut signifies that the perspective of the character has deviated far enough from normal or from that of the other characters around her so as to disrupt her sense of ordinary time or space.

In the very mainstream film *Erin Brokovich* (Steven Soderbergh, 2000), when Erin (Julia Roberts) gets bad news on the telephone, there is a series of jump cuts that convey her emotional distress at what she is hearing and, although all of the shots are objective, it is possible to understand from the jump cutting that her subjective experience is intense enough to have disrupted her ordinary feeling for time and space.

A far more extreme, revolutionary version of this intensified subjectivity occurs in Oliver Stone's *Natural Born Killers* (1994), in which Woody Harrelson and Juliet Lewis play characters who live so far outside of the rules of civilization that they are unstuck in time and space. Their subjectivities rule the construction of their worlds, which blink rapidly, almost compulsively, through colors, textures, framings, and media. There is, to quote Dr. Jane Mills, film scholar, "visual anarchy".[7] Point of view and perspective bounce from the inner realities to the objective actualities of the central characters, and everyone they encounter, so swiftly and colorfully that the two soon blur and take on a new, mixed, version of reality. The continuity of time and space is creative and variegated in its contraction and expansion.

Natural Born Killers remains a watershed in the "in your face" editing style. It paved the way for sequences and films such as *21 Grams* (Alejandro Gonzalez Inarritu, 2003) that come completely unstuck in continuous time and space even though they portray events that could be depicted in the Hollywood continuity style.

But the style rubric of the intersecting spectra of thematic montage to continuity cutting and collision to linkage remains useful for describing these "new" editing approaches, because their newness is in fact a variation on the old styles and develops in reaction to the concerns

FIGURE 9.13
Woody Harrelson as the radically subjective Mickey living in his own perception of time and space in Natural Born Killers *(Oliver Stone, 1994). [Photo credit: Warner Bros; The Kobal Collection; Sydney Baldwin]*

of the more traditional forms. To experience these editing styles as revolutionary, we have to experience them in relation to the traditions they disrupt, traditions that, of course, were at one point quite revolutionary themselves. Perhaps Oliver Stone and the editors of *Natural Born Killers*, Brian Berdan and Hank Corwin, see a smooth linkage as a wasted opportunity, just as Eisenstein did, but take it to farther extremes.

SUMMARY

If we say that style is the result of a set of choices and define those choices as sitting within a range from thematic montage to continuity cutting and from collision to linkage, then it is possible to say that style choices are choices about the shaping of a film's time, space, and energy, three things by now familiar to the reader as core components of rhythm. In films from the 1920s to the present, style choices and their consequent editing rhythms shape the movement of images, events, and emotions to give rise to ideas and distinctive perceptual experiences in film.

ENDNOTES

1. Giannetti, L., *Understanding Movies,* p. 133.
2. Eisenstein, S., *Film Form: Essays in Film Theory,* p. 50.
3. Pudovkin, V. I., *On Film Technique and Film Acting,* p. 31.
4. Dancyger, K., *The Technique of Film and Video Editing, Theory and Practice,* p. 132.
5. Ibid.
6. Cecile Decugis as quoted in McGrath, D., *Screencraft: Editing & Post-Production,* p. 75.
7. Cited from a conversation about the film in class at University of Technology, Sydney in 2008.

CHAPTER 10

Devices

A device, for our purposes, is something that "complicates the formal patterning . . . providing form with variations."[1] It is a way of constructing a moment or a passage that varies the unfolding of a story from direct, linear cause-and-effect chains to more complicated and potentially more expressive patterns of telling. An editing device varies form by playing with some of the unique capacities of cinema to shape time, space, energy, and movement.

Before talking about devices and their uses, it is important to note here something editors often say when trying to make generalizations about their working processes, which is, "It depends on the story." These editors are, of course, absolutely right. Every decision made in the edit suite needs to be made with reference to the unique story being told, whether that story is narrative drama, abstract meditation, investigative journalism, or some other form.

But devices, unlike individual decisions or processes, can be discussed out of the context of any particular production and applied to any story. This chapter looks at two devices: parallel action and motion effects. It presents some case studies on how they have been used effectively and offers some principles about them that may be useful for any production. But ultimately it will be up to the individual editor to make use of them, and their particular applications will be unique to their stories.

The following case studies on parallel action and slow/fast motion discuss each of these devices. Case studies are used to illustrate principles about how they might work affectively, or not work if they become clichés.

PARALLEL ACTION

Another way of saying "parallel action" is to say "meanwhile." "Meanwhile" is a literary device that was very fashionable in the early years of film. The grandfather of many film devices and conventions, filmmaker D.W. Griffith, says that he was heavily influenced by Charles Dickens, the king of plotting "meanwhiles,"[2] but actually this use of meanwhile can be found all over literature. Ironically, just as Dickens is credited as an authority for a device that is really "common to fiction at large," D.W. Griffith was later credited with devices that were common, even intrinsic, to the development of narrative film form at large.[3] Whether invented by Griffith or having evolved as the aggregate of filmmaking knowledge developed and spread from country to country, parallel action is one of the earliest cinematic storytelling devices to be explored and continues to be used as an extremely effective, efficient, and exciting way of moving story events, creating feelings, revealing information, and heightening tension.

As a film-editing device, parallel action essentially leaves one character or story in progress and turns to look at what is happening elsewhere at the same time. Why do this? One reason is, as Eisenstein said, to relieve boredom. But I would put that in the positive and say that one of the primary purposes of parallel action is to create excitement. From the point of view of shaping cycles of tension and release, the device of cutting parallel action opens questions. How will the two things that are happening in two different places at the same time impact each other? And *when* will they?

The nuances of "when" are the editors' domain. As editors, we know from the script that the two sides of the parallel action will eventually connect and that the plot events that are the result of their convergence will occur. Contemporary audiences are pretty well aware of this, too. If you were screening a dramatic film in which a fireman was racing to save a child in a burning building and paused the film midway through the action to ask, "Will the fireman get there in time?" the audience would most likely say, "Yes, probably." But audiences are not really in the theater just to experience the unfolding of events. They also come to the cinema to have the psychosomatic experience of *how* the events unfold. It is their empathetic experience with the characters on their journeys, and their feeling with the movement of image, sound, emotions, and events, that they also come to the movies for. They may be confident the fireman will save the child from the burning building but still come to the movies to enjoy the tension of the open questions. How close will he get to missing? How much tension will there be? How well will the editor cut the parallel action sequence? How well will she modulate the rate and angle of convergence to create a satisfying tension, a satisfying unfolding of the action in time, a satisfying rhythm?

PRACTICAL EXERCISE

Parallel Action Part 1

Activate the principles of parallel action by setting up a practical exercise for yourself now and then adding to it after each short case study.

The exercise is to write a parallel action sequence based on the premise that a detective is hunting for a fugitive.

First decide on the facts of the case: what, where, when, who, and why. There is no requirement that your characters or problem be of a particular type. Your detective might be the good guy or the bad guy. She might be a down-to-earth sheriff in Minnesota or he might be an adrenalin junkie secret agent in another galaxy. The device is useful in all genres, in all kinds of screen stories.

Next, decide on the story action in your first sequence of shots. Describe what is happening in one place and time; for example, where and when the fugitive begins the story, and "meanwhile," what is happening in the detective's location.

Now, before going on to read the case studies, decide how your sequence is going to end. Will the fugitive be caught or escape?

Once you've jotted some notes on all of these points, go on to read the case studies, and, if possible, see the films they describe. After each case study add another set of shots to your sequence, deciding on the shot sizes and contents and cuts. In other words, decide what the viewer will see and hear and *when* we will see and hear it using the cutting principles each case study reveals.

PARALLEL ACTION CASE STUDIES

The Great Train Robbery (Edwin Porter, 1903)

This first case study of parallel action is not a study of true parallel action but of an innovation in film form that is an important precursor of parallel action.

In 1903, Elliot Porter made *The Great Train Robbery*, a film that was innovative in length, subject matter, and structure. It depicts the story of a robbery and the subsequent escape and capture of the thieves, mostly in a linear timeline: first the robbers enter the train station, knock out the station master, and tie him up so he can't warn the train conductor; then they rob the train and escape. But as the robbers are escaping we see something that has not yet been seen in film in 1903: Porter cuts back to the train station, where we see the station master recovering and sounding the alarm. It looks as though Porter is saying, "The robbers are escaping, and *meanwhile* the station master is waking up." In *Film Editing, History, Theory and Practice*[4] Don Fairservice argues that this is not really a "meanwhile." In fact, he claims that what Porter is doing is more complicated: he is taking us back to an earlier point in time and showing us the continuation of action that would have happened earlier in the story. However, whether it is a true parallel action or not, for our purposes it does something that sets a precedent for parallel action: it cuts from the experience of one time, place, and character action in progress to another, revealing to us, as an audience, something that none of the characters could know. We move ahead of the characters in the story, knowing more than they do and experiencing the tension of the questions: How will these two strands of action impact each other? And when?

To contemporary eyes it is a bit tricky to see this story as tension-filled, but this is not a fault of the plotting or the structure. Rather, it just takes too long, and it happens in long shots only, no close-ups. So the rhythm relies solely on performance and plot, the story showing is hampered, to our sensibility, by being out of sync with contemporary

FIGURE 10.1

The Great Train Robbery *(Edwin Porter, 1903)*, at about 16 minutes, was roughly four times as long as almost any film up to then and told a tension-filled tale of the American frontier. [Photo credit: Edison; The Kobal Collection]

rhythms. However, it is a useful example of how much the contemporary audience experience of story relies on cinematic aspects of editing and shooting to create understanding and empathetic engagement. And it also reveals the impact the editor can have on story experience by modulating the rate and angle of convergence of the two parallel events.

Strangers on a Train (Alfred Hitchcock, 1951)

The opening sequence of *Strangers on a Train*[5] is a close-range parallel action sequence. We see two pairs of feet, one with flashy two-toned shoes and one with sensible brown shoes and a tennis racquet, stepping out of taxis at a train station. The shoes' owners are unaware of each other but, as the editor (William H. Zeigler) cuts back and forth

PRACTICAL EXERCISE

Parallel Action Part 2

The questions raised by Porter's structural innovation of cutting away from one action to see another are: How will these two events impact on each other? And when? When writing the ending or the scenario about the detective chasing the fugitive, you wrote the facts that tell *how* the two sides of your parallel action will impact on each other. The opportunity now is to think about *when* the two sides of the action in the story will converge.

Will the convergence be prolonged by complications or come to a quick and decisive end? How much time will we spend with each character, getting to know them and care about them?

Make a decision about how long you would like your parallel action sequence to be, how long the overall production will be, and how much weight or emphasis this sequence has in the overall film. It could be the entire plot or only a small part of it. Now write the next series of cuts, adding in a complication to each character's objectives that could prolong the sequence. Later you will have to decide whether to keep this subplot, when you decide if you've got the rhythm of the sequence right.

between them, we are aware of both walking on what appears to be a direct collision course toward each other. We are, consciously or unconsciously, caught up in the question: How will these two characters, about whom we have already made a series of judgments based on their shoes, impact each other? And when?

Hitchcock, being a master filmmaker, knows that these are the questions he has created and chooses to make use of our expectations to create a twist. The two pairs of feet walk toward each other (apparently) at an accelerating pace; the cuts also accelerate, and the music by Dimitri Tiomkin emphasizes the connection and tension between the two images as they appear to come closer and closer, faster and faster. Just when we expect them to collide, Zeigler cuts to a wide shot of the turnstile at the train track entrance, and the two sets of shoes walk in, one at a time, without noticing each other. It turns out that "brown shoes" was farther away from the entrance than "flashy shoes," but the tight framing and accelerating cutting played right into the expectations of the audience that they would crash into each other. Hitchcock uses his knowledge of the audience's expectations to set up some underlying themes of the whole film, that things don't unfold as you might expect, life takes unexpected pathways and can turn to the left or the right in an instant.

After the turnstile shot comes a dissolve to a shot of the train tracks diverging at a crossing. The train stays on the straight track until the last possible second and then moves onto the track that veers off in another direction, affording us another metaphor for the lives of the two key characters whose paths cross each other's on this journey. Only then does the parallel action between the two pairs of shoes come back into play; the shoes walk along the corridor of the train, sit, cross their legs, bump each other, and that's when faces are finally revealed: when the strangers meet.

In this example of parallel action we get some important informa-tion from the mise-en-scène: our judgments about the characters come from the style of shoes, our sense that they are going to crash comes from the screen direction and pace at which they apparently walk toward each other. But it is the cutting that creates the possibility for us to surmise the story. The cutting is what creates the impact of the sequence because it makes us think that these two events will impact each other, and soon. This is an excellent example of cutting creating the story. It allows us to surmise things that in fact are not part of the plot; it gets us to, in a sense, tell ourselves the story by giving us the opportunity to make a connection between two things. The cutting allows us to think we know more than the characters. We think we are moving ahead of them and feel tension about the impending collision. The cutting then reveals we are just like the characters, we only know what they know, except that we also know that things are not what they seem.

Gallipoli (Peter Weir, 1981)

Parallel action is frequently about time pressure. As discussed earlier, the tension is not only about whether two people or events will intersect, but when, and if it will be soon enough. The audience's

PRACTICAL EXERCISE

Parallel Action Part 3

Hitchcock and Zeigler's parallel action sequence in *Strangers on a Train* demonstrates some valuable principles about frame exclusion and inclusion that can apply to the scenario you are writing: What will be seen in your fugitive/detective scenario? And what information will be withheld? It is also possible to extrapolate from this sequence that accelerating pace and cutting between things moving right to left and things moving left to right will create an expectation that they will collide. Further, on a more sophisticated level, it is possible for you to use that expectation in your sequence to give us the expectation that things are about to converge and then to twist that expectation to reveal something else.

Write the next sequence of shots in your scenario and give some attention to what is seen and for how long, and what is not seen but which we might surmise is just outside the frame. Note, also, screen direction. At this point in your scenario, do the characters appear to be moving toward each other or away? More quickly or less? What expectations can you create with timing, pacing, and trajectory phrasing?

experience of how the time passes, how the pressure mounts on each side of the action creates their understanding of the story.

Peter Weir's *Gallipoli* tells the story of Australian soldiers fighting in Turkey for the British Empire in World War I. This story occupies an interesting place in Australia's national mythology, being a horrible defeat and terrible loss of lives and, at the same time, a moment when Australians asserted their ability to stand up for themselves and not just be minions of the British. So the ending had to convey both. It had to make us care about the soldiers and mourn their loss, but not see it as a simple, ignominious defeat.

The ending of the film is a parallel action sequence in which one soldier (Frank Dunne, played by Mel Gibson) runs toward the trenches to deliver a message that could save all of the men's lives. The sequence starts 9 minutes before the climactic ending, but at first it doesn't feel much like classical parallel action. Frank leaves the trenches with a note for the officer in charge and we go with him, following him as he talks, first to one officer, then another, and cutting only occasionally back to the trenches to see what is going on there. The emphasis of time is on Frank's journey and his obstacles, actions, and emotions.

FIGURE 10.2

Mel Gibson as Frank Dunne, running, pressured by time and responsibilities, in Gallipoli *(Peter Wier, 1981). The other side of the parallel action in this sequence shows us what he is responsible for and increases our anxiety about his run. [Photo credit: Associated R & R Films/Paramount; The Kobal Collection]*

The questions are: Will he get killed on the way? Will the snobbish British officer defeat his initiative? Will the Australian superior officer do the right thing and stand up for his men? And, as Frank stands in the tent of the Australian general, holding his breath on a knife's edge of anticipation (a beautifully cut moment), we hold our breath too and silently wish for the general to make up his mind, be decisive, give the order in time!

But just as Frank gets the all-important message to delay the attack, the sergeant back in the trenches gets the opposite message by telephone, and now the emphasis of the cutting shifts.

Frank begins his run back up the hill, through the other soldiers, under enemy fire, and against the clock. But, although his journey is action packed and filled with tension, there are only seven short shots of it between this point and when the film ends 4½ minutes later. The rest of the time is spent in the trenches, mostly in intimate, lyrical shots of the young men whose lives will be lost if Frank doesn't make it in time. The very sensitive and clever editor, William Anderson, understands that this is no longer just Frank's story. He has shown us how hard and important Frank's struggle is, but now the emphasis is shifted from Frank's journey to what is at stake. In other words, the emphasis has shifted from action to emotion. The editor makes a very well-judged choice to spend the balance of his time on investing our emotions and making us care, so that the ending is not just "oh, too bad, he didn't make it," it is a devastating experience of loss for the audience.

The lesson to take away from this sequence (once you get over its overwhelming impact) is that in a parallel action sequence it is often possible to identify one side of the sequence as "action" and the other as "emotion." In other words, one side might be under time pressure or pursuing a goal or moving events along in some way, whereas the other side is what's at stake. In this case the men in the trenches are at stake, and the editing is structured in such a way as to immerse us deeply in feeling for and with them. It favors emotion over action and consequently, when they are gunned down, we feel loss.

So the question an editor can ask herself when cutting parallel action is: Where is action and where is emotion? And what is the balance I need to achieve between them?

PRACTICAL EXERCISE

Parallel Action Part 4

The question for an editor is sometimes whether to create parallel action if it didn't exist in the script, but more often there are likely to be questions of emphasis, as in: Which side of the story do I show, when, and for how long? Which actual cutting points will slant the stories in the way I want? These questions also lead us back to, Whose story is it? As in: Who do I want the audience to care about and sympathize with, and who do I want them to hope wins?

In the scenario you are creating, it might be possible to say that one side is action and one is emotion or to say who is driving the action and what is at stake. If your detective's job is at stake and the fugitive keeps out-maneuvering her, then action is with the fugitive and emotion is with the detective. It could just as easily be the opposite, or it could be that the detective is trying to catch the fugitive to warn him of the great danger he is in. No matter what the plot events are, the question of balancing action and emotion could be available for the editor to play with.

The next question for the editor is: If one side is action and one side is emotion, how much time do we need to spend in each place to raise the stakes and the tensions? If one or the other side were seen for longer, how would that change the balance?

As you sketch out the next part of your parallel action sequence, try to make notes that reveal the balance of action and emotion you will create. It is a matter of shaping the timing, pacing, and trajectory phrasing into a rhythm that puts emphasis in the right place.

The Godfather (Francis Ford Coppola, 1972)

I return now to *The Godfather*, which was also discussed in Chapter 8, to look in more detail at the baptism sequence and the parallel action between Michael Corleone (Al Pacino), a young man on the cusp of becoming the Godfather of the New York underworld, and a series of murders his henchmen are executing around the city.

In this famous sequence Michael is in church taking on the role of being a spiritually responsible godfather to his sister's newborn baby. But this baptism is a metaphor; the baby is not the only one being baptized, Michael is too. The baby's baptism is ceremonial, sonorous, and richly decorated in lace and ritual, but the new Godfather's baptism is in blood.

This parallel action sequence has been very carefully planned, and its efficacy relies a great deal on the composition of the shots and the action to draw the metaphor between the two baptisms. The editors, William Reynolds and Peter Zinner, cut from the priest's action of preparing the baby for baptism to a hitman preparing his gun, from the priest anointing the baby's chin with a holy ointment to a barber anointing a hitman's chin with shaving cream. These are physical indicators of the metaphor, images and movements from which the audience can draw a metaphoric connection between the two sides of the action. The emotional connection between the two sides of the parallel action comes from two things: 1. the sounds of the service, which are artfully cut across from the grand church to the sordid sites

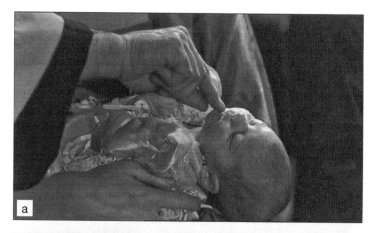

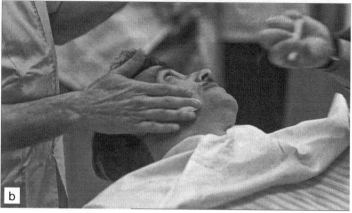

FIGURE 10.3

The comparison of the similarities of these two figures having their chins anointed in the baptism/murder sequence of The Godfather *(Francis Ford Coppola, 1972) highlights the irony of their differences.*
[Photo credit: Paramount Pictures, Alfran Productions]

of violence, and 2. the precise timing of image cuts to cue the audience that Michael Corleone knows what is going on and condones it.

The music imbues the whole sequence with the association of the holy, the sanctified, and the just, which of course is ironic because only half of the action is sanctified by God; the other half is a series of brutal, sudden, and alarming murders. The sound of the baby crying is heard only over shots of hitmen getting ready to kill. In shots inside the church the baby is sleepy and peaceful. The sound of the dialog is drawn over shots in disparate locations. When the priest asks Michael if he accepts God, we see Michael reply affirmatively. But the priest presses the point, in accordance with the ritual, asking Michael if he believes in Jesus and if he believes in the Holy Spirit. When Michael replies to these questions, we hear his affirmation, but we see something different: images of his thugs going about their work. Later, when Michael is asked repeatedly if he renounces the devil and his work, the questions are heard over images of someone being gunned down; their terror and spurting blood are then juxtaposed immediately with a close-up of Michael, looking down and inward, affirming that he does renounce the devil.

A very important part of making this ironic and metaphoric cutting work is the editors' timing of cuts on Al Pacino's performance. It is the precise timing that allows us to surmise that Michael is fully aware of the violent action taking place, knows it is taking place at his behest, and both regrets and sanctions it.

The first close-up of Michael in the sequence is a slightly high-angle shot looking at Michael from roughly the perspective of the priest, who is standing a step above Michael on the altar. At the beginning of this shot Michael is looking down and appears to be listening to the priest, gazing at the baby (Fig. 10.4a). He then looks up toward the priest (Fig. 10.4b), then his eyes shift to the middle distance and glaze over slightly, as he looks into his own thoughts (Fig. 10.4c). Once his inward gaze is established, there is another shot of the baby, but

FIGURE 10.4

Just before the killings start in the baptism/murder sequence of The Godfather *(Francis Ford Coppola, 1972), there is a shot of Michael (Al Pacino) that tells us, just through the shifts of his eyes, that his mind is in two places at once: here with the holy ritual in the church and away with the unholy ritual taking place at his behest. [Photo credit: Paramount Pictures, Alfran Productions]*

Michael is not looking at him, Michael's gaze is on the images in his mind's eye: the preparations for the killings. Had the editors left the shot 46 frames, or 1½ seconds earlier, they would have left us with the impression that Michael's thoughts were with the baptism. Instead, the timing leaves us with the impression that his thoughts are far away.

From there forward, as both the music and the mayhem escalate throughout the sequence, the editors use a repeating pattern of cutting back to Michael as he is looking inward and then holding on the shot as he responds to the priest. The response is performed calmly, even beatifically, and allows us to align with his thoughts, to believe, with him, that he can be both good and bad at the same time. It is the timing of the cut to Michael as he looks inward that tells us he knows what is going on, the holding on the shot as he responds that aligns us with him emotionally, and then the cutting back to the violence that creates the irony: we are emotionally aligned with the perpetrator of inhuman acts, who is reflective, sorrowful, and imbued with the righteousness of the Church. And this is the irony of the entire film. The good people in the film, the ones we understand, like, and feel with in the cycles of tension and release, are the monsters. The film form, including performances, shooting, cutting, sound, music, and devices, moves our understanding, caring, and allegiance toward the protagonist at the same time it reveals his stately, mindful, even responsible descent into base thuggery.

The Borgias (Neil Jordon, series creator, 2011–2013)

Parallel action is a core device in the structures of complex television series where multiple plot lines run in parallel to each other over many episodes and seasons. The Borgias is just one example of this kind of construction, but it is one where the parallel action is particularly energized, especially near the end of season three. Apparently the series was abruptly cancelled by Showtime, one season short of its intended four-season arc. This may explain why the parallel cutting is so pronounced in season three. There were many plots and relationships

PRACTICAL EXERCISE

Parallel Action Part 5

Three very useful principles are demonstrated in *The Godfather's* parallel action:

1. Metaphoric connections between the two sides of the action are made by choreographing the juxtaposition of actions and images to imply relationships;

2. Overlapping sound and music reshape our understanding of the relationship between the two sides of the action completely; and

3. Timing of cuts throws the energy from one shot to the next and shapes our empathetic responses.

As you write the next sequence of shots, try to make use of these three principles to shape your story. Even if the images are not being placed to mirror each other directly the way they are in *The Godfather*, it is important to think about how they build a sequence of ideas when juxtaposed. Cutting a shot of the desert from one side of the action with a shot of a swimming pool on the other side will contrast the two sides. Cutting bird wings flapping with tissues fluttering will compare them. This is, of course also a stylistic question. As discussed in Chapter 9, if you make collisions of screen direction, energy, line, or movement, the two sides of the parallel action will read in a relationship to each other that is different than if you make smooth linkages.

The overlapping of sound or music will draw the emotional color from one side of the action to the other, which can be used ironically. But overlapping sound in parallel action can also be used to create an emotional resonance or stronger alliance with one side of the action. It may even create a sense of premonition: we might feel that one character knows what is happening somewhere else in the story.

Is there one side of your scenario you would take the sound from at this point and draw it over the other?

The timing of your cuts will, as discussed in Chapter 7, throw the energy or intention of one shot to the next shot, making the energy or action of the second shot feel as though it is responding to the first shot. This sense of timing is how the editors of *The Godfather* align us with Michael in the Baptism sequence. It would be useful to you now to make sure you know who you want the audience to be aligned with in your sequence (it could be more than one figure) and to think about how timing of the cuts will strengthen that alignment.

As you write the final convergence of the two sides of your parallel action, you may want to think about style, metaphor, and sound connecting the two sides. Consider how you might play with the timing of cuts to shape responses as convergence occurs.

Having come to the final convergence for your sequence, you now have the opportunity to do the most fun part of filmmaking: editing! As this is a written, not a shot, sequence, you will have to imagine the flow rather than experience it, but this still provides an opportunity for you to sing the rhythms in your head as you read through your scenario. Listen to the song for a modulated build of tension and be aware of release points as you, for example, introduce complications or dwell on emotional moments. The releases are as important as the builds of tension in creating a compelling rhythm. You might go back to your scenario at this point and exclude some information from the earlier parts of the sequence so you can have a "reveal" later. Think about cutting points throughout and how you can use them to align the audience with the characters.

that had to be closed and cutting them in parallel creates efficiencies and impact.

This is not the only function of parallel cutting in this series though. The editors Lisa Grootenboer and Wendy Hallam Martin synthesize all

FIGURE 10.5
Rogerigo (Jeremy Irons), Lucrezia (Holliday Grainger) and Cesare Borgia (François Arnaud) have competing plans and ambitions. The complex parallel cutting of season three of The Borgias *keeps each of their plots moving forward rapidly and adds energy to the drama with sharp juxtapositions of actions and emotions. [Photo credit: Showtime Networks]*

of the purposes and techniques of parallel action as they swirl us through the season's climax.

- They bring excitement of rapid movement from place to place to what could otherwise become a staid period drama.

- They plant the questions: How will these multiple strands of action impact each other?

- They develop tension by revealing characters plans but withholding information about execution.

- They use "meanwhile" to complicate the plots with other characters' intentions.

- They keep all of the characters' stories present in the viewer's minds.

- They balance "action" and "emotion" so that we care about what is at stake for each.

- They make metaphoric connections, use overlapping sound and music, and throw the energy from one shot to the next so that we stay synchronized with the movement of events, emotions, images and sound.

Snatch (Guy Ritchie, 2000)

The parallel action sequence in *Snatch* is, like *The Great Train Robbery*, not really parallel action. In fact, Guy Ritchie takes filmmaking back almost 100 years and makes a slyly winking sequence that brings the viewer in on three "parallel" sides of a story by taking us backward and forward in time, just as Edwin Porter did in 1903.

FIGURE 10.6
Dennis Farina and Vinnie Jones get ready to go on more than just a car ride in Snatch *(Guy Ritchie, 2000). [Photo credit: Columbia/SKA Films; The Kobal Collection; Sebastian Pearson]*

In *Snatch*, as three sets of interests converge on their common objective, they collide, literally, in a violently fatal car crash that is absurd and clever. We see the crash three times, as though we can see all points of view, not in parallel, but sequentially.

The absurdity of this sequence arises from the dialog and the situation. The cleverness arises from the sequential way that information is revealed. Just as Hitchcock makes use of our expectations to subvert them in *Strangers on a Train*, Ritchie knows we know what to expect from parallel action. And he plays with our expectations, thwarting them by manipulating the conventions of the device. One set of characters goes forward to a certain point in time and space, and then the edit jumps back to an earlier time and shows another set of characters on their journey to converge, not just in space, but in time. This manipulation of linear time makes the viewer feel like a God. As well as showing information the characters would not know about things going on at the same time but in another place, it reveals information that the characters could not know about their own futures.

This playing with the device shifts our allegiance; it takes us outside of the story so that we do not feel with any of the characters, exactly; it is as though we feel allegiance with the filmmaker instead. We stand in his shoes, playing with time and space. We feel clever, omniscient, just as the director might feel because he, of course, like a God, knows more about the story than any of his characters could.

French film theorist Christian Metz proposed that cinematic space and time allow the audience a kind of godlike quality, of always being in the right place at the right time. Parallel action allows spectators to be where the actions are even if the two actions are taking place worlds apart. In this way, parallel action creates one of the unique and enjoyable sensations of the movies. Unlike life, in the movies we can always be where the action is. If this unique sensation is not, to quote singer/songwriter Paul Simon, "why God made the movies," it is certainly one reason the device of parallel action arose so early in the development of film form and remains so robust. This function of placing the spectator in the right place at the right time gives rise to a final and very useful question an editor can ask herself when putting together a parallel action sequence: Where is the action? Because that, of course, whether it is physical, emotional, or event action, is where the audience wants to be.

SLOW MOTION

Why make something slow motion? The major function of slow motion is to prolong for the purpose of heightening, whatever effect the gesture or action covered is meant to have; i.e., to make it more poetic, romantic, glorious, horrifying, or otherwise heighten the emotionality or importance of a moment.

Why would seeing something for a longer time make us more emotional about it? There are, I believe, at least two answers to this question. The first is a simple matter of temporal emphasis. If an emotion or action is in progress and it is portrayed in slow motion, then it will automatically have more "emphasis by duration" than it would normally have. The other reason slow motion heightens affect is "emphasis by stress." As discussed in Chapter 3, the emphasis by stress is the accent or emphasis created by the energy or quality of movement, not by its duration.

Slow motion changes the energy or quality of a normal movement and thus gives it a greater emphasis. It increases the magnitude of an occurrence in our perception and changes the quality of our kinaesthetic empathy, I believe, because it creates an image of a greater effort of bodies in motion. Bodies (and these could be human bodies, bodies of water, bodies of objects) expend greater energy to do an action when they appear not just to push against obstacles on their journeys but also to be pushing the resistance of time. This "resistance of time" can, in some cases, also create the opposite quality of

FIGURE 10.7

The elegiac opening of Lars von Trier's Melancholia *(2011) takes the idea of "time in close-up" and gives it an extended aesthetic and emotional life. The framing positions us as though we are looking at a painting, but as it sustains over nearly 10 minutes we feel, like the characters, that we are straining against time or floating within it, unable or unwilling to break free. [Photo credit: Zentropa Entertainments]*

movement; not greater strain but a floating, buoyant quality can be created by that temporal resistance. In this case, time becomes a sort of cushion of air holding a body up as it moves in slow motion. As viewers, our kinaesthetic response to the effort involved is heightened as the bodies appear to strain against time or float within it, unable or unwilling to break free and move with normal gravity and tempo. The great Soviet documentary filmmaker Dziga Vertov[6] is quoted as saying that "slow motion is time in close-up." This suggests that slow motion does for time what the close-up does for space, which is make us more intimate with it, more cognizant of it, and more sensually affected by it.

The following case studies look at a few examples of slow motion in films to extract some principles about how and why it is used, what the particular effects of our heightened kinaesthetic empathy may be, and when slow motion might be cliché or overused.

SLOW MOTION CASE STUDIES

Chariots of Fire (Hugh Hudson, 1981)

Chariots of Fire is the Best Picture Academy Award-winning tale of the religious and ethical conflicts experienced by members of the British track team in the 1924 Olympics in Germany. The races that take place in the film are very important ways of showing the story. They show us the characters in competition with each other, with other teams, and with themselves, drawing a physical metaphor between running a race and the competitions and co-operations of life. Variations on speed of motion are often used in depicting these races to underline, enhance, or create emotional impact, the tensions of the conflict, and most importantly, the kinaesthetic empathy required for us, the viewers, to have a felt experience of the runners' stories.

In the climactic gold medal-winning race there is the use of a couple of different speeds of slow motion in the sequence, all done in-camera, by speeding up the rate at which film runs through it. There is a range of slow motions in the athletes' bodies, but the crowd is in normal time. This signals that the athletes are having a special kinaesthetic experience. Some athletes are slower and more glorious or expending more effort than others, as they prepare for the race, line up on their marks, get set into their starting postures, and go. But the race itself, the first time we see it, is mostly in long shot and normal time. Given that these are Olympic athletes running a mere 100 meters, it is very quick—under 6 seconds, including the win.

Given that this is a climactic moment of the film and many of the emotional and plot lines are riding on its outcomes, running it in under 6 seconds is a very interesting choice and one which, I believe, was probably made in the edit suite. As soon as the race ends, in fact as it is won, the editor, Terry Rawlings, returns to slow motion. The winner, our hero, Harold Abrahams (played by Ben Cross), breaks the tape in a surge of effort against time that seems as though his chest is literally pushing the weight of time in front of him as he pushes across

FIGURE 10.8

Ben Cross as Harold Abrahams pushes against time to reach the finish line in Chariots of Fire *(Hugh Hudson, 1981). [Photo credit: 20th Century Fox/Allied Stars/Enigma; The Kobal Collection]*

the finish line (Fig. 10.8). His friends and teammates in the crowd run down to congratulate him in slow motion, and then the editor makes another interesting choice: he replays the race, this time in slow motion. One could surmise that this is the memory of the race as it was felt by the characters, but the shots are not really set up to encourage us to infer that. There is no shot of Abrahams's head or face or gaze that would imply we are shifting into his memory. So to me, this replay of the race feels as though it is for my benefit as an audience, so that I can feel the effort, this time in slow motion, feel the physical and psychological exertion as Abrahams strains against time and circumstances toward victory. In short, the race is replayed so that I can have the experience of kinaesthetic empathy that can be created by slow motion. When I watch the race the first time, the tension of the question of who will win is foremost in my experience. Slow motion here might have the effect of making me impatient rather than making me empathetic. Also, the extreme quickness of the race is, to my mind, a more accurate representation of what it might feel like to the athletes. After all the build up, the training, the tensions, the politics of getting to this point, that race would feel very quick indeed. The second time allows me the kinaesthetic experience of being in the race as a value in itself, a heightened, more glorious, more effort-filled experience than anything in my real life.

The Navigator (Vincent Ward, 1988)

Another very useful aspect of slow motion has to do with prolonging the occurrence of an event for storytelling purposes. Slow motion prolongs the sensation of an action occurring rather than having occurred. To clarify this point, I refer to screenwriting teacher Robert McKee's book *Story: Structure, Substance, Style and the Principles of Screenwriting*. McKee discusses the idea that emotion is something an audience experiences *while* something is going on.[7] We experience feeling as something is occurring, not once it is over and we already know the result. This of course is similar to the tension of the open question I have been referring to throughout the book, and it is also a way of describing the kinaesthetic empathy that occurs while the question is open. Not only do we feel tension about what will happen, but we feel with the characters as they go through an event. Once an event is resolved, their emotions and ours dissipate.

McKee says there are only two emotions: pleasure and pain. They each have a lot of variations—joy, love, happiness, rapture, fun, ecstasy, etc., or misery, stress, grief, humiliation, remorse, etc.—but they all come back to pleasure and pain.

> As audiences we experience emotion when the telling takes us through a transition of values. As soon as the plateau is reached, however, emotion quickly dissipates. An emotion is a relatively short-term, energetic experience. Now the audience is thinking, great, he got what he wanted, what happens next?[8]

So if we experience the emotion during the journey, but as soon as we get there, we stop feeling the energy of the emotion, then slow motion, quite simply, prolongs the journey, so that we either can pay more attention to it or feel it for longer.

At the end of Vincent Ward's moving and inventive film *The Navigator*, the protagonists have reached a very hard fought objective, which is to raise a cross on the steeple of a church. Because it is a mythical parable being told in two time frames, present-day New Zealand and medieval plague-ridden Europe, the storyteller, a young boy, knows that there will be a great triumph but also a terrible tragedy once the goal is reached. He doesn't know what the tragedy is, and neither do we, until the cross has been raised and the boy starts to fall from the spire. There are a series of jump cuts that repeat and prolong the action of the boy falling away from the spire, and then there is a slow motion shot, not of the boy, but of his glove, drifting gracefully across the sky, never quite reaching the ground.

The slow motion is necessary to prolong the occurrence of the event, to give us time to realize who is falling and what the story implications of that fall are. It is also very necessary emotionally. A quick fall would change the emotional quality of the event from a lyrical sacrifice to a bad accident. But what I think is really interesting is that the slow motion shot of the fall is not a shot of the boy, but of the glove. I think that the editor, John Scott, and director, Vincent Ward, knew that putting in a slow motion shot of the boy falling would be too much. It might be maudlin or sentimental, it would almost certainly be a cliché, and it could never be lyrical, because it's just too awful. Using the glove as a metonym allows us to see the beauty of the fall, to feel suspension of the moment as the glove is suspended by time, and to experience the grace of its movement as the grace of letting go.

Thelma and Louise (Ridley Scott, 1991)

This case study on slow motion is from the end of *Thelma and Louise*, the 1991 Academy Award nominee for editing by Thom Noble. *Thelma and Louise* was a controversial film when it was released. The controversy was over the feminist credentials, or lack thereof, of the story, and one aspect of the controversy centered on the end: When the two women drive off the edge of a cliff rather than surrender to the law, is it defiant liberation or just suicidal wreckage and waste?

The use of slow motion, music, and a slow fade to white in the last shot are aspects of form that fuel the controversy. As the two women drive off the cliff's edge, the car soars in a glorious, triumphant, arc in the air, in a gracious slow-motion suspension of time. The car doesn't fall. Ever. Rather, the editor stops time and motion with a freeze-frame, and then the slow fade to white, timed with the rising cadence of the music, leaves us with the impression that the protagonists are flying, not falling. The very upbeat tune continues into a credit sequence montage of all of the happiest moments of the film. All of these techniques are used to convince us of one thing: a happy ending. And they succeed, largely owing to the physiological responses we can be depended on to have when we see smiling faces and graceful flows and hear happy music that synchronizes us to its infectious beat. It is only on a cognitive level that this film's ending is sad. Only if you think about the wreckage and dead bodies that, of course, you never see, do you think about the waste and horror the events imply. How different would this movie have felt if the car had flown at regular speed? What if it had actually crashed?

This film uses slow motion at the end of the story to sustain the emotional energy generated by the action. Placed at the end, the slow motion sustains our emotional energy as we leave the cinema and, even more importantly, sustains the emotion we feel about the action in progress rather than having the feeling that freedom and flight have come to an end.

FAST MOTION

Technically speaking, fast motion is the opposite of slow motion. It can be created either by running the film more slowly through the

FIGURE 10.9
Geena Davis and Susan Sarandon as the title characters in Thelma and Louise *(Ridley Scott, 1991). When they make the decision to go forward rather than surrender, is their decision noble, lyrical, and redemptive or ignominious and wasteful? The filmmaker relies on slow motion and a few other editing devices to show his perspective. [Photo credit: MGM/Pathe; The Kobal Collection]*

camera or by dropping out frames in the edit suite. Unlike slow motion, there is no perceptual difference in using one of these techniques or the other. Running the film through the camera more slowly means that the action is covered in fewer frames, which is the same effect as dropping frames out in editing so that action goes by more quickly.

Affectively speaking, the function of fast motion may also be the opposite of slow motion. If the function of slow motion has been to make something more poetic, romantic, glorious, horrifying, or otherwise heighten the emotionality of a moment, then is the function of fast motion to make you feel less?

In many cases, we laugh at fast motion or experience it as a light moment. By being too speeded up to be real, fast motion is kinaesthetically comic; it creates absurdity by ellipses.

According to Robert McKee, comedy is predicated on the audience feeling that no one gets hurt. So, if fast motion makes us feel less, perhaps it does so by leaving the impression that the characters feel less. Our kinaesthetic empathy is activated by the recognition of an onscreen figure's kinaesthetic experience, so if those figures don't feel an event, we don't either.

This kinaesthetic effect could be said to be drawn from the technical means of production of fast motion. It is almost as though, by dropping out frames, you eliminate the points of contact at which the body would normally feel pain. The frame where the body actually crashes to the ground is left out, or the crash occurs too quickly to hurt. Instead of straining against time or feeling it as a force of support or cushioning, bodies onscreen slip through time with very little contact, too little to have an impact.

TWO QUICK FAST MOTION CASE STUDIES

- *Romeo and Juliet* (Baz Lurhmann, 1996)

- *Two for the Road* (Stanley Donen, 1967)

In Baz Luhrmann's 1996 version of Shakespeare's *Romeo and Juliet*, editing rhythms and style do a great deal to update the story to contemporary Southern California. In the scene in which Juliet's mother asks Juliet if she would like to marry Paris, the editor, the audacious and daring Jill Bilcock, conveys a great deal about the mother's character and her relationship with her daughter by use of fast motion. The scene is cut with absolute respect for the rules of classical continuity cutting. There are no jump cuts or even jarring cuts from long to close-up shots. Shot sizes and composition progress from wide to medium to close in an orderly and reliable way.

As Juliet, Claire Danes's performance is unaffected and sincere. Meanwhile, however, her mother (played by Diane Venora) is getting ready for a costume party, which she intends to go to as a Las

Vegas-style Cleopatra in a gold wig and sequins. She is chain smoking, barking at servants, and stressing equally about her daughter's future prospects and her own appearance. Bilcock supports and conveys the mother's manic energy and scatterbrained approach to life by speeding up her action, so that by contrast with Juliet she appears silly, slightly insane, and, even more importantly, utterly lacking in feeling. The point of the scene is that Juliet's mother is oblivious to Juliet's emotions, and this is conveyed through use of fast motion. She dashes, spins, and slips through the scene feeling nothing, being impacted on by no one, and letting nothing touch her.

In *Two for the Road* Albert Finney and Audrey Hepburn play lovers on a road trip to explore Europe and their love. The couple inadvertently meet up with some old friends of Finney's character and get dragged along on a tourist trip to see a chateau somewhere in France. The whole sequence of visiting the chateau, taking photos, getting ice creams, and attending to other needs takes place in under two minutes, all in fast motion. The players look, exclaim, pose, snap, eat, smile, and carry on just as tourists ought to but at such a rate that none of the experiences has any meaning whatsoever, and this, of course, is the point. This tourists' view of an antique culture is a kind of desecration of time, the friends' grotesque parody of family living is a warning to the young lovers, the whole event is a travesty of a felt experience, but a funny one because although they miss the actual meaning of anything they are doing, they don't feel bad. At this rate of fast motion, they don't feel anything.

MIXED MOTIONS AND SPEED RAMPING

One exception to fast motion being funny is that it can be confusing or about confusion. Fast motion can be used to create a head space in which things are moving so quickly that a crisis is precipitated. But this use of fast motion is quite often mixed with slow motion and various speeds in between, the effect being one of disorientation in time and therefore a loss of one's sense of place in the world. A useful reference for this is the ending of Arthur Penn's 1967 film *Bonnie and Clyde*. When Bonnie and Clyde are suddenly and very gorily gunned down, Penn and the editor Dede Allen use a rapid-fire mix of slow and faster shot speeds to convey the confusion, panic, and depths of feeling of the characters.

More recently, mixed motion speeds are used in action films to convey a kind of superhuman control and power in fight scenes. The hero might slip into a slow motion preparation, creating tension, a heightened sense of his gravitas and the power of the obstacle he faces, a feeling that he not only has to push against his enemy, but push against time itself. Then he will spin into a faster-than-the-speed-of-light kick, signaling his incredible dexterity and mastery of the elements of time, space, and gravity. Then he'll land in a perfectly controlled normal speed, re-grounding us in real time and space and preparing us for the next onslaught.

SUMMARY

There are many more devices available to editors and filmmakers to vary their storytelling and rhythms, and very likely some still to be invented. The two discussed herein, motion effects and parallel action, were chosen because they have an easy accessibility to editors. It is possible for an editor to create parallel action in a story that is plodding along or to create motion effects to change the texture and feel of time—characters' time and movie time. Both of these will complicate the unfolding of a story and, if used well, enhance expression as well as providing interest or variation.

Parallel action is particularly interesting as well, not just because it is one of the oldest devices, but because, in a sense, any cutting that uses a shot–reverse shot is parallel action. If there are two people in a conversation and the editor cuts between them, she is very often showing us not just what the action and reaction are—in other words, just what is happening sequentially—but is subtly manipulating time to show us what is going on meanwhile. If she cuts from a man drumming his fingers impatiently to a woman staring out the window she could be saying "he is impatient; meanwhile, she is lost in her thoughts." If there are two characters, there are two stories, and the questions for the editor will be the same in handling any two stories running parallel to each other: questions of emphasis, of where is action and where is emotion, and which one needs to be emphasized more to give this story the right balance.

ENDNOTES

1. Turim, M., *Flashbacks in Film: Memory & History,* p. 5.
2. See Eisenstein, S., "Dickens, Griffith and the film today," in *Film Form,* p. 205.
3. See Fairservice, D., *Film Editing: History, Theory and Practice,* for more information on the evolution and development of practices and devices in editing.
4. Ibid., pp. 42–48.
5. This example of great editing technique first came to my attention when I was reading *The Technique of Film and Video Editing: Theory and Practice,* by Ken Dancyger. So rich are the innovations that Hitchcock brought to the film form that Chapter 6 of that book is completely devoted to experiments in editing by this master filmmaker.
6. Vertov is quoted in the DVD commentary by film scholar and Soviet film expert Yuri Tsivian on Vertov's masterpiece *Man with a Movie Camera.*
7. For more information on McKee's ideas about emotional transitions, see pp. 33 and 34 in *Story: Structure, Substance, Style and the Principles of Screenwriting.*
8. Ibid.

CHAPTER 11

Collaboration and The Vulcan Mind Meld

In the long running television series *Star Trek*, the highly evolved alien race known as Vulcans can do a very cool maneuver called a "Vulcan Mind Meld." They place their fingers against someone's head and sonorously chant "your thoughts to mine," thus downloading the relevant memories, experiences, and thoughts to solve the problem at hand, direct from the other person's brain to their own.

This chapter is going to propose that an editor/director collaboration at its best, is like a Vulcan Mind Meld, without the laying on of hands, or the sonorous cliché chanting. And that the editor is the Vulcan.

This chapter is near the end of this book because it relies on the ideas that have come before it about what an editor does in shaping the film edit. Its "meld" theory relies on agreement, in the first instance, that the work of an editor is not just the mechanics of editing, as in chopping bits of sound and image into a timeline. The work of an editor is creative. Editors create structure and rhythm. They do this by manipulating movement. They manipulate the movement of the film from one shot to another, from one idea to another, one performance to another, and so on. The editor shapes the movement of story, the movement of emotion, and the movement of image and sound.

Recognition of this underlying action of an editor, the shaping of movement, is key to understanding how editors make decisions, and also how they collaborate. In the intuitive process of shaping a film's movement, editors persuasively and skillfully extract the thoughts of directors, producers, and audiences and filter them through their own perspectives and intuitions, to shape the structure and rhythm of the cinematic story.

THE MIND MELD

One might be forgiven for thinking that this next section is going to be about the finer sensibilities and listening skills of the editor. Their incredible patience and good humor, exalted capacities for working steadily, quietly, sensitively for long hours with little reward and less credit, and so on. But it isn't. It is about cognition and the neurology discussed in Chapter 1.

Specifically it is about extended mind theory and mirror neurons.

First a brief re-cap on mirror neurons: these neurons are parts of the brain that mirror movement that you see, allowing you to interpret what you see based on your own feeling for movement or kinaesthetic empathy. These special neurons allow you to understand meaning in movement. Scientists have hypothesized[1] that they are the key to how we understand each other: through mirror neurons we recognize the intentions in moving bodies and images and know how they feel.

So, when an editor is shaping the movement of the rushes, she is literally feeling it, empathizing with the movement onscreen as she cuts, and if it doesn't feel right, if it doesn't mirror in her body in the right rhythm or dynamic for the meaning she is trying to construct, she moves the cuts and watches again, to see if it feels right the next time.

What does this have to do with collaboration?

Extended Mind

The editor isn't just feeling the movement of the rushes through her own sensibility, she is also channeling the director's sense of rhythm, flow, story, and emotion. She shapes the release of information, the emphasis, the emotional qualities by tuning to the movement feeling that the director has brought to the material and that he or she is bringing into the suite. This is where the mind meld comes in. It is unspoken. It is literally felt, through the mirror neurons and the bodies of the collaborators, not discussed or processed consciously. One could say that this is an instance of what cognitive philosophers call "extended mind."

Chalmers and Clark's influential 1998 essay "The extended mind" proposes that the mind is not bounded by brain and body. Thinking, they assert, is an activity located in brain, body, and world. By way of illustration they propose, for example, that the re-arrangement of tiles on the scrabble board is "not part of action, it is part of *thought*."[2] Film editing, is like a scrabble board in this way—you need the pieces in order to have thoughts or make decisions about them.

The "extended mind" of a director, an editor, and the film they are working on relies on what collective cognition advocates call "complementarity." "Complementarity," cognitive scientist John Sutton writes, is what happens when "biological and non-biological resources . . . work together, coalescing into integrated larger cognitive systems."[3] This then is a more scientific explanation (with all due respect to the science officer of the Starship Enterprise, the Vulcan Mr. Spock), of the director–editor "mind meld." The mind of the director, with its feeling for story, emotion, image, and sound, works with the mind of the editor in a complementary way so that the two minds coalesce, with the filmed material, into an integrated cognitive system.

Heightened Sensitivity

Even in an integrated cognitive system, the editor's mirror neurons have a particular impact on collaboration because the editor's are more sensitive or more trained, or both. When this is true, then the editor has a special talent for shaping movement. Great editors have highly refined capacities to see and feel movement. They use it to shape the release of information and ideas into a compelling pattern;

to breathe the movement of emotions into a dynamic the viewer can synchronize with immediately, viscerally. They use it to sculpt the movement of images and sound into an aesthetic composition that energizes the sight, carries the emotional dynamic, and conveys the story information with elegance and grace as need be, or with violent collisions should the need be. Editors are trained. They have years of experience. Their intuitions for this particular part of the process, shaping the flow of movement, are sharper, more specialist, more honed than anyone else's, even the director's.

What is interesting to me is that this last point may be contentious. But why would it potentially be a put-down of a director to say that someone on the team has a greater talent for some part of the filmmaking process than they do? Why do editors hide this special skill, much the way Vulcans—when in the company of humans on Star Trek—would often hide their pointy Vulcan ears? Are they trying to make the directors/humans feel more comfortable? It is not hard to imagine that the Vulcan Mind Meld may be a bit unnerving for a director to acknowledge. The Vulcan Mind Meld is definitely a ceding of some control, and that, I'm sure, is scary. Especially if the Vulcans are invading your planet. But the trick to collaboration is to realize that the Vulcans are not invading your planet, they are collaborating.

So what does "collaborating" mean? Some people say "working together" is not "collaboration"—if the director is making all of the decisions. But what about decisions made intuitively? Decisions that arise from complementary cognitive processes working as an integrated system? Unspoken decisions that are the result of sensitized neurological and embodied processes rather than discussion? There are also questions about "creativity" that come into the debates on collaboration. I contend that in order to understand the creative collaboration between the director and editor it is necessary to understand that there are different kinds of creativity, some are responsive and some are generative, but all of them are significant. These questions of responsive and generative creativity lead on to questions of power and hierarchies and to consideration of the value to the film, to the process, and to the collaboration, of the editor's intuitive work.

DECISION MAKING

Like the director, the editor's job is making decisions. Editors don't necessarily see or make decisions about anything before it is shot. But they do about absolutely everything after. In fact they may be the only crew members who see and make decisions about everything once it is shot. Editors look at the rushes and start making decisions about three things: which shot, where, and for how long. They look at scenes, sequences, and acts with the same questions. They look at flow of events and ideas, are they clear? Have the decisions made metaphors or just statements of fact as is appropriate to the moment? Do the juxtapositions, moment to moment, create collision or linkage of ideas, emotions, and images? Is time, to paraphrase the title of Yvette Biro's book on the subject, turbulent or flowing?[4] The editor's work is, in some sense, the most "theoretical" work of any crew member, especially if we take the word "theory" from its ancient Greek origins, theoria meaning "contemplation, speculation, a looking at, things looked at."[5] Editors see it all, they see what it might be if put together in a certain way and they try it out. The first cut is a hypothesis, it asks "does it all fit together like this?" The editor looks at it, it isn't quite right, she refines the hypothesis, makes another theory of how it all fits together.

Where is the director through all of this? Doesn't the director make these decisions about what works and what doesn't? Well yes, absolutely, and no, certainly not. But this is where the questions of "working with" or "working for" comes in, and we'll get to that in a moment. First, while the director is still on set, or even while she is getting a coffee, or talking on the phone or sitting right next to the editor, the editor makes thousands and thousands of decisions, at the speed of light. Think about it. There are, depending on the country in which you are cutting, 25 or 29+ frames per second. Sixty seconds per minute. There may be three angles on every important minute, and three takes of each angle, nine shots, each lasting roughly a minute, and the editor decides which shot, where, and for how long. Or more precisely, which frame of the possible 1500 of each shot will connect to which frame of the possible 1500 of any other shot from a combined pool of some 15,000 possible frames each of which could be put together, theoretically, with any of the others in any possible combination. Thousands of decisions, made before showing the director anything and asking: "how about this?" so that the director can make one yes or no decision, or perhaps even just "wait and see."

RESPONSIVE CREATIVITY

I turn now to first-hand experience to try to explain the somewhat inexplicable workings of the Vulcan Mind Meld. I recently had two experiences with a director on the same day; they weren't particular to that director, they were the same two experiences any editor has had countless times.

First, the director comes in and says: "Move this shot before that one". A few minutes later when I have smoothed the edges of the shot-to-shot relation, so that the cut itself works, the overall flow still isn't right, it doesn't feel right. The director suggests that I try putting in ten more frames. I suggest, "Could we try another approach? Rather than telling me what to do, try telling me what you are looking for and I'll figure out how to do it." My theory is that allowing an editor this space for responsive creativity is a way of galvanizing the editor's skill, knowledge, and kinaesthetic intelligence to create what the director is looking for.

The other common experience is when the director gives seven general notes and walks away. Four of them are about shots he wants put back in the cut somewhere and two are about structure; one is telling me what to do and I diplomatically ignore it. (Diplomacy in the director/

editor collaboration is not being nice, it is being tough, nicely.) Hours later the director comes back, all of the shots he wanted are back in, and the structure is working. But not the way he expected. I have made, over the few hours he was away, literally hundreds and hundreds of decisions about which shot, where and for how long, which frames to cut on, where to dissolve, how sound and music would create a dynamic with image. When he comes back, he is pleased. He feels his choices have been good ones. "Good notes," I say. "Good cutting," says he, acknowledging that cutting and directing are not the same thing.

The editor/director collaboration is interpretive, and it requires editors' intelligence to be activated, their decision-making capacities to be engaged, and their particular talents to be given space to stretch their legs. As Cate Blanchett said, in an interview in *The Sydney Morning Herald*, "It is not the director's job to connect the dots for you. The director makes a proposition and you complete the sentence—that's the actor's job."[6] Later down the track it's the editor's job, too, and just like actors, editors do a better job if they are given recognition of their unique capacities to do it, without anyone being afraid that their decision-making authority is being stripped away.

POWER AND HIERARCHY

So are the director and the editor equal? That is the wrong question. They are not "equals" in the hierarchy—if they irrevocably disagree, the director gets the final say.

Are they both decision-makers? Both creative? Clearly. They are equally creative and occupy different spheres of creativity. Interpretive creativity is not "less" than generative creativity and does not involve less decision making, it comes at a different phase in the process and takes its directions from a different source.

Generative creativity collaborates with interpretive creativity or perishes. Interpretive creativity makes decisions, applies skills, knowledge, wisdoms, experiences, artistry that the generator does not have and so cannot apply.

I have elsewhere argued that editors are like dancers; now I'll make the analogy with singers. Composers can't necessarily sing, and if they can't, they are stuffed without singers. Which is "higher": composing or singing? Which is more "valuable"? Which is more creative? Which brings more to the project? Why ask such stupid questions? They need each other, and we need both.

The question of equality has a bit of a mind–body-split whiff around it. Why do we say there is unevenness of "thought" if one person is making the decisions and another is setting up the material to be decided upon, that one is a labor more exalted or important, that one is art and the other craft?

What if we were to ask the movie—were you made by one mind or many? Are you the sum of your parts or greater? If each "collaborator" thinks that their creative contribution to the film is 50 percent, and there are ten key creatives or heads of department, then how do we account for the whole being 500 percent collaborators contributions? Why doesn't it add up? Are these people deluded about how important their role is? No. It just isn't a quantifiable equation.

Australian film industry analysts Simon Molloy and David Court have written about the value of "psychic income" to the film industry. ("Psychic income" being an economist's term for what we used to call meaning or camaraderie or the satisfaction of doing your best, or being creative). Molloy and Court suggest that "consumers of Australian screen content . . . are the beneficiaries of a 150–295 million dollar annual subsidy based on the passion and commitment of workers in the sector."[7] I would like to suggest that it is not just the audience but the film itself that benefits from the psychic contributions, made by mind meld or otherwise, of creative personnel, and this is why the equation can't be quantified. Everyone gives 100 percent and still the film is greater than the sum of its parts.

SYNCHRONIZING WITH THE DIRECTOR

Sometimes tensions arise between directors and editors who "feel" things differently, and the editor has some tricky judgment calls to make in these situations. If a director feels the rise and fall of tension and release or the flow of movement in a different way from the editor, it could be because he is not seeing what is really there, but what he hoped would be there, or what he intended to have captured but didn't. In these cases, it is up to the editor to bring the director around to a new way of seeing the material. This may mean working without the director present for a while and shaping something that has its own integrity. Then, when the director sees it, there is an opportunity for him to say, "That's not how I intended it, but it really works."

On the other hand, sometimes directors and editors feel things differently because the director is deeply tuned to the material and the performances, and the editor doesn't yet see its potential to go in a particular direction. In these cases, it is really important to try to synchronize *through* the director. Use his sense of how things flow rather than your own—see with his eyes, feel with his heart rate, tune your kinaesthetic empathy to his feeling for the rise and fall of tension in a scene or across the whole film.

In either case, it's essential not to make too big a deal of things too early. Much will change over the course of an edit and if there is a showdown over who is right about a given moment, then that moment will always be a sore point, no matter who wins. Furthermore, both the editor

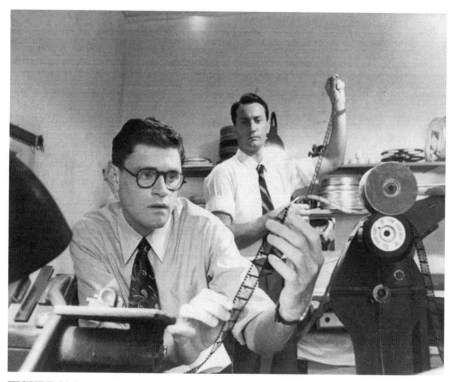

FIGURE 11.1
Working collaboratively in the edit suite under pressure, as seen in Phillip Noyce's classic Australian drama Newsfront *(1978). [Photo credit: Palm Beach Pictures; The Kobal Collection]*

and the director actually lose in these showdowns because their experience of the contentious moment shifts from being a direct experience of the material to an indirect one: instead of seeing the moment, they remember the argument and impasse it caused and see it as a problem. Diplomacy skills are emphasized in the teaching of editing, and this is one example of where those skills can be used to good effect. If no standoff is created by the editor, then, later, when things have cooled down, it will always be possible to come back and have another go at the moment in question.

A cautionary note for both editors and directors: Editors hate it when directors snap their fingers or hit the table to indicate where they want a cut because these gestures, as well as expressing a kind of dictatorship or distrust of the editor's intuition, can actually jump between the editor and her own feeling for the material. On the other hand, these directorial gestures are very immediate physical responses and could save lots of time and discussion about how the material should be shaped. If the editor can just step back and not take them personally, the director's gestures can be a great guide to how he feels the material. My advice to directors is: Try not to snap your fingers, as that seems imperious, but do make the gestures that will clue the editor in to how you feel the material; that way, at least she'll know what she's working with.

In the end, understanding the Vulcan Mind Meld of editing as intuitive, unspoken collaboration requires understanding minds as physical and cultural entities. Minds are not just functions of brain and body; they are integrated systems of brain, body, and world. They are not just neurons flashing in patterns, responding to and creating movement, memory and emotion; they are also an endless cultural inheritance.

The mix of the physical and the cultural, the blend that makes decisions and shapes artworks is what we call "intuition". As the Vulcan in this metaphor, the editor is not taking power from the director, they are using their intuition to interpret the material. They are "making it their own" by investing their "psychic money". They are not taking anything away by being creative, they are collaborating.

ENDNOTES

1 Gallese, V., and Goldman, A., "Mirror neurons and the simulation theory of mind-reading."

2. Clark, A., and Chalmers, D., "The extended mind."

3. Sutton, J. (2010). "Exograms and interdisciplinarity: History, the extended mind, and the civilizing process."

4. Biro, Y., *Turbulence and Flow in Film, The Rhythmic Design*.

5. Definition, from www.etymonline.com/index.php?term=theory (accessed 2 November, 2012).

6. Blake, E., "A theatrical masterclass."

7. Molly, S., and Court, D., "For love and money: Estimating the value of psychic income in Australia."

CHAPTER 12

Editing Thinking and Onscreen Drafting

This chapter is new to the second edition of *Cutting Rhythms*. It is based on experiments I have been doing with teaching and screen production since the first edition came out in 2009 and creative research done through the support of a 2014 Macquarie University grant.

Since 2009, digital tools for screen production have continued to proliferate, becoming cheaper, higher in quality, and more accessible. They seem set to continue on that trajectory into the future. But have production pathways shifted to recognize these possibilities? Or are we mostly still emulating the Hollywood "factory" model that was set up when we were shooting on film? Do linear production models reflect the constraints of the old tools rather than the opportunities of new tools for capture, cutting, and exhibition?

The idea of an onscreen draft is a response to these questions. I am taking the notion of "camera stylo"[1] or camera-as-pen literally and asking: Can cheap digital technology—the camera and editing program on your iPhone for example—be a script development tool? Can we add a creative, embodied, rapid prototyping phase to script writing and production development with these digital tools?

Before discussing what an onscreen draft is, and why it may be useful, I will introduce an idea that underpins the onscreen drafting process: Editing Thinking.

EDITING THINKING

The idea that expert practitioners develop special kinds of thinking has lead to the terms "design thinking" (thinking like a designer in approaching problem solving)[2] and "studio thinking" (habits of mind taught through studio art)[3] I propose that editing thinking is another such kind of thinking, and that not only is it developed by gaining expertise in the craft of editing, but it can be developed by people other than film editors who wish to enjoy its benefits and uses. Editing thinking is what editors do, but it can also be a capacity developed by other people. Further, editors who have editing thinking skills can transfer these skills to other fields of practice.

Editing thinking is the intuitive process of sensing, hypothesizing, and realizing structure and rhythm.[4]

Editing thinking begins with the editor's mirror neurons responding to movement in unedited film material (see Chapter 1). Editing thinking is the editor using her own "embodied simulation response"[5] to guide decisions that create the optimal embodied simulation response of viewers. This decision making is often attributed solely to directors. However as editing practice shows us clearly, the editor makes thousands of decisions about form and flow before the director makes ratifying decisions about the editor's choices.

Editing thinking is thinking by doing. Editing thinking can be applied to any mass of material that is available for the shaping of structure and rhythm. Editing thinking, therefore, is what editors do when faced with a mass of film rushes, but it could also be a description of what, for example, curators do when pulling together exhibitions, or educators do when designing a unit of study. Conference organizers use editing thinking to create coherent structure and rhythm of events and ideas. Writers use editing thinking when converting their masses of creative ideas from sprawling notes into poems, novels, or screenplays.

EDITING THINKING

Practical Exercise

The practical exercise for editing thinking is simple: organize something and give it flow. It could be anything—beads in a chain or tiles in a mosaic are good places to start. Design a pattern that alternates or has blocks of color, shape, and texture. This is a structure. Refine your design so that it has flow—your eye moves across it and you can feel its coherence and its dynamics. This is a rhythm.

From there move on to something that actually moves—a game or an event. Variables come into your organization now. Timing, pacing, and trajectory phrasing are your tools, just like in a film. The task of creating structure and rhythm is the same, just more complex. Your "editing thinking" has to juggle the challenges of movement and emotion, tastes and personalities. But a strong structure and a coherent rhythm turns these challenges into strengths—the experience is richer and stronger for them.

Editing thinking is an intuitive form of thinking. It is physical, embodied thinking. It responds creatively to pressures and possibilities. Editing thinking is a transferable skill. It shapes coherent narratives and experiences from what is otherwise a mass of material. The best practical exercise for developing editing thinking is editing: take a mass of material and give it structure and rhythm.

Editing thinking relies on developed sensitivities and expertise. In the case of film editing, the sensitivity is to movement and the expertise is in movement of story, emotion, image, and sound. Most of this book looks at how editors can develop these sensitivities and areas of expertise. This chapter will look at a new use of the expert editor's editing thinking: Onscreen drafting.

WHAT IS AN ONSCREEN DRAFT?

It is a truism to say that the "editor writes the last draft of the script." Anyone who has ever been to an editing class has probably heard it, and anyone who has ever edited a film has almost definitely experienced it. The editor writes the last draft of the script partly because of all of the inspirations, improvisations, contingencies, and disasters that can befall a shooting script as it makes its way from page to screen. For example, the director might have gotten new ideas on set and added them into the captured material. Or interpreted the script differently than was expected by the writer. In fact, the interpretation by many collaborators may have changed the script's intention or design in some way. The actors may or may not have done the lines exactly as written. The money or time may have run out before all of the script could be captured and so cuts were made or moments compressed or amalgamated. For all of these material reasons the shooting script is never exactly the same as the final film. But this is only partly why the editor writes the last draft of the script.

The editor is the creative collaborator with an expert knowledge of movement of story, emotion, image, and sound. When ideas that started out as words on a page become moving images and sounds, the editor's developed sensitivity to movement kicks in and she writes the last draft of the script in movement. Editing thinking is applied to things that seemed as though they would work when they were on the page, but which simply don't create a coherent experience when edited as a flow of movement. There are many reasons why this could happen. Perhaps the captured material doesn't create a solid structure—it produces an experience that has repetition or digression, extraneous bits or gaps. Perhaps performances have shaped the subtext and emphasis differently than the script may have implied, so the editor might adjust characters' dialogue, action, or even whole journeys. Perhaps there are metaphors or sensations that can be got out of the juxtaposition of filmed images and sounds that weren't fully exploited or designed in the script. Perhaps the script just wasn't that great and the editor's thinking is needed to make it better.

Here is where the principle of onscreen drafting has its genesis. When we understand how and why the editor writes the last draft of the script and add this to the fact that digital filmmaking tools could introduce new processes of filmmaking, we have to ask: why not create an onscreen draft? Why not bring editing thinking into the creative process much earlier and see how that might benefit story, emotion, image, and sound?

In his seminal article on design thinking Tim Brown writes: "Historically, design has been treated as a downstream step in the development process—the point where designers, who have played no earlier role in the substantive work of innovation, come along and put a beautiful wrapper around the idea."[6]

Editing has also traditionally been treated as a "downstream" step in the filmmaking process, the point where editors, who have played no earlier role in the substantive work of storytelling, come along and put a beautiful wrapper around the idea. But digital tools can change that. We can use the camera and the laptop as sketchpads and use editing thinking to improve scripts and films by making onscreen drafts.

Here is how it works:

An "onscreen draft" is a no-budget digital rendering of a whole story or screenplay that gets created somewhere in between the first and final drafts of the script.

It does not replace a script draft; it is part of the script development process.

It includes digital shooting and cutting, though the cut may also incorporate some found footage, just as it will incorporate things like temp sound and music.

An onscreen draft is ugly. This is important. If it is going to be part of script development it *cannot* be polished in its production values.

It is testing things like thematic coherence, information clarity or redundancy, dramatic questions and whether they sustain interest, plots, and whether they complicate or just repeat, as well as character's motivations, relationships, and emotional dynamics.

It can test shots, frames, staging, texture, and color but only if it is testing these in relation to the script, in order to reveal something about the script for a re-writing process.

An onscreen draft *must* be cut together. An onscreen draft is testing the relationship of the scripted actions to real ones. The question is: Will this script make an onscreen experience of image, sound, movement, and time that tells a story with strong structure and engaging rhythm? In other words, will this script work onscreen? This question can only be answered by cutting image, sound, and movement together.

So, an onscreen draft is not the final film, it is a draft of the film that the editor writes. It uses the editor's special skills to shape movement *onscreen* of story, emotion, image, and sound cheaply and in sketch form, before shooting the final version of the film. Onscreen drafting is, above all, a chance to test ideas, to fail and learn. It is writing as a digital, embodied, editing thinking process.

What an Onscreen Draft Isn't

Onscreen drafting is not improvised cinema. Improvisation can also be used in developing script ideas, as it is, for example, in British director Mike Leigh's process. But onscreen drafting is intended to actually be part of a scripting process, shooting of a draft of the script as written in order to test its current soundness and recognize what needs to be re-written.

Onscreen drafting is also not the same as the digital cinema process of "no-frills cinema," as was promoted by the Danish Dogme 95 manifesto, or as seen in American "mumblecore" movies. In fact in some ways it is the opposite. It is done on no budget to ensure that when money is spent on high production values, design, actors, lights, and so on, it is spent to good purpose, with clear intent.[7]

WHY DRAFT?

Screen storytelling is an art. There is no other art that is made without first making a draft in the art form's media.

For example, no one would ever write a symphony just on paper. In the pre-digital age they would have written a piano reduction. In the digital age they write music with software that can play back an approximation, a draft *in sound, not in writing,* of the large scale, complex idea being developed.

Similarly large scale and complex visual art works are sketched first.

I spoke to Australian painter Michelle Hiscock about why she sketches and she was very clear. She said: "you sketch to know." Without sketching you can imagine what something might be on the canvas, but you don't really know what your imaginings are until you begin to sketch. As they take form on paper they reveal themselves. They also reveal the delusions and illusions of the conceptual phase. Sketching corrects these through trial and error and gets the material to match the imaginings, or vice versa.

Hiscock also said, in our conversation, that "you sketch to see" and this is a very important idea for onscreen drafting. What she is "seeing" as she drafts is how the trees and the skyline actually sit in relation to each other, as opposed to fuzzy, optimistic, hopeful but ungrounded seeing—the kind of "seeing" we call envisioning when we read through a script. Doing an onscreen draft is a way of seeing the script differently. Seeing it as a set of decisions to be made and rehearsing decision making by making decisions, not by imagining options. This is a key thing for filmmakers, especially film students.

Drafting teaches you things about your work that you need to be able to do without thinking about it when you get to the oil paints or orchestras. It teaches you about form, anatomy, pattern, composition, time, space, energy, style, and so on, all in relation to the particular content you are trying to create.

So, now that the tools are available, why wouldn't we do the same with cinema?

RAPID PROTOTYPING

A screenplay is not an onscreen draft. Screenplays do go through multiple drafts from scribbles on the backs of napkins to fully funded shooting scripts. But a screenplay is often described as being like a blueprint, and a blueprint is not film. Cinema is an art of performance, dynamics, images, and sounds, not of words on paper. If a screenplay is analogous to an architectural blueprint, an onscreen draft would be analogous to a 3D print of the building.

3D prints are the same relationship to buildings as the onscreen drafts I propose are to films. They are relatively cheap. They test the theory that is the blueprint or script. They come at a stage in the process where there is still time to change and refine ideas and their expression. Yet they would never be mistaken for buildings themselves. They are mediated drafts, a step closer to the real thing, but still revisable.

With this 3D model or "rapid prototype" in mind, I turn now to look at some variations of onscreen drafting which are common practice in some parts of the screen industries to see how they are similar to the onscreen drafting process I propose, and how they are different.

The first of these is the "rapid prototyping" process commonly used in digital game development. A rapid prototype is defined as a visual and sometimes experiential manifestation of an intangible concept.[8] In their feature article "How to prototype a game in under 7 days" published by the online magazine Gamasutra,[9] Gray et al. write about some principles of rapid prototyping, which could equally well apply to onscreen drafting of film. These are:

1. "Embrace the possibility of failure, it encourages risk taking"

   In rapid prototyping, as with onscreen drafts, there is little to lose and off the wall ideas can be tried and learned from, even if they fail. This is beneficial for a team: it allows them to risk and fail. It is also empowering: shorthand is developed, ideas are demonstrated, processes are refined so that everything can be done more effectively when the big money is being spent.

2. "Enforce short development cycles"

   More time does not necessarily mean more quality. At this phase of scripting, a film project could spend many, many hours chasing an idea that isn't necessarily very good, down a hypothetical rabbit hole. Why not throw it up onscreen and, as Hiscock said in relation to sketching with charcoal, really see it.

3. "Constrain Creativity"

   Rapid prototyping sets some kinds of rules or boundaries on the project in order to nourish creative possibilities that are focused rather than sprawling. In an onscreen drafting phase of a film project, the key constraint on creativity would be money. In a no-budget draft, ingenuity for realizing ideas would be given a chance to flourish.

EMBODIED DECISION MAKING

Embodied decision making means making decisions in practice, not just in theory. We have a lot of embodied metaphors that apply to the high pressure decision making that occurs on set, such as: thinking on your feet, shooting from the hip, or running with it. In an onscreen draft, these are the capacities that get some exercise. Drafting gives them a workout rather than waiting until the big day when the clock is ticking and the money is draining away to see whether you are physically up to the task.

There are lots of pressures on a film set—lots of people and not much time and lots of things that are not exactly as expected. At this point, under pressure, decisions are made that have huge downstream implications. Embodied decision making is learning about the decisions that will need to be made through making them. Onscreen drafting means getting a chance to discover the implications of your decisions in an early draft.

Animated films have long been using an embodied onscreen drafting process to develop scripts. In this process very rough drawings and sound are gradually replaced with more and more refined versions from line drawings to wireframes, to block 3D versions until the final version of the script and images are literally built on top of the first sketches. The discipline required to make this work is to not become distracted by the possibilities for beautiful images too early, but to sketch and script until the flow of story and emotional dynamics over time makes sense and feels right.

This principle of failing early, failing fast, or failing forward is one of the keys to onscreen drafting and it is also something that is perhaps misunderstood in creativity. Filmmakers need permission to fail, because this is a key to creative risk taking, and something that is most likely to produce fresh, innovative ideas. But nobody really wants to fail in the end. There is a tension between wanting to encourage risk and wanting to produce successes. Onscreen drafting can reduce this tension. Instead of asking whether to fail it asks when to fail. The answer is: fail when you have time to learn and then to succeed. Fail in a draft, not in a final film.

An onscreen draft is an exercise that builds the muscles of decision making and of resilience. It builds the collaborative vocabulary of teams and it activates the usually untapped intelligence of the editor in an early editing thinking process.

CASE STUDY: *WOMAN WITH AN EDITING BENCH*

In 2012/2015 I worked an onscreen drafting process supported by a research grant from Macquarie University in Sydney, Australia. The title of the research was: *The role of "editing thinking" in innovative models of screen development and production practice.*

This research was testing the strategy of using editing thinking to prototype ideas while they are still at script draft stage. It applied editing thinking strategies to the production of a short film inspired by the life and work of Soviet Montage era editor Elizaveta Svilova (1900–1975). The film, *Woman with an Editing Bench*, models editing thinking as a process and is also about Svilova's editing thinking.

Here is a quick plot summary:

> *Woman with an Editing Bench* is about the fight for creativity in the face of repression.
>
> In the 1930s Soviet Union Stalin has personal approval over all films and film scripts. Dziga Vertov and his editor Elizaveta Svilova make radical and groundbreaking documentaries (*Man with a Movie Camera*, 1929). Stalin is threatened by their formal innovations; he wants his henchmen to shut down their creativity.
>
> Vertov, unhappy and artistically constrained, is inept at understanding how to work within the bureaucracy. Svilova is savvy and knows how to work the system laterally and from behind the scenes—as all great editors do. She is also adept at working with Vertov's mind, understanding what he wants to say and how he wants to say it. Svilova's editing makes Vertov's genius possible. Vertov's eccentricity makes Svilova's editing genius indispensable. When Svilova finally wrangles approval to shoot a film, the two of them are seen in their element, making the vibrant montage that justifies their struggle to create. They work together and think together. They almost become part of the footage they are taking.
>
> But when the shoot is finished, and they review the footage, they find some of it is missing. The bureaucrat in charge reveals that the footage isn't missing, it has been withheld. Vertov's clumsy attempt to challenge the bureaucrat gets his project cancelled. Vertov seems to give up and be dying a metaphorical death. But Svilova saves the key footage and pushes on, attempting to save Vertov through the completion of their film.

Making *Woman with an Editing Bench* as a research project, I shot and cut together an onscreen draft; in fact I cut three versions of it, and learned something from each of them.[10] Here are just some of the things I learned.

The Stakes Were Too Conceptual

In the first draft of the script, as in the final draft, Svilova is all that stands between Vertov and the bureaucracy that wants to block him. But in the first draft being blocked from making films was just a concept. When I screened the first cut of the onscreen draft for the producers, Lyn Norfor and Richard James Allen, they picked up on this right away (see Fig. 12.1 and Fig. 12.2).

FIGURE 12.1

In this screen grab of Beth Aubrey, Richard James Allen and Jardine Patten from the Draft Shoot *we can see that Vertov (Allen) and the Bureaucrat (Patten) are arguing, but we don't know what they are arguing about. Also, Svilova (Aubrey), who is supposed to be the hero, the one who stands between Vertov and his nemesis, is sidelined. [Photo credit: Screen shot from* Draft Shoot, *cinematographer: Michi Marosszeky for The Physical TV Company]*

FIGURE 12.2

In this screen shot of Richard James Allen (Vertov), Leanna Walsman (Svilova) and Marcus Graham (the Bureaucrat) from Woman with an Editing Bench *we can see what they are fighting for: the camera. We can also see that Svilova is the one doing the fighting. Vertov is distracted by his own ideas. Svilova is literally between Vertov and the Bureaucrat. [Photo credit: screen shot from* Woman with an Editing Bench, *cinematographer Kieran Fowler for The Physical TV Company]*

Tone Was Too Light

In the first draft of the script the tone of the relationships between Vertov and Svilova was playful, and Vertov's ebullient physicality was often described in terms of dance. Once onscreen it became clear that the tone of the relationship did not match the circumstances. Vertov needed to be seen struggling and Svilova needed to be seen working things out, making decisions and taking actions. This had an impact on the way I re-wrote the characters and the way I directed them, which also extended to Svilova's relationships with the Bureaucrat and his henchmen, the guards (see Fig. 12.3 and Fig. 12.4).

FIGURE 12.3

In the Draft Shoot, *I invented a backstory for Svilova (Beth Aubrey) in which she had known the guards (played by Kim Anderberg and Ivan Germano) since they were kids, so she didn't take them seriously as a threat. [Photo credit: screen shot from* Draft Shoot, *cinematographer: Michi Marosszeky for The Physical TV Company]*

FIGURE 12.4

In the final version of Woman with an Editing Bench, *the guards are a real threat, and Svilova (Leanna Walsman) hides under the rewind bench when they invade the edit suite to shut it down. [Photo credit: Jonathan Grace for The Physical TV Company]*

Perspective Was Unclear

As soon as I had put together the first version of an edit of the onscreen draft it was possible to see that perspective was a problem. Whose story is it? What is the filmmaker saying about the story? The perspective I had in my head was not on the screen, except in one moment: the last one. Once I saw the last shot in context of the story leading up to it, I knew I had to work backwards from there to re-design all of the action to lead to it.

After shooting and cutting the onscreen draft, every event in the script was ultimately re-written either partially or completely. Stakes were clarified. Tone was modified. Things that were too general were made specific. The problems and actions were redesigned to build to the resolution.

It is possible that all of these things could have been done on paper, but I think it unlikely. The conversations I had with the producers

FIGURE 12.5

In the onscreen draft version, Vertov (Richard James Allen) jumps out of a window on what seems like a whim. [Screen shot from Draft Shoot, *cinematographer: Michi Marosszeky for The Physical TV Company]*

FIGURE 12.6

In the final version of Woman with an Editing Bench, *Vertov's (Richard James Allen's) jump is a logical but surprising development of his earlier actions and it leads inevitably to Svilova's actions at the end of the film. [Photo credit: Jonathan Grace for The Physical TV Company]*

when looking at cuts were conversations I have had with producers in edit suites many times before, on many projects. But on this project, for the first time, I was having them at draft stage. Usually when we have those conversations the editor is trying to fix the problems of the script and the production with editing. This time we were able to go back and re-write the script using the insight we'd gotten from editing thinking and the onscreen draft.

ENDNOTES

1. "The Birth of a New Avant-Garde: La Caméra-Stylo," is an influential 1948 essay by Alexandre Astruc in which coins the phrase "camera stylo" meaning camera as pen. It has been reprinted in *The French New Wave: Critical Landmarks* edited by Ginette Vincendeau and Peter Graham.

2. Brown, T., "Design thinking."

3. Hetland, L., Winner, E., Veenema, S., and Sheridan, K.M., *Studio Thinking—The Real Benefits Of Visual Arts Education.*

4. I am undertaking further research through Macquarie University in Sydney into the areas of cognitive science and creative practice to continue to develop this hypothesis. For the purposes of this chapter, the definition relies on research into editing partnerships such as that of Dziga Vertov and Elizaveta Svilova, my own experience as an editor, and my students' experiences in making "onscreen drafts" of films and using these drafts to strengthen the structure and flow of scripts and productions. My thanks, particularly to the enthusiastic and willing students of Macquarie University who did onscreen drafts and production assignments, and to Genevieve Clay-Smith who embraced onscreen drafting as part of her process at AFTRS.

5. Gallese, V., and Guerra, M., "Embodying movies: Embodied simulation and film studies."

6. Brown, T., "Design thinking."

7. I recently heard from a Hollywood feature film editor that it took him six weeks of working alone with the director to solve structural problems in a film that weren't evident in the script. Many of the scenes that were shot were dropped in that process and there was a lot of ADR recorded to make it work. Wouldn't it have been cheaper to shoot and cut an onscreen draft and find out before spending all of the money on huge stars, huge crews and huge schedules?

8. Coughlan, P., and Canales, K., "Prototypes as (design) tools for behavioral and organizational change a design-based approach to help organizations change work behaviors."

9. Gray, K. et al., "How to prototype a game in under 7 days."

10. The cast and crews on both versions were fantastic—I couldn't have asked for better. I am indebted to all of them for being such great collaborators, especially Michi Marosszeky and Beth Aubrey, two fearless women who dove into the drafting process without judgment and brought extraordinary energy, talent, conviction and skill. Thank you!

Bibliography

Allen, R.J., *Out of the Labyrinth of the Mind: Manifesting a Spiritual Art beyond Dualism*, D.C.A. thesis, University of Technology, Sydney, 2004.

Allen, R., and Smith, M., editors, *Film Theory and Philosophy*, Oxford University Press, Oxford, 1999.

Allman, W.F., *Apprentices of Wonder: Inside the Neural Network Revolution*, Bantam Books, New York/London/Toronto/Sydney/Auckland, 1989.

Arnheim, R., *Film as Art*, University of California Press, Berkeley, Los Angeles/London, 1957.

Aronson, L., *Scriptwriting Updated: New and Conventional Ways of Writing for the Screen*, AFTRS Publishing/Allen & Unwin, Sydney, 2000.

Astruc, A., "The birth of a new Avant-Garde: La Caméra-Stylo," 1948. Reprinted in *The French New Wave: Critical Landmarks* edited by Ginette Vincendeau and Peter Graham, British Film Institute, London, 2009.

Bartenieff, I., with Lewis, D., *Body Movement: Coping with the Environment*, Gordon & Breach, New York/London/Paris, 1980.

Barthes, R., "Musica Practica," in *Image—Music—Text*, essays selected and translated by Heath, S., Fontana–Collins, London, 1979.

Bazin, A., *What Is Cinema?* essays selected and translated by H. Gray, foreword by J. Renoir, new forward by D. Andrew, University of California Press, Berkeley, 2004.

Benedetti, J., *Stanislavski: An Introduction*, Methuen Drama, London, 1990.

Bergen, R., *Sergei Eisenstein: A Life in Conflict*, Overlook Press, Woodstock/New York, 1999.

Berger, J., *Ways of Seeing*, British Broadcasting Corp./Penguin, London, 1972.

Bergson, H., *Introduction to Metaphysics*, translated by M.A. Anderson, Philosophical Library, New York, 1961.

Bergson, H., *Matter and Memory*, translated by N.M. Paul and W.S. Palmer, Zone Books, New York, 1991.

Blake, E., "A theatrical masterclass," *Sydney Morning Herald*, Entertainment, 2011, Available at www.smh.com.au/entertainment/theatre/a-theatricalmasterclass-20111110-1n7ud.html#ixzz2B2MBKiwA (accessed April 11, 2015).

Biro, Y., *Turbulence and Flow in Film, The Rhythmic Design*, Indiana University Press, Bloomington, 2012.

Bogue, R., *Deleuze on Cinema*, Routledge, New York/London, 2003.

Bordwell, D., *The Cinema of Eisenstein*, Routledge, New York, 2005.

Bordwell, D., "Intensified continuity: Visual style in contemporary American film—Critical essay," *Film Quarterly*, Spring 2002, 55(3), pp. 16–28.

Bordwell, D., *Narration in the Fiction Film*, University of Wisconsin Press, Madison, 1985.

Bordwell, D., *On the History of Film Style*, Harvard University Press, Cambridge, MA/London, 1997.

Bordwell, D., and Carroll, N., *Post-Theory: Reconstructing Film Studies*, University of Wisconsin Press, Madison/London, 1996.

Bordwell, D., Staiger, J., and Thompson, K., *The Classical Hollywood Cinema*, Routledge, London, 1985.

Bordwell, D., and Thompson, K., *Film Art: An Introduction*, 5th edition, McGraw–Hill, New York, 1997.

Bottomore, S., "Shots in the dark: The real origins of film editing," in *Early Cinema: Space, Frame, Narrative*, edited by T. Elsaesser, with A. Barker, BFI Publishing, London, 1994.

Bottomore, S., "The panicking audience? Early cinema and the 'train effect'," *Historical Journal of Film, Radio, and Television*, June 1999, Volume 19, Issue 2, p. 177.

Brannigan, E., *Dancefilm: Choreography and the Moving Image*, Oxford University Press, Oxford, New York, et al., 2011, p. 240.

Brogan, T.V.F., "Rhythm," in *The Princeton Encyclopedia of Poetry and Poetics*, edited by A. Preminger and T.V.F. Brogan, Princeton University Press, Princeton, NJ, 1993.

Brown, T., "Design thinking," *Harvard Business Review*, 2008, 86(6), pp. 84–92, 141. Available at www.ncbi.nlm.nih.gov/pubmed/18605031 (accessed April 11, 2015).

Carroll, N., *Theorizing the Moving Image*, Cambridge University Press, Cambridge, UK/New York/Melbourne, 1996.

Clark, A., and Chalmers, D., "The extended mind," *The Philosopher's Annual*, 1998, XXI, pp. 59–74. Available at www.jstor.org/stable/3328150 (accessed April 11, 2015).

Claxton, G., "The anatomy of intuition," in *The Intuitive Practitioner*, editors T. Atkinson and G. Claxton, Open University Press, Buckinghamshire/Philadelphia, 2000.

Cook, D., *A History of Narrative Film*, Norton, London/New York, 1996.

Coughlan, P., and Canales, K., "Prototypes as (design) tools for behavioral and organizational change a design-based approach to help organizations change work behaviors," *The Journal of Applied Behavioral Science*, 2007, 43(1), pp. 1–13.

Crittenden, R., *Fine Cuts: The Art of European Film Editing*, Taylor & Francis, London et al., 2006, p. 400.

Dancyger, K., *The Technique of Film and Video Editing: Theory and Practice*, 2nd edition, Focal Press, Boston/Oxford/Johannesburg/Melbourne/NewDelhi/Singapore, 1997.

Dancyger, K., and Rush, J., *Alternative Scriptwriting*, Focal Press, Boston/Oxford/Johannesburg/Melbourne/New Delhi/Singapore, 1995.

Deleuze, G., *Cinema 1: The Movement Image*, translated by H. Tomlinson and B. Habberjam, University of Minnesota Press, Minneapolis, 2003.

Deleuze, G., *Cinema 2: The Time Image*, translated by H. Tomlinson and R. Galeta, University of Minnesota Press, Minneapolis, 2003.

Deren, M., "The visual arts today," in *Film Theory and Criticism*, editors G. Mast and M. Cohen, Oxford University Press, New York/Oxford, 1985.

Durr, W., Gerstenberg, W., and Harvey, J., "Rhythm," in *The New Grove Dictionary of Music and Musicians*, editor S. Sadie, Macmillan, London/Washington, DC/Hong Kong, 1980.

Dymtryk, E., *On Film Editing*, Focal Press, London, 1984.

Eikhenbaum, B., "Problems of cine stylistics" (1927), translated by R. Sherwood, edited by R. Taylor, in *The Poetics of Cinema*, Special Issue, *Russian Poetics in Translation*, RPT Publications, Oxford, 1982, pp. 5–18.

Eisenstein, S., *Film Form: Essays in Film Theory*, edited and translated by J. Leyda, Harcourt Brace, San Diego/New York/London, 1977.

Fairservice, D., *Film Editing: History, Theory and Practice*, Manchester University Press, Manchester/New York, 2001.

Feuerstein, G., *The Yoga-Sutras of Pata ñ jali: A New Translation and Commentary*, Inner-Traditions International, Rochester, VT, 1989.

Feury, P., *New Developments in Film Theory*, Macmillan, Hampshire/London, 2000.

Fisher, L., "Film editing," in *A Companion to Film Theory*, editors T. Miller and R. Stam, Blackwell, Malden, MA/Oxford/Carlton, VIC, 2004.

Fraleigh, S.H., *Dance and the Lived Body: A Descriptive Aesthetics*, University of Pittsburgh Press, Pittsburgh, 1996.

Gallese, V., "Intentional attunement : A neurophysiological perspective on social cognition," *Cognitive Brain Research*, 2006, 1079(1), pp. 15–24.

Gallese, V., and Goldman, A., "Mirror neurons and the simulation theory of mind-reading," *Trends in Cognitive Science*, 1998, 2 (12).

Gallese, V., and Guerra, M., "Embodying movies: Embodied simulation and film studies," *Cinema: Journal of Philosophy and the Moving Image*, 2012, 3, pp.183–210.

Gannon, S., and Life, D., *Jivamukti Yoga*, Ballantine Books, New York, 2002.

Giannetti, L., *Understanding Movies*, 4th edition, Prentice–Hall, Upper Saddle River, NJ, 1987.

Gibson, R., "Acting and breathing," in *Falling for You: Essays on Cinema and Performance*, editors L. Stern and G. Kouvaros, Power Publications, Sydney, 1999.

Goddard, J.-L., "Montage mon beau souci," in *Godard on Godard: Critical Writings*, editors J. Narboni and T. Milne, Secker & Warburg, London, 1972.

Gray, K. et al., "How to prototype a game in under 7 days," *Gamasutra*, 2005. Available at www.gamasutra.com/view/feature/130848/how_to_prototype_a_game_in_under_7_.php (accessed April 11, 2015).

Greenfield, A., "Filmdance: Space, time and energy," *Filmdance Catalogue*, Elaine Summers Experimental Intermediate Foundation, New York, 1983.

Grodal, T.K., *Moving Pictures: A New Theory of Film Genres, Feelings and Cognition*, Clarendon Press, Oxford, 1997.

Henderson, B., "The long take," in *Movies and Methods: An Anthology*, editor B. Nichols, University of California Press, Berkeley, 1976.

Hetland, L., Winner, E., Veenema, S., and Sheridan, K.M., *Studio Thinking—The Real Benefits of Visual Arts Education*, Teachers College Press, New York, 2007.

Hooper, G., "Science and the fear of 20th century art," *Real Time + On Screen*, Number 60, April–May 2004. Available at www.rt.airstrip.com.au/article/60/7376 (accessed April 15, 2004).

Humphrey, D., *The Art of Making Dances*, Grove Press, New York, 1959.

Kennedy, B.M., *Deleuze and Cinema: The Aesthetics of Sensation*, Edinburgh University Press, Edinburgh, 2004.

Kimergard, L.B., "Editing in the depth of the surface: A few basic principles of graphic editing," *P.O.V.*, 6, "The Art of Film Editing." Available at http://imv.au.dk/publikationer/pov/Issue_06/section_1/artc6A.html (accessed April 11, 2015).

Kivy, P., "Music in the movies: A philosophical inquiry," in *Film Theory and Philosophy*, editors R. Allen and M. Smith, Clarendon Press, Oxford, 1997.

Kuleshov, L.V., *Kuleshov on Film*, selected, translated, and edited, with an introduction by R. Levaco, University of California Press, Berkeley, 1974.

Le Fanu, M., "On editing," *P.O.V.*, 6, "The Art of Film Editing." Available at http://imv.au.dk/publikationer/pov/Issue_06/section_1/artc1A.html (accessed April 11, 2015).

Leyda, J., *Kino: A History of the Russian and Soviet Film*, 3rd edition, Princeton University Press, Princeton, NJ, 1983.

Malloch, S.N., "Mothers and infants in communicative musicality," *Musicae Scientiae*, Special Issue, *Rhythm, Musical Narrative and Origins of Human Communication*, 1999–2000, pp. 13–28.

Malloch, S.N., and Trevathen, C., "The dance of wellbeing: Defining the musical therapeutic effect," *Nordic Journal of Music Therapy*, 2000, 9(2), pp. 3–17.

McGrath, D., *Screencraft: Editing & Post-Production*, Rotovision, Crans-Pres-Celigny, Switzerland, 2002.

McKechnie, S., Grove, R., and Stevens, K., *Conceiving Connections: Further Choreographic Research*, Australian Research Council, Canberra. Available at www.ausdance.org/au/connections (accessed April 11, 2015).

McKechnie, S., Grove, R., and Stevens, K., *Unspoken Knowledges: New Choreographic Research*, Australian Research Council, Canberra. Available at www.ausdance.org/au/unspoken (accessed April 11, 2015).

McKee, R., *Story: Substance, Structure, Style and the Principles of Screenwriting*, Methuen, London, 1999.

McLean, A.L., "Feeling and the filmed body," *Film Quarterly*, Spring 2002, 55(3), pp. 2–15.

Menary, R., *The Extended Mind*, editor R. Menary, MIT Press, Boston, 2010, p. 382.

Meyerhold, V., *Meyerhold on Theatre*, translated and edited with a critical commentary by E. Braun, Methuen Drama, London, 1998.

Michotte, A., *The Perception of Causality*, Basic Books, New York, 1963.

Mitoma, J., Zimmer, E., and Steiber, D.A., editors, *Envisioning Dance on Film and Video*, Routledge, New York/London, 2002.

Mitry, J., *The Aesthetics and Psychology of Cinema*, translated by C. King, Athalone Press, London, 1998.

Modell, A.H., *Imagination and the Meaningful Brain*, MIT Press, Cambridge, MA/London, 2003.

Molly, S., and Court, D., "For love and money: Estimating the value of psychic income in Australia," *Lumina* 10, AFTRS, 2012.

Motion Picture Editors Guild Newsletter. Available at www.editorsguild.com/newsletter/SpecialJun97/directors.html (accessed April 11, 2015).

Mundal, S., "Notes of an editing teacher," *P.O.V.*, 6, "The Art of Film Editing," http://imv.au.dk/publikationer/pov/Issue_06/section_1/artc4A.html (accessed April 11, 2015).

Murch, W., *In the Blink of an Eye*, AFTRS Publishing, Sydney, 1992.

Murch, W., *In the Blink of an Eye*, 2nd edition, Silman–James Press, Los Angeles, 2001.

Neill, A., "Empathy and (film) fiction", in *Post-Theory*, editors D. Bordwell and N. Carroll, University of Wisconsin Press, Madison, 1996.

Newlove, J., and Dalby, J., *Laban for All*, Routledge, New York/Nick Hern Books, London, 2004.

Noddings, N., and Shore, P.J., *Awakening the Inner Eye: Intuition in Education*, Teachers College Press, Columbia University, New York/London, 1984.

O'Steen, S., *Cut to the Chase: Forty-five Years of Editing America's Favorite Movies*, as told to B. O'Steen, Michael Wiese Productions, Studio City, CA, 2002.

Oldham, G., *First Cut: Conversations with Film Editors*, University of California Press, Berkeley/Los Angeles/Oxford, 1992.

Ondaatje, M., *The Conversations: Walter Murch and the Art of Editing Film*, Bloomsbury Publishing, London, 2002.

Orpen, V., *Film Editing: The Art of the Expressive*, Wallflower, London/New York, 2003.

Panikkar, K.N., "Rhythm and its applications," in *Creative Arts in Modern India (Essays in Comparative Criticism)*, editors R. Parimoo and I. Sharma, Books & Books, New Delhi, 1995.

Panofsky, E., "Style and medium in the motion pictures," reprinted from "Bulletin from the Department of Art and Archeology," in *Film Theory and Criticism: Introductory Readings*, 3rd edition, editors G. Mast and M. Cohen, Oxford University Press, Oxford/New York, 1985.

Pearlman, K., and Allen, R.J., *New Life on the 2nd Floor*, Tasdance, Launceston, 1996.

Pearlman, K., and Allen, R.J., editors, *Performing the Unnameable: An Anthology of Australian Performance Texts*, Currency Press and *RealTime*, Sydney, 1999.

Pepperman, R.D., *The Eye Is Quicker: Film Editing: Making a Good Film Better*, Michael Weise Productions, Studio City, CA, 2004.

Pitches, J., *Vsevolod Meyerhold*, Routledge, London/New York, 2003.

Preminger, A., and Brogan, T.V.F., editors, *The New Princeton Encyclopedia of Poetry and Poetics*, Princeton University Press, Princeton, NJ, 1993.

Pudovkin, V., "Film technique," reprinted in *Film Theory and Criticism*, 3rd edition, editors G. Mast and M. Cohen, Oxford University Press, Oxford/New York, 1985.

Pudovkin, V.I., *On Film Technique and Film Acting* (revised memorial edition, 1st edition 1929), Vision Press, London, 1974.

Ramachandran, V.S., "Mirror neuron and imitation learning as the driving force behind 'the great leap forward' in human evolution." Available at www.edge.org/3rd_culture/ramachandran/ramachandran_p2.html (accessed April 8, 2015).

Reisz, K., and Millar, G., *The Technique of Film Editing*, Focal Press, London/Boston, 1984.

Restak, R., *The New Brain: How the Modern Age Is Rewiring Your Mind*, Rodale, Emmaus, PA, 2003.

Rosenblum, R., *When the Shooting Stops, the Cutting Begins: A Film Editor's Story*, Penguin, New York, 1979.

Rowe, K., "Dany Cooper interview," *Inside Film Magazine*, November 2004, 71, pp. 43–44.

Salt, B., *Film Style and Technology: History and Analysis*, Starwood, London, 1983.

Sayles, J., *Thinking in Pictures: The Making of the Movie "Matewan,"* Houghton Mifflin, Boston, 1987.

Schmidt, M.R., and Stivers, C., "You know more than you can say: In memory of Donald A. Schon (1930–1997)," *Public Administration Review*, May 2000, 60(3), pp. 265–274.

Schmidt, P., "Introduction," in *Meyerhold at Work*, editor P. Schmidt, Applause, New York/London, 1996.

Scholes, P.A., *The Oxford Companion to Music*, 10th edition, edited by J.O. Ward, Oxford University Press, Oxford, 2000.

Schon, D., *The Reflective Practitioner: How Professionals Think in Action*, Basic Books, London, 1991.

Sheets, M., "Phenomenology: An approach to dance," in *The Dance Experience*, editors M.H. Nadel and C.N. Miller, Universe Books, New York, 1978.

Smith, M., *Engaging Characters: Fiction, Emotion and the Cinema*, Clarendon Press, Oxford, 1995.

Smith, M., "Imagining from the inside," in *Film Theory and Philosophy*, editors R. Allen and M. Smith, Clarendon Press, Oxford, 1997.

Sobchak, V., *The Address of the Eye: A Phenomenology of Film Experience*, Princeton University Press, Princeton, NJ, 1992.

Sokolowski, R., *Introduction to Phenomenology*, Cambridge University Press, Cambridge, UK/New York/Melbourne/Madrid, 2000.

Sollberger, A., *Biological Rhythm Research*, Elsevier, Amsterdam/New York/London, 1965.

Stam, R., *Film Theory: An Introduction*, Blackwell, Malden, MA/Oxford/Carlton, VIC, 2000.

Stein, J., and Urdang, L., editors, *The Random House Dictionary of the English Language*, unabridged version, Random House, New York, 1966.

Stevens, K., McKechnie, S., Malloch, S., and Petocz, A., "Choreographic cognition: Composing time and space," in *Proceedings of the 6th International Conference on Music Perception & Cognition*, edited by C. Woods, G. Luck, R. Brochard, F. Seddon, J.A. Sloboda, and S. O'Neill, Keele University, Keele, UK, August 2000.

Sutton, J., "Exograms and interdisciplinarity: History, the extended mind, and the civilizing process." 2010. *The Extended Mind*, pp. 189–225. Available at http://www.johnsutton.net/Exograms_Sutton.pdf (accessed April 11, 2015).

Tarkovsky, A., *Sculpting in Time*, translated by K. Blair-Hunter, University of Texas Press, Austin, 1986.

Tobias, J., "Cinema, scored: Toward a comparative methodology for music in media," *Film Quarterly*, 2004, 57(2), pp. 26–36.

Todd, M.E., *The Thinking Body: A Study of the Balancing Forces of Dynamic Man*, Dance Horizons, Hightstown, NJ, 1973.

Turim, M., *Flashbacks in Film: Memory & History*, Routledge, New York/London, 1989.

Van Leeuwen, T., "Rhythmic structure of the film text," in *Discourse and Communication: New Approaches to the Analysis of Mass Media Discourse and Communication*, editor T.A van Dijk, de Gruyter, Berlin/New York, 1985.

Van Leeuwen, T., *Introducing Social Semiotics*, Routledge, New York, 2005.

Vertov, D., *Kino-Eye: the Writings of Dziga Vertov*, edited by A. Michelson, translated by K. O'Brien, University of California Press, Berkeley/Los Angeles/London, 1984.

Wartenburg, T.E., and Curran, A., *The Philosophy of Film: Introductory Text and Readings*, Blackwell, Malden, MA/Cambridge, UK/Carlton, VIC, 2005.

Weidman, V., "Film editing—A hidden art?" *P.O.V.*, 6, *The Art of Film Editing.* Available at http://imv.au.dk/publikationer/pov/Issue_06/section_1artc2A.html (accessed April 11, 2015).

Weiss, E., and Belton, J., editors, *Film Sound: Theory and Practice*, Columbia University Press, New York, 1985. Available at www.moviemaker.com/hop/vol3/02/editing2.html (accessed April 11, 2015).

Index

The letter 'f' following a page number refers to an illustration; the letter 'n' refers to a note.